Cooperative Learning in Physical Education

Cooperative Learning is a dynamic instructional model that can teach diverse content to students at different grade levels, with students working together in small, structured, heterogeneous groups to master subject content. It has a strong research tradition, is used frequently as a professional development tool in general education and is now emerging in physical education.

This book defines Cooperative Learning in physical education and examines how to implement it in a variety of educational settings. It explores Cooperative Learning in physical education from three main perspectives. The first, context of learning, provides descriptions of Cooperative Learning in different levels of education (elementary school, secondary school and university physical education). The second, Cooperative Learning in the curriculum, offers case studies from teachers and researchers of their experiences of implementing Cooperative Learning within their own national context. The third perspective, key aspects of Cooperative Learning, examines how the different elements of the model have been foregrounded in efforts to enhance learning in physical education.

As the only text to provide international perspectives, from eight different countries, of Cooperative Learning in physical education, this book is important reading for any student, researcher or teacher with an interest in physical education, sport education, sport pedagogy, curriculum development or methods for learning and teaching.

Ben Dyson is Associate Professor in the School of Critical Studies in Education at the University of Auckland, New Zealand. He has taught for over 20 years in universities in Canada, the USA and New Zealand. His research focuses on curriculum and instruction, innovative pedagogical practices in schools and physical education policy research.

Ashley Casey is course leader for Sport and Physical Education at the University of Bedfordshire, UK. He has worked as a secondary-school physical education teacher for 15 years, during which time he completed his PhD. His research is around sustained curriculum renewal in physical education through models-based practices such as Cooperative Learning. He has published work on school-based interventions using these approaches.

Routledge Studies in Physical Education and Youth Sport

Series editor: David Kirk
University of Bedfordshire, UK

The Routledge Studies in Physical Education and Youth Sport series is a forum for the discussion of the latest and most important ideas and issues in physical education, sport, and active leisure for young people across school, club and recreational settings. The series presents the work of the best well-established and emerging scholars from around the world, offering a truly international perspective on policy and practice. It aims to enhance our understanding of key challenges, to inform academic debate and to have a high impact on both policy and practice, and is thus an essential resource for all serious students of physical education and youth sport.

Also available in this series

Cooperative Learning in Physical Education

A research-based approach

**Edited by
Ben Dyson and Ashley Casey**

Routledge
Taylor & Francis Group

LONDON AND NEW YORK

First published 2012
by Routledge
2 Park Square, Milton Park, Abingdon, Oxon OX14 4RN

Simultaneously published in the USA and Canada
by Routledge
711 Third Avenue, New York, NY 10017

Routledge is an imprint of the Taylor & Francis Group, an informa
business

British Library Cataloguing in Publication Data
A catalogue record for this book is available from the British Library

Library of Congress Cataloging in Publication Data
Cooperative learning in physical education : an international perspective /
edited by Ben Dyson and Ashley Casey.
    p. cm. -- (Routledge studies in physical education and youth sport)
    1. Physical education and training--Study and teaching. 2. Group work
in education--United States. I. Dyson, Ben. II. Casey, Ashley.
    GV361.C654 2012   796.071--dc23
    2011048159

ISBN: 978-0-415-66738-8 (hbk)
ISBN: 978-0-203-13298-2 (ebk)

Typeset in Times New Roman
by Bookcraft Limited, Stroud, Gloucestershire

Ben: This work is dedicated to Lisa, Brennan and Lily who continue to be my inspiration.

Ashley: For Sarah, Thomas and Maddie, who made this possible.

Contents

Figures

Tables

Contributors

Ingrid Bähr PhD studied physical education, art and educational science before she joined the scientific staff at the University of Bremen and did her doctoral thesis in 2004. She works in research in the field of Cooperative Learning in physical education and is now Professor for Didactics of Physical Education at the University of Hamburg.

Ashley Casey PhD is a former physical education teacher now working in the Institute of Sport and Physical Activity Research at the University of Bedfordshire. His research interests are pedagogical models, professional learning and practitioner research.

Rona Cohen PhD works at the School of Education and School of Physical Education in the College of Physical Education and Sport Sciences at the Wingate Institute, Israel. Her research interests are in motor development, Cooperative Learning and sports and gender.

Wendy Dowler is currently completing her PhD and working in Education at the University of Wollongong, Australia. Her research interests are exploring pedagogical models that promote inclusive physical education.

Ben Dyson PhD has taught for over 20 years in universities in Canada, the USA and New Zealand. His research focuses on curriculum and instruction, innovative pedagogical practices in schools and physical education policy research.

Javier Fernández-Río PhD is a Professor in the Faculty of Teacher Training and Education at the University of Oviedo in Spain.

Michelle Grenier PhD is an Assistant Professor at the University of New Hampshire, USA. Her research interests include school practices that promote effective inclusionary instruction.

Lucile Lafont PhD is Professeur des Universités in Bordeaux Segalen University, France, where she is in charge of the research team Vie sportive (LACES). Her research is concerned with social interactions and motor skills acquisition (Cooperative Learning, tutoring and modelling).

Antonio Méndez-Giménez is a former Head of Physical Education in a secondary school and now teaches at the University of Oviedo in Spain.

Alan Ovens is a Principal Lecturer in Physical Education in Critical Studies in Education at the University of Auckland. His research interests are centred on critical pedagogy, teacher education, and theorizing complexity in physical education.

Wayne Smith is a Senior Lecturer in Physical Education in Critical Studies in Education at the University of Auckland. His research interests are centred on skill development, critical pedagogy and teacher education in physical education.

Sue Sutherland PhD is an Assistant Professor in Physical Education at Ohio State University. Her scholarly interests are in the areas of student-centred pedagogy and PETE doctoral education in the USA.

Carlos Velázquez-Callado is a primary teacher who is also enrolled in a PhD programme at the University of Valladolid. He is a strong advocate for Cooperative Learning in his school, at the university level and throughout Spain.

Jonas Wibowo is a postgraduate now working in the Didactics of Physical Education section at the University of Hamburg. He is working on his doctoral thesis in teacher–student interaction in group lessons in physical education.

Pat Yeaton is a physical education teacher at North Hampton School, USA. She is also an Affiliate Professor at the University of New Hampshire.

Sima Zach PhD is the Head of the School of Education in the College of Physical Education and Sport Sciences at the Wingate Institute, Israel. She is also the head of the teacher education programme. Her research interests are in sport and physical education psychology.

Foreword

Throughout the field of education, and physical education in particular, there is an enduring interest in the idea of cooperative learning. In this edited collection, Ben Dyson and Ashley Casey have put together an impressive international perspective on Cooperative Learning in physical education. The collection covers primary, secondary and university contexts with chapters from Spain, Germany, France, Australia, Israel, the USA, the UK and New Zealand. It is through their collaborative efforts with researchers internationally that such a collection has been made possible.

While the concept of cooperative learning is not new, it is enjoying considerable attention at this time, because as a concept it is a sympathetic 'fit' with contemporary educational discourse that advocates student-centred, reflexive, problem-based teaching methods. Moreover, educators have been drawn to the pedagogical potential of cooperation because they recognize that when a number of individuals work together they can achieve more than if they work independently. For example, in physical education, much of the curriculum content focuses on sport. Sport, while competitive in its fundamental logic, requires a high degree of cooperation between the participants to ensure the game 'works' and teams are successful.

What was originally conceived as cooperative learning pedagogy (Dyson, 2001) has now evolved into the cooperative learning model. Although we are not given an explanation as to why the term 'model' is chosen in preference to 'pedagogy', it does hint at a way of thinking about pedagogy that is underpinned by current discourses of performativity. Models tend to bring up questions of fidelity of treatment. Is the model being implemented 'correctly'? Efficacy of treatment regarding specified outcomes becomes important. Models are, or at least seem to be, important for physical education pedagogy. This book will answer some of the questions regarding pedagogies for cooperative learning raised by teachers and researchers in the field.

The editors argue in their Introduction that 'teachers should be equipped to use a number of pedagogical models in physical education (Direct Instruction, Sport Education, Teaching Games for Understanding, Adventure-Based Learning, Personal and Social Responsibility and so on)'. Implicit in this statement is the idea that instructional models can be thought of as different tools that teachers should have in their 'tool box' and can employ when necessary. It is a worthy objective for teachers to learn how to employ different pedagogies to bring about a variety of student learning outcomes. This makes a change from the 'traditional methodology' that Hoffman (1971) claimed 'was the most widely used pedagogical method in PE'.

According to Hoffman, 'traditional methodology' consisted of teacher explanation of what is to be learned, teacher demonstration (or perhaps a pupil demonstration), followed by organized class practice. This teaching method was (and maybe still is), for many teachers and pupils alike, *the* way to teach physical activity. Hoffman suggested that the method had its origins 'not in science or even theory, but in the unglamorous realities of life' (Hoffman, 1971, p. 57). The cooperative learning model is clearly a welcome break from this tradition, and not only can it 'deliver' worthwhile outcomes in terms of social learning, it can also be a vehicle for professional renewal for many teachers who choose to try it. Based on constructivist epistemologies, the chapters in this collection provide ample evidence of the success of cooperative learning pedagogies in enhancing student learning.

Unlike previous books, such as Grineski's *Cooperative Learning in Physical Education* (1996), which are more focused on practical ways to teach for cooperative learning, this collection is explicitly research-informed and practice-oriented. Although focused on physical education, *Cooperative Learning in Physical Education: a research-based approach* would also be relevant to anyone who teaches physical activity and sport. This is a book that deserves a place on the shelves of all physical educators. It will be a valuable resource for student teachers, practising PE teachers, teacher educators and graduate students alike.

Professor Richard Tinning
University of Auckland and *University of Queensland*

References

Dyson, B. (2001). Cooperative Learning in an elementary school physical education program. *Journal of Teaching in Physical Education* 20: 264–81.

Grineski, S. (1996). *Cooperative Learning in Physical Education*. Champaign, IL: Human Kinetics.

Hoffman, S. (1971). Traditional methodology: prospects for change. *Quest* 15: 51–7.

Introduction
Cooperative Learning as a pedagogical model in physical education

Ben Dyson and Ashley Casey

Key terms: pedagogical model, approaches to Cooperative Learning, elements of Cooperative Learning, Cooperative Learning in physical education

Typically, Cooperative Learning has been defined as a dynamic instructional model that can teach diverse content to students at different grade levels. Students work together in small, structured, heterogeneous groups to master subject matter content (Dyson *et al.*, 2010). However, one of the current gaps in the literature is a definition of Cooperative Learning that specifically relates to physical education. One of the primary aims of this book, therefore, is to consider that gap.

This chapter begins the book's consideration of Cooperative Learning in physical education through an exploration of the most current research. The subsequent chapters form the heart of the book. These chapters will develop the expanding literature around Cooperative Learning in physical education and ask the reader and the wider academic community to consider the model in alternative ways. In the final chapter we will present our definition of Cooperative Learning in physical education derived from our experiences, the experiences of teachers and research of the chapter authors (which explore inquiry in eight different countries) and the current literature. We believe that the richness of this book will emerge from the similarities and differences in the varied global contexts that these leading educators and authors are working in. The authors have described their particular context so that the reader will have a sense of where they are coming from and what the specific situation is that they are working in.

Cooperative Learning is an extensive field of inquiry that was the subject of laboratory research into the effects of cooperation on performance as early as the 1940s (Deutsch, 1949). Research dating back to the late nineteenth century has shown that working cooperatively is beneficial to learning (Deutsch, 1949; Johnson and Johnson, 1994), yet it was only in the 1970s that it was linked with and used in education as a pedagogical approach to learning through empirical work in the fields of social relationships, group dynamics, learning and instruction and as a result has experienced something of a revival (Antil *et al.*, 1998;

Slavin, 1986). Teachers frequently use groups in their teaching, and pupils have naturally formed, or have been formed into, formal and informal learning groups, yet it was not until 'a set of principles and methods' (Slavin, 1990, p. xi) were developed for use over an extended period of time that Cooperative Learning was defined and recognized as a model of instruction.

Cooperative Learning is a model of instruction that, although starting from a single root, developed along four separate lines: the conceptual approach, the curricular approach, the structural approach and the complex approach. As might be expected, each of these interpretations of Cooperative Learning has developed its own methods and criteria that differ one from another, an explanation of which will enable the reader to appreciate the different connotations of the term 'Cooperative Learning'. The *conceptual approach* was developed following the establishment of the Cooperative Learning Center by David and Roger Johnson at the University of Minnesota. It has been called the conceptual approach because it assumes that teachers can learn the key principles of structuring Cooperative Learning and then adapt these to fit their own situations and classrooms. Robert Slavin and his colleagues at Johns Hopkins University in Baltimore developed the *curricular approach* as a means of helping teachers to deliver specific learning outcomes in their classrooms. It was created with the purpose of developing curriculum-specific structures that have been designed to support learning in heterogeneous classrooms. *Structural Cooperative Learning*, in contrast, was based upon the work of Spencer Kagan, who designed it to be content-independent, that is, to be used in different situations such as in the achievement of mastering content, or developing concept development or team building, rather than in different curriculum areas such as mathematics and English. The *complex approach* was developed by Elizabeth Cohen, the Director of the Stanford Program for Complex Instruction at Stanford University. Cohen and her colleagues developed a model of Cooperative Learning that sought to increase the thinking, linguistic and academic skills of under-served children through the use of heterogeneous groups.

Utilizing Cooperative Learning as a pedagogical model (Haerens *et al.*, 2011, p. 324) represents a deliberate act of teaching. In their recent propositional piece Haerens *et al.* (2011) proposed the term 'pedagogical model' as a more comprehensive approach compared to the previously employed 'instructional model' (Metzler, 2005), because 'the term pedagogical model highlights the interdependence and irreducibility of learning, teaching, subject matter and context' (p. 324). We therefore define Cooperative Learning as a pedagogical model because the emphasis on 'instruction' inherent in traditional physical education practices is replaced by focus on a more inclusive and comprehensive nature of learning that, as Casey proposes in Chapter 5, positions the teacher and the students as co-learners.

The use of heterogeneous groups is an example of how traditional teacher-focused instruction is changed in an effort to make learning, teaching, subject matter and context equal components of a Cooperative Learning classroom. However, Johnson and Johnson (1999, p. 68) warned that the performance of any small group depends on how it is structured:

Seating people together and calling them a cooperative group does not make them one. Study groups, project groups, lab groups, home-rooms, and reading groups are groups, but they are not necessarily cooperative. Even with the best of intentions, teachers may be using traditional classroom learning groups rather than cooperative learning groups. To ensure that a group is cooperative, educators must understand the different ways cooperative learning may be used and the basic elements that need to be used and the basic elements that need to be carefully structured within every cooperative activity.

There are many occasions when students are grouped together or asked to work together, but these are not structured to be Cooperative Learning groups (Kagan, 1998). In our experience there is a prevalence of such random groupings in physical education that is far in excess of any other subject. Yet these are not often (or deliberately) structured to be cooperative. For a teacher to use the Cooperative Learning model he or she must (a) make deliberate choices to use the model and (b) ensure that certain conditions are in place, for only with their deliberate inclusion can Cooperative Learning be expected to be more effective than other forms of instruction. The elements that make learning cooperative are defined by Johnson and Johnson (1994, p. 2, our emphasis) as:

1   clearly perceived positive interdependence;
2   considerable promotive (face-to-face) interaction;
3   clearly perceived *individual accountability* and personal responsibility to achieve the group's goals;
4   frequent use of the relevant interpersonal and small-group skills;
5   frequent and regular *group processing* of current functioning to improve the group's future effectiveness.

There are therefore considered to be five critical elements of Cooperative Learning both in mainstream classrooms and in physical education: (i) positive interdependence, (ii) individual accountability, (iii) promotive face-to-face interaction, (iv) interpersonal skills and small-group skills, and (v) group processing. These elements will be examined in detail throughout this volume, and examples will be drawn from the physical education literature and practical examples given from teachers and students in school- and university-based programmes.

Positive interdependence exists when students perceive that they are linked to group members in such a way that they cannot succeed unless other group members do. That is, students rely on each other to complete the predesigned task. *Individual accountability* refers to students taking responsibility for completing their part of the task for their group. Accountability mechanisms like student task sheets hold students individually accountable and create a situation where assigned tasks are more explicit for students. These accountability strategies attempt to ensure there are no 'free riders' (Slavin, 1996) or 'competent bystanders' (Tousignant and Siedentop, 1983). *Promotive face-to-face interaction* is literally head-to-head discussion within the group while group members are in close proximity to each other. *Interpersonal and small-group skills* are student behaviours that allow free and easy communication between group-mates. They are developed through the tasks in which students participate and may include listening, shared decision-making, taking responsibility, giving and receiving feedback and encouraging each other. *Group processing* is usually in the form of an open dialogue or group discussion related to the lesson content that can occur at any time during the lesson (Dyson, 2002).

The Cooperative Learning model

In this section we have undertaken a brief review of current research on Cooperative Learning in physical education, for which there is now an emerging body of literature. However, in physical education we have derived our initial definitions and support for our work from research in many different subject areas. Research in general education has demonstrated that use of the Cooperative Learning model has been shown to improve academic achievement, active learning, social skill development and classroom equity (Cohen, 1994; Gillies, 2006; Johnson and Johnson, 1989, 2009; Slavin, 1996). Gillies (2006) suggested that Cooperative Learning can provide instruction that leads the student to more authentic learning experiences, allows for more active participation, is more meaningful and empowers students to learn complex content, previously proposed by Cohen (1994). Cooperative Learning has a dual learning emphasis on social and academic goals (Antil *et al.*, 1998; Cohen, 1994). In addition to this dual focus, when Cooperative Learning is used as a pedagogical practice in physical education, the psychomotor domain of learning is added as a learning priority (Metzler, 2005).

One teaching strategy that is unique to Cooperative Learning is 'the Cooperative Learning structure'. In lessons the teacher purposefully designs Cooperative Learning structures to enhance students' psychomotor domain of learning. Cooperative Learning structures are ways of managing the inter-action of individuals in a classroom. Structures provide the step-by-step procedures that are used to present, practise and review tasks. Some regulate interaction between pairs, some are best for small groups and others involve the whole class (Kagan, 1992). In many of the chapters the authors discuss different kinds of Cooperative Learning structures, such as: Learning Teams, Jigsaw, or Think–Pair–Share (Johnson and Johnson, 1989; Kagan 1992). For example, Learning Teams is based on Slavin's (1996) Student Teams-Achievement Division and Learning Together (Johnson and Johnson, 1989). Learning Teams give students the opportunity for responsibility and shared leadership. These are generally used for teaching motor skills and tactics but can be applied to any physical education content. Students begin to work in pairs and progress to working in small teams of four to six. Each student is assigned a different role to help each team-mate learn (e.g. recorder, encour-ager, coach, equipment manager). Positive interdependence is realized by each student taking on a specific role to complete the group task (Dyson, 2001,

Dyson and Grineski, 2001). Many of these structures are common to PETE (physical education teacher education) programmes and teachers in schools. These will be presented as different structures or ways to teach Cooperative Learning. We will challenge the reader to try different structures in their teaching and learning process.

Lafont *et al.* (2007) reported that motor and tactical skills can be developed through oral discussions among peers regarding the goals and strategies in basketball units. In other research Casey *et al.* (2009) studied the implementation of Cooperative Learning with 11–12-year-old students. This research argued that Cooperative Learning allowed the teacher to have a similar emphasis on social and academic learning goals, allowing students to understand and improve their small-group and interpersonal skill in conjunction with their athletics skills. However, while some have argued that psychomotor learning could be seen as the academic learning achieved through Cooperative Learning in physical education, the development of social skill is a key element of this pedagogical model (Metzler, 2011).

For many years social skill development has received a great deal of attention in the Cooperative Learning literature – Cooperative Learning methods (Slavin, 1990) improve social skills and social relations among students (Slavin *et al.*, 1985). Research has supported the notion that social skills need to be taught explicitly (Sapon-Shevin, 1994). Teachers must plan specific social skills, such as listening, working together and providing appropriate feedback to each other, to enhance students' interpersonal skills. Students make the greatest gains in learning when teachers delegate responsibility so that more students can talk and work together at multiple learning centres (Cohen, 1994). In physical education Cooperative Learning develops interpersonal and social skills in a positive and supportive learning environment (Barrett, 2005; Casey *et al.*, 2009; Dyson, 2002; Goudas and Magotsiou, 2009; Lafont *et al.*, 2007).

Barrett (2005) studied sixth-grade physical education classes' use of a structure called Performer and Coach Earn Rewards (PACER), which was grounded in Slavin's (1996) work and used three elements of Cooperative Learning: cooperative interaction, individual accountability and group contingency (this was previously referred to as positive interdependence by Johnson and Johnson, 1989). Barrett reported that the Cooperative Learning structure PACER increased students' percentage of correct trials during practice with task cards, compared to whole-group instruction. PACER motivated students to be involved in more motor-appropriate practice. 'PACER was successful in creating an environment in which students performed a substantially higher percentage of correct trials during student practice while performing at least as many trials (on average) as they did during whole-group instruction' (Barrett, 2005, p. 99).

Goudas and Magotsiou (2009) reported the effect of a cooperative physical education programme on the development of students' social skills and attitudes toward group work. Students in a Cooperative Learning programme enhanced their social skills and attitudes toward group work compared to a control group. Goudas and Magotsiou found that the Cooperative Learning groups not only developed motor skills but empathy to other students, and decreased their disruptive behaviours. In addition, these students increased their preference for working in groups.

In a recent study, Dyson *et al.* (2010) used multiple methods to analyse the ecology of Cooperative Learning in physical education classes. T-tests of the quantitative data revealed that instruction time, management time, transitions and wait time decreased significantly during the Cooperative Learning units, and refining, extending and applying tasks increased significantly. Cognitive/ social tasks (group processing) were observed consistently in every lesson and contributed to student learning. The researchers identified four main categories from the qualitative data: organization and management of students, roles, skill development and strategizing. To promote individual accountability, the teacher used task sheets, assigned Cooperative Learning roles, kept group sizes small, randomly chose students to demonstrate their competence and asked students to teach their team-mates skills and tactics.

Another key contribution of the Cooperative Learning model is that it has the propensity to assist students with disabilities. Grenier (2006) reported that teachers can use purposeful strategies to accommodate students with disabilities. Teachers must consider the context and group dynamics when planning instruction, and develop the 'ability to create an environment of acceptance while developing tasks in ways that enhance learning through positive social interactions for students with disabilities' (Grenier, 2006, p. 257).

Interestingly, in the general education literature Stanne *et al.* (1999) examined the influence of cooperation, competition or individualistic situational structures on motor performance. Stanne *et al.* (1999) reported in their meta-analysis of 64 studies that cooperation promotes higher motor skills performance than individualistic effort or competition (effect sizes 0.53 for cooperation; 0.36 for competitive or individualistic efforts). For the physical educators this finding suggests that cooperation can enhance the development of motor skills.

The school-based research in physical education validates the use of Cooperative Learning (Barrett, 2005; Casey *et al.*, 2009; Casey and Dyson, 2009; Dyson, 2002; Dyson *et al.*, 2010; Goudas and Magotsiou, 2009; Lafont *et al.*, 2007). More importantly, now we provide a rationale from leading scholars in the field for the utility of Cooperative Learning as a pedagogical model in physical education. Recently, many futurists in physical education pedagogy or sport pedagogy have argued for the increased use of instructional models or pedagogical models in physical education (Metzler, 2005; Metzler and McCullick, 2008; Kirk 2010). In this book we argue that teachers should be equipped to use a number of pedagogical models in physical education (Direct Instruction, Sport Education, Teaching Games for Understanding, Adventure-Based Learning, Personal and Social Responsibility, and so on). In Dyson *et al.* (2004) Cooperative Learning, Sport Education and Tactical Games were compared and contrasted as pedagogical models in physical education. This text provides a deep insight into one of many pedagogical models, that is, Cooperative Learning in physical education.

An introduction to the chapters

The contents of this volume are divided into three parts: Part 1: Contexts of learning; Part 2: Cooperative Learning in the curriculum; Part 3: Key aspects of Cooperative Learning. Part 1 includes chapters from school-based curriculum foci in New Zealand, Germany and Spain. Part 2 offers studies from the primary (elementary), intermediate and college level. Part 3 discusses key aspects of Cooperative Learning in chapters exploring group processing, student interactions and the application of Cooperative Learning for persons with disabilities.

Part 1: Contexts of learning

In the first chapter, Ovens, Dyson and Smith present research from a school-based project in New Zealand that implemented Cooperative Learning in two primary and three secondary schools. This chapter presents a study that explored the co-construction of Cooperative Learning programmes in schools with university academics supporting school-based teachers. They argue that teachers need to be able to utilize innovative pedagogical practices that are congruent with current research findings, such as Cooperative Learning, in order to support student success. This chapter discusses how Cooperative Learning can facilitate the integration of the recently revised New Zealand curriculum (Ministry of Education, 2007) into physical education practices. It explores particularly the process of collaborative professional development in presenting and supporting the use of innovative pedagogical practices. In addition, the authors present the constraints on and enablers of research on teaching in physical education in the New Zealand context. Ovens *et al.* attempted to develop a professional learning community based on Cooperative Learning as a pedagogical practice in physical education programmes. They found that Cooperative Learning was a feasible pedagogical model to meet the social-critical curriculum presented in the recently revised New Zealand curriculum.

In Chapter 2 Bähr and Wibowo present two driving forces for Cooperative Learning in physical education in Germany. First, there is an explanation of how Cooperative Learning is understood in German sport pedagogy following the idea of *Bildung*. This term, or more accurately this philosophy, is used to describe a student-centred instructional process where the teacher is a 'guide', not a leader. The student is the leader in his or her own learning. Their educational philosophy argues for 'as much leeway as possible but also as much structure as necessary'. In addition to the current sport and movement culture that focuses on motor achievement ('education *to* sport') in German sport pedagogy, the Cooperative Learning model allows for personality development to move into an equal focus ('education *by* sport'). The method of Cooperative Learning offers itself as a possibility to realize this 'dual task' of physical education formulated in the nationwide reformation of the new curricula in Germany. The authors present a 'sport concept' that includes learning 'in' and 'through' the physical as an embedded part of the physical education curriculum. Bähr and Wibowo report on an empirical study regarding the quality of the learning process and learning effects in Cooperative Learning in physical education, using the example of learning a handstand. In addition, Bähr and Wibowo draw our attention to the 'Socratic method' of teaching and propose that in physical education we could expand our research in this area of, setting up problems and asking students questions, in order to improve the relationship between the teacher and the student.

In Chapter 3 Fernández-Río and Méndez-Giménez explore students designing and making their own equipment. The first underlying concept or pillar they explain is to increase the students' consciousness of the physical environment, in order to become more sustainability orientated and environmentally responsible. The second pillar is the construction of equipment with the needs of individual students firmly in mind. The third pillar of this approach was the scarcity of materials available in physical education as a result of limited budgets. The fourth and final pillar of this perspective refers to the individual who builds the materials. When students are asked to build a 'cardboard ringo' (similar to a frisbee) in small groups, they are forced into a promotive face-to-face interaction. Consequently, interpersonal skills are developed through the activity, and group processing is used to solve possible behaviour problems. The challenge of the task is designed to demonstrated individual accountability, because students must create low-cost, efficient equipment for the group. Fernández-Río and Méndez-Giménez suggest that this context helps develop positive interdependence among students when they play different roles (building, presenting and/or assessing their equipment). In promoting the creation of homemade or self-made materials their intention is that students, with the help of their peers or their family, should construct at least some pieces of their physical education equipment. Once built, these homemade materials can be integrated in the physical education sessions like conventional equipment but with more creative possibilities.

Part 2: Cooperative Learning in the curriculum

In Chapter 4 Velázquez-Callado explores and interprets the practical application of Cooperative Learning methods and physical activity at the primary-school level. He presents Cooperative Learning structures and several teaching strategies such as working in groups, cooperative games or team-building activities. As Dyson and colleagues have reported (Dyson, 2001, 2002; Dyson *et al.*, 2004; Dyson *et al.*, 2010), Velázquez-Callado presents strategies and techniques to help students learn to analyse skills, correct errors, in a supportive, encouraging environment, and solve their own problems within Cooperative Learning structures. The Cooperative Learning model provides an equitable learning environment where both academic and social learning can be achieved. Velázquez-Callado argues that in physical education it is the connection between the cognitive and the psychomotor domain that becomes the academic learning. He suggests that this interconnection is highlighted by the social and emotional learning in the affective domain that typifies his understanding of Cooperative Learning in physical education. We would like to emphasize, as Velázquez-Callado states, that Cooperative Learning is not just students working in groups, playing cooperative games or being involved in team-building activities. He emphasizes that teachers need to learn what Cooperative Learning is before they can use it as a pedagogical practice with their students in a positive and inclusive learning environment.

In Chapter 5 Casey presents the notion of our current education system as an 'anaesthetizing' one. In an honest and frank manner, Casey paints a vivid picture: 'As a young teacher I now believe that was I was guilty of putting the content (the sport) and the teacher (myself) before the learning and the learner.' Casey describes his journey as a teacher and how Cooperative Learning has facilitated a conceptual shift in the way he teaches. For Casey it is not business as usual but a 'seismic shift' in his personal philosophy. Casey's main contribution is an ability to connect his pedagogy with his students in a meaningful and purposeful manner while they co-construct the physical education curriculum. Defining Cooperative Learning in physical education as a 'pedagogical model that explores the social-cultural significance of human movement' he argues that teachers and students must learn together if they are to successfully engage with new pedagogical models.

In Chapter 6 Zach and Cohen argue that social interaction and social activities should be structured into the physical education teacher education (PETE) processes. They suggest that many teacher preparation programmes throughout the world utilize various pedagogical models and/or approaches but rightly point out that there is a paucity of research exploring these practices in PETE. Zach and Cohen strongly advocate for teaching and practice for pre-service teachers in a wide range of pedagogical models. They present both theoretical and practical knowledge and understanding of Cooperative Learning in physical education in general and in PETE in particular, presenting examples of how positive interdependence can be explained to PETE majors in gymnastics, orienteering and basketball. They highlight that one of the major challenges of teacher education programmes is to guide pre-service teachers' knowledge and practical opportunities. Zach and Cohen discuss their work in relation to academic knowledge and practical knowledge in PETE but remind us of the age-old challenges of the theory–practice gap. They point out that fostering the social domain is a major purpose of the physical education curriculum designed by the Ministry of Education in Israel. Nevertheless, Cooperative Learning as a pedagogical model in physical education in Israel is not commonly utilized. Zach and Cohen report that pre-service teachers acknowledged the importance of the social domain, but had difficulties in setting attainable objectives, or planning relevant tasks in order to achieve these objectives. They argue that physical education is one of the most appropriate and relevant subjects in the school curriculum and that the Cooperative Learning model can help improve the quality of instruction.

Part 3: Key aspects of Cooperative Learning

In Chapter 7 Sutherland examines the value of 'group processing' from an adventure-based learning perspective. Sutherland presents a comprehensive definition of 'group processing' and provides a useful metaphor of the 'Sunday drive' as a way of elucidating the complex nature of group processing. She discusses the inherent value of group processing that our colleagues in adventure education (Miles and Priest, 1990) have written about for years, but points out the problematic nature of quality group processing and the time constraints on the teacher. Group processing is presented in PETE in the USA within the adventure-based learning part of the programme. Practical strategies are presented for Cooperative Learning to promote a physical and emotional environment conducive to reflective and introspective discussion. Sutherland argues that without incorporating group processing the full benefit of Cooperative Learning is diminished.

In Chapter 8 Grenier (a university faculty member) and Yeaton (a physical education teacher) team up to write their story of the implementation of Cooperative Learning for students with disabilities. In their chapter they promote Cooperative Learning as a potent pedagogical model enriched by the task-related processes that facilitate student engagement, particularly for students lacking age-appropriate physical or social skill competencies. Differentiated learning is promoted through explicit, concrete direction while a balanced mentor–mentee process of support emerges from the completion of group goals.

Grenier and Yeaton emphasize that the implementation of Cooperative Learning for students with disabilities requires commitment to the pedagogical process of instruction. At the elementary level they present the STEPS (student, task, equipment, peer support and safety) process and then tell the story of Joey (who has cerebral palsy) and how through the use of STEPS he is truly integrated into the physical education class. Grenier and Yeaton argue that within the Cooperative Learning model, students can work together towards group goals through the natural support of peers and a shared understanding of the outcomes of their actions. That is, Cooperative Learning promotes cultural sensitivity through the integrally bound relationships of the group.

In Chapter 9 Lafont presents a French physical education perspective and demonstrates how the Cooperative Learning model can help physical education teachers meet the requirements of the French national curriculum. Lafont reports on how the implementation of Cooperative Learning structures can enhance students' social skill development through their work in small groups. Lafont presents how a European theoretical framework can elucidate our understanding of peer interactions and how they are developed in a series of projects from her research and the work of her colleagues in France. This perspective of Cooperative Learning refers to developmental or functional social psychology. This perspective, applied to physical education specifically in France, supports the analysis of 'verbal interactions' and 'debate of ideas' in small groups or dyads. The research from a variety of content areas strengthens that case that appropriate verbal exchanges in small groups can allow students to develop both increased understanding and acquisition of games and performance strategies (for example in basketball, handball, acrobatics and table tennis). Lafont contends that in the Cooperative Learning classroom, the analysis of interactive dynamics, speaking turns and contents of verbal exchanges in small groups or in dyads is a complementary means to understanding the benefits of Cooperative Learning in relation to different social roles in a physical education class.

In Chapter 10 Dowler presents Cooperative Learning and interactions within an inclusive secondary school physical education programme. Her chapter explores the possibility of utilizing the Cooperative Learning model as a pedagogical practice to enhance social interaction between students with a mild intellectual disability and their peers without a disability. Dowler focuses our attention on explicit examples from her current research in the Australian context. She highlights the challenges of implementing Cooperative Learning in a secondary-school inclusive physical education class with outcomes that may well promote or discourage students' interactions. Dowler presents several useful definitions related to inclusion in physical education. Her detailed observations provide an in-depth understanding of teachers' and students' interactions within Cooperative Learning as a pedagogical practice. Teaching strategies that encourage and discourage social interactions are presented. Dowler concludes that the Cooperative Learning model shows potential to improve interactions between students with a mild intellectual disability and their peers without a disability. Importantly, equal status interactions are promoted when students contribute equally, sharing roles and resources as they pursue common goals in a Cooperative Learning task. Dowler argues that in the Cooperative Learning model students are supported by the teacher and other students authorizing the use of equal status interactions.

References

Antil, L.R., Jenkins, J.R., Wayne, S.K. and Vadasy, P.F. (1998). Cooperative Learning: prevalence, conceptualizations, and the relation between research and practice. *American Educational Research Journal* 35: 419–54.

Barrett, T. (2005). Effects of Cooperative Learning on the performance of sixth-grade physical education students. *Journal of Teaching in Physical Education* 24: 88–102.

Casey, A. and Dyson, B. (2009). One teacher's attempts, through action research, to use models-based practice. *European Physical Education Review* 15(2): 175–99.

Casey, A., Dyson, B. and Campbell, A. (2009). Action research in physical education: focusing beyond myself through Cooperative Learning. *Educational Action Research* 17: 407–23.

Cohen, E.G. (1994). Restructuring in the classroom: conditions for productive small groups. *Review of Educational Research* 64: 1–35.

Deutsch, M. (1949). A theory of cooperation and competition. *Human Relations* 2: 129–51.

Dyson, B. (2001). Cooperative Learning in an elementary physical education program. *Journal of Teaching in Physical Education* 20: 264–81.

Dyson, B. (2002). The implementation of Cooperative Learning in an elementary physical education program. *Journal of Teaching Physical Education* 22: 69–85.

Dyson, B., Griffin, L. and Hastie, P. (2004). Sport education, tactical games, and Cooperative Learning: theoretical and pedagogical considerations. *Quest* 56: 226–40.

Dyson, B. and Grineski, S. (2001). Using Cooperative Learning structures in physical education. *Journal of Physical Education, Recreation and Dance* 72: 28–31.

Dyson, B.P., Linehan, N.R. and Hastie, P.A. (2010). The ecology of Cooperative Learning in elementary school physical education classes. *Journal of Teaching in Physical Education* 29: 113–30.

Gillies, R.M. (2006). Teachers' and students' verbal behaviours during cooperative and small-group learning. *British Journal of Educational Psychology* 76: 271–87.

Grenier, M. (2006). A social constructionist perspective of teaching and learning in inclusive physical education. *Adapted Physical Activity Quarterly* 23: 245–60.

Goudas, M. and Magotsiou, E. (2009). The effects of a cooperative physical education program on students' social skills. *Journal of Applied Sport Psychology* 21: 356–64.

Haerens, L., Kirk, D., Cardon, G. and De Bourdeaudhuij, I. (2011). Toward the development of a pedagogical model for health-based physical education. *Quest* 63: 321–38.

Johnson, D.W. and Johnson, R.T. (1989). *Cooperation and competition: theory and research*. Edina, MN: Interaction Books.

Johnson, D.W. and Johnson, R.T. (1999). *Learning together and alone: cooperative, competitive, and individualistic learning*, 5th edn. Boston: Allyn & Bacon.

Johnson, D.W. and Johnson, R.T. (2009). An educational psychology success story: social interdependence theory and Cooperative Learning. *Educational Researcher* 38: 365–79.

Johnson, R.T. and Johnson, D.W. (1994). An overview of Cooperative Learning. In J.S. Thousand, R.A. Villa and A.I. Nevin (eds), *Creativity and collaborative learning*, 31–44. Baltimore, MD: Paul H. Brookes Publishing Co.

Kagan, S. (1992). *Cooperative Learning*, 2nd edn. San Clemente, CA: Kagan Publishing.

Kagan, S. (1998). Teams of four are magic! *Cooperative Learning and College Teaching* 9(1): 9.

Kirk, D. (2010). *Physical education futures*. London: Routledge.

Lafont, L., Proeres, M. and Vallet, C. (2007). Cooperative group learning in a team game: role of verbal exchanges among peers. *Social Psychology of Education* 10: 93–113

Metzler, M.W. (2005). *Instructional models for physical education*, 2nd edn. Scottsdale, AZ: Holcomb Hathaway.

Metzler, M.W. (2011). *Instructional models for physical education*, 3rd edn. Scottsdale, AZ: Holcomb Hathaway

Metzler, M.W. and McCullick, B.A. (2008). Introducing innovation to those who matter most: the P-12 pupils' perceptions of the model-based instruction. *Journal of Teaching in Physical Education* 27: 512–28.

Miles, J.C. and Priest, S. (1990). *Adventure programming*. State College, PA: Venture.

Ministry of Education. (2007). *The New Zealand curriculum*. Wellington: Learning Media Limited.

Sapon-Shevin, M. (1994). Cooperative Learning and middle schools: what would it take to really do it right? *Theory into Practice* 33(3): 183–90.

Slavin, R.E. (1986). *Using team Learning*. Baltimore, MD: Center for Social Organization of Schools, The Johns Hopkins University.

Slavin, R.E. (1990). *Cooperative learning: theory, research and practice*. Boston: Allyn and Bacon.

Slavin, R.E. (1996). Research on Cooperative Learning and achievement: what we know, what we need to know. *Contemporary Educational Psychology* 21: 43–69.

Slavin, R.E., Sharan, S., Kagan, S., Hertz Lazarowitz, R., Webb, C. and Schmuck, R. (eds) (1985). *Learning to cooperate, cooperating to learn*. New York: Plenum.

Stanne, M.B., Johnson, D.W. and Johnson, R.T. (1999). Does competition enhance or inhibit motor performance? a meta-analysis. *Psychological Bulletin* 125: 133–54.

Tousignant, M. and Siedentop, D. (1983). A qualitative analysis of task structure in required secondary physical education classes. *Journal of Teaching in Physical Education* 3: 47–57.

Part 1
Context of learning

1 Implementing the Cooperative Learning model in physical education

The experience of New Zealand teachers

Alan Ovens, Ben Dyson and Wayne Smith

> Key terms: school-based research, change in pedagogical practice, student-centred pedagogy, continual professional development

In this chapter we discuss how we, a group of three university faculty, worked with a small group of New Zealand teachers to support their use of the Cooperative Learning model to restructure their teaching of physical education. By working with teachers, we were able to appreciate the complexity of contemporary educational settings and gain a valuable insight into educational practice. This collaborative approach provided valuable insights into the ongoing feasibility of using the Cooperative Learning model in physical education and the factors that enable and constrain teachers' use of Cooperative Learning. We begin with an overview of recent New Zealand curricular reforms particularly with respect to how Cooperative Learning may be a valuable resource for such reforms and their efforts to support the development of quality teaching.

The educational context in New Zealand

Like education in many other Western democracies, the New Zealand education system has undergone significant reform over the past 20 years. Amongst the many changes has been the introduction of a new national curriculum, which introduced a radically different conceptualization of health and physical education (Ministry of Education, 2007). Under this new curriculum health and physical education changed in focus from a more traditional multidisciplinary approach underpinned by performance discourses and social development to one that included a more holistic approach, embracing socio-cultural and critical perspectives (Ovens, 2010). Teachers have been at the forefront of implementing these changes, with an expectation that they place greater emphasis on critical perspectives and inquiry-focused learning approaches.

Another aspect of the reforms has been an increased focus on teaching quality. Evidence of this has been the Ministry of Education-sponsored Best Evidence

Synthesis project (BES), which aims to provide an ongoing synthesis of research information in a manner that can inform educational policy and practice, and has been central to this focus on improving teaching quality. The effect has been an increased attention on how teachers teach. For example, the New Zealand curriculum (NZC) states that, 'students learn best when teachers: create a supportive learning environment; encourage reflective thought and action; enhance the relevance of new learning; facilitate shared learning; make connections to prior learning and experience; provide sufficient opportunities to learn; and inquire into the teaching-learning relationship' (Ministry of Education, 2007, p. 34). Many of these teaching qualities can be found in the Cooperative Learning model (Alton-Lee, 2011), and led us to believe that Cooperative Learning as a pedagogical model would be appropriate to use in the New Zealand school physical education context.

Evidence gathered through the BES shows that 'task design plays a central role in structuring and developing an effective learning community' (Alton-Lee, 2003, p. 27). Mirroring the Cooperative Learning model, the BES suggests that an effective task design should recognize that the social and the cognitive are not distinct domains in practice, and therefore should be integrated and embedded in task design and classroom organization. The BES contends that the most effective and appropriate pedagogical approaches are those that create a learning environment that works like a community. This involves building a sense of cohesion, where care and support are generated through the practices and interactions of teachers and students. It is one in which students feel accepted and encouraged to actively engage in shared activities and conversations with other students. 'The learning community concept emphasises not only the role the teacher takes in directly interacting with students, but also the key role the teacher's pedagogical approaches have in shaping peer culture' (Alton-Lee, 2003, p. 22). An active, engaged community learning approach is enhanced when teachers' organization and task designs develop a learning community in which students learn how to support the learning of each member of the community. Difference and diversity become central to our understanding of community. Such a community recognizes and utilizes students' skills to manage complementary problem-solving roles with boys and girls of different ethnicities.

> The learning community concept places importance on the interdependence of socio-cultural and cognitive dimensions of individual accountability. It is one that encourages students to develop effective co-operative and other social skills to enable group processing to facilitate learning for all participants.
>
> (Alton-Lee, 2003, p. 22)

The NZC and BES also support teaching and learning approaches that encourage reflective learners and a reflective teaching approach labelled 'teaching as inquiry' (Sinnema *et al.*, 2011; Ministry of Education, 2007). A teaching-as-inquiry approach requires teachers to reflect on the impact of their teaching on their students (Sinnema *et al.*, 2011). 'The teacher uses evidence from research and their own past practice and that of their colleagues to plan teaching and learning opportunities aimed at achieving the outcomes prioritised in the focusing inquiry' (Alton-Lee, 2003, p. 35). In the same way that teachers are encouraged to reflect on their practice, learners are encouraged to develop the ability to pause and consider the nature of what they are learning from an experience. The evidence suggests that teachers encourage this when they design tasks and create opportunities that require students to critically evaluate the material they use. In this research project we adopted a community-of-researchers approach that sought to embrace a collegial, inquiry-focused, reflexive teaching and teacher-as-researcher context (Stenhouse, 1975).

The above overview reflects how contemporary curriculum and pedagogical developments in New Zealand, and by inclusion health and physical education (HPE), provided a supportive environment to trial this Cooperative Learning research project. The questions asked in the project were not only *if* the Cooperative Learning model was appropriate in the New Zealand school HPE context but also what enabling and constraining factors impacted on its success in terms of student learning. The significance of the research was in gaining an understanding of the context-dependent complexities that impact on physical education teachers' ability to employ the model in their school HPE lessons. In the presentation of the data and analysis of findings we seek to answer how the teacher-researchers adapted the model to meet their particular situated context. To this end, we highlight the situation-specific complexities the teachers negotiated in their implementation of the Cooperative Learning model in their school.

Methodology

The project employed the idea of a professional learning community to conceptualize how the project participants worked together to implement Cooperative Learning as a pedagogical model. The advantage of thinking of ourselves as a learning community was that it broke down the traditional hierarchies associated with researcher–participant relationships and respected the knowledge each participant brought to the project. Inquiry and professional learning were critical in this approach, and to facilitate this each participant teacher was supported to undertake action research into their own teaching (Elliot, 1991; Groundwater-Smith and Mockler, 2005). The university-based members of the school group acted as 'critical friends' to this teacher inquiry through workshops and visits. In this way, one outcome of the project was a series of individual case studies of the receptivity and innovation of each teacher's involvement. A second outcome was the analysis of the collective experiences of the research group and the teachers' experiences implementing the Cooperative Learning model. Regular meetings allowed the participants to share their individual experiences and engage in a collective analysis of themes and issues.

The project itself was divided into three phases. Phase one focused on building the learning community, as this was central to the idea that we wished to 'research with' teachers rather than do 'research on' teachers. A purposive sampling approach (Patton, 2002) was used to identify and select the teacher participants.

We sought to work with participant teachers who were experienced teachers and capable of implementing a new pedagogical model within their teaching. We also sought teachers who were working with different year levels, from both primary and secondary schools. The teachers were identified through our discussion with a professional development support unit who worked regularly with teachers in the Auckland region. Once identified, the teachers were invited to participate through email.

At the start of the project our professional learning community was composed of 14 people: three university researchers, three teachers working at the primary-school level, six teachers working at the junior secondary level and one working at the senior secondary level, and a research assistant. Of the participant teachers, eight were female and two were male. This provided a group small enough to meet regularly and have everyone's input into discussion while also providing a diverse mix of participants. One teacher, Kaye, had used Cooperative Learning to teach dance to Year 7 and 8 students, a year before this study. During the course of the project, three of the teachers withdrew. As part of the initial phase of the study, everyone was involved in a series of three workshops to outline the project, assess participants' needs, deepen participants' understanding of Cooperative Learning as a pedagogical practice and support the development of their individual lesson plans and units of instruction.

The second phase of the project involved supporting the participant teachers to implement the Cooperative Learning model in their own teaching as a case study of their own inquiry and reflection. The aim was for the teachers to implement at least two cycles of action research, which, in practice, roughly equated to a unit of work of four to six weeks. To facilitate this, each participant teacher was paired with a university researcher who acted as the teacher's critical friend. The intention was that this pairing would meet weekly to discuss and plan the lessons, and set goals for the following week. However, in practice, this varied depending on the needs of the teacher and the exigencies of the unit of work being taught. In addition, extreme bad weather during the winter term meant that the project was put on hold for several participants until the spring term.

As part of their action research, the participant teachers were asked to collate evidence of their experiences with the Cooperative Learning model as it related to the pedagogical and content issues they encountered. Evidence collected and reflected on by the teachers could include lesson plans, teaching resources, examples of student work or peer observations. Selected lessons were observed by the university researchers using a Cooperative Learning verification sheet to check coherence with the pedagogical model. These observations, both formal and informal, were then shared with the teacher to help the teachers to critically reflect on their teaching process. In addition, each teacher was interviewed at the start of, mid-way through and at the end of the project.

The final phase of the project involved evaluating the key outcomes of the study. This involved both collective and individual meetings that were audio-taped and transcribed. For group meetings, the participant teachers were asked to share elements of their school-based experiences of the Cooperative Learning model, which were then collectively discussed by the group.

The researchers analysed all the data produced from the project using constant comparison and inductive analysis (Denzin and Lincoln, 2005; Lincoln and Guba, 1985) to develop and consider emergent themes. For this chapter, the data were analysed in relation to two questions:

1   What are teachers' perspectives of the feasibility of the Cooperative Learning model as a pedagogy for the New Zealand curriculum?
2   What factors enable and constrain teachers' ability to implement the Cooperative Learning model?

Findings and discussion

The project supported the participating teachers to implement the Cooperative Learning model into their own diverse teaching situations. In the following discussion we initially consider data in relation to the feasibility of Cooperative Learning as a pedagogical model for implementing the New Zealand curriculum. In relation to this, the teachers' perspectives were grouped into two categories relating to personal philosophy and changing pedagogy. We then consider the factors that enabled and constrained teachers' ability to implement the Cooperative Learning into their teaching.

Feasibility

Discussions with the participant teachers supported the view that Cooperative Learning, as a pedagogical model, was compatible with current educational reforms in New Zealand and more importantly their philosophical perspective. In the teachers' view, the Cooperative Learning model provided a teaching approach that supported the ideas in the New Zealand curriculum, overlapped with many of the professional development initiatives undertaken in schools and resonated with teachers' own personal philosophies about good teaching. In other words, in the teachers' view, there was a strong coherence between the ideas being promoted in the New Zealand reform movement and this Cooperative Learning model.

Two examples of this can be read in the comments made by two of the teachers in their final interviews. For Sally, who taught Year 4 students in a primary school, the Cooperative Learning model aligned with both the national curriculum and the way her school was developing their specific school curriculum. In her opinion, the Cooperative Learning model

> links to inquiry learning and the children being principled learners and being risk takers and inquirers and reflectors and thinkers. Those are the key elements of the learner profile and that's linked to the key competencies of the New Zealand Curriculum as well, so it's all related.

For Jackson, working with senior secondary students (Year 11 and 12), the emphasis was on improving the educational outcomes for Maori students (the indigenous race of New Zealand). He saw the explicit connection between the school scheme of work and the Cooperative Learning model's pedagogical practices that he was implementing in his lessons. He observed social skill development and classroom equity similar to that presented in the published literature (Cohen, 1994; Johnson and Johnson, 2009). For example, he commented that Cooperative Learning 'seems to be making the classroom a positive place for the students to socialise and work and develop their understanding of things and limit their behaviour problems in classes'. For Jackson, this related directly to the aim of raising Maori achievement.

Related to this was the belief that the Cooperative Learning model enabled teachers to create a positive learning environment. Teachers felt that the model allowed them to become more student-centred in their teaching, allowing them to shift more responsibility to the students while simultaneously providing opportunities for students to be more included, supported and focused in their learning, which is similar to findings in other research (Casey *et al.*, 2009; Dyson *et al.*, 2010). As Sally revealed, 'I think that the kids are getting a lot out of it, particularly socially and cognitively.'

A strong factor in shaping the teachers' opinions was the positive outcomes they could see happening in the lessons. Similar to the findings of Johnson and Johnson (2009), a salient feature was the teachers' perspectives that the quality of student learning had improved. For example, Kay, who worked at the primary-school level as a specialist dance educator, explained that the implementation of the Cooperative Learning model

> meant that my dance programme was much more interesting for them [the students] and I think their level of work improved as a result, whereas in parts, I've done solo warm ups right throughout the whole cycle but now I put those in half way through, and the work I've had from the students has been outstanding. ... Much higher standard and a deeper standard.

The teachers also spoke of a range of other improvement in the quality of learning, such as enhanced student motivation, improved behaviour, higher-quality cognitive and physical involvement, improved social interaction and an increased sense of empowerment and responsibility. These benefits reflect a more positive learning environment.

Another benefit reported by the teachers was the increased sense of empowerment and responsibility for the student learning it enabled; this finding supports the concepts presented in the literature (Dyson *et al.*, 2004). This belief is evident in the comment Kay made in respect to her dance lessons. She reported that she was 'giving them more independence, giving them a bigger role ... realising that the students have the ability, more ability than I allow them or expect them to have'. Several of the teachers were impressed by the way their students engaged in the lessons. There were no 'freeriders' (Slavin, 1996) in their classes or 'competent bystanders' (Tousignant and Siedentop, 1983).

Enabling conditions

Schools are not blank contexts in which innovative curriculum or new ideas are easily implemented (Casey, 2010; Kemmis and Grootenboer, 2008). On the contrary, and in the midst of current reforms, schools are inundated with ideas that create real tensions and dilemmas for teachers. Schools are required to run their own professional development programmes to revise and test new teaching ideas. Viewed in this way, understanding the key factors that enabled and constrained teachers' efforts to implement the Cooperative Learning model becomes salient, not only because of the social and situated nature of teaching, but also because understanding those aspects that enable the Cooperative Learning model are important in order to support its successful implementation (Dyson *et al.*, 2004; Fullan, 2005).

The teachers consistently commented that an enabling factor was their philosophical alignment. That is, Cooperative Learning needed to align with their teaching and learning philosophy. This alignment, or lack of alignment, underpins the reasons why teachers are adopters or non-adopters of a new pedagogical practice. Philosophical alignment appears to provide teachers with the resilience to work through the various constraints present in their work situations and use the model in a generative sense to guide their teaching (Casey *et al.*, 2009).

The teacher's philosophy was important because the Cooperative Learning model had to resonate with their own ideas about good teaching in order for them to experiment with, revise and learn from implementing the model. Sally's comment from her final interview was typical of how the participant teachers viewed an alignment with their own philosophy. First, Sally saw the link between her beliefs about teaching and those implicit in the Cooperative Learning model when she stated that, 'children should be active and interactive … they'll learn best by doing and trying out for themselves and just creating things themselves and problem-solving'. In addition, she stated that the Cooperative Learning model provided the means for students to learn from each other and to problem-solve. Notably Sally also commented that implementing the Cooperative Learning model and being part of the research project has not changed her philosophy, rather, the Cooperative Learning model is coherent within her teaching philosophy.

Alignment of philosophy within the teacher's professional community was also important and this included the department, school and other colleagues such as the visiting researchers. Of particular interest was the way the participating teachers were able to see an alignment between the Cooperative Learning model and the other initiatives the school was prioritizing. This can be seen in the following comment from Michelle in relation to how she integrated Cooperative Learning with her school's emphasis on thinking and differentiation. She comments:

> [T]he thinking skills is embedded in Cooperative Learning through the group processing. I did include the PMS, which is a structure of critical thinking. So I have tried to put a lot in. Differentiation was probably the hardest one. They did choose what level they wanted to work at, but because of the structure of the unit, they were often pushed.

Associated with this concept, the teachers also acknowledged they needed buy-in from the students. Discussing her junior-high class, Jemma reflected, 'If they've bought into it then their motivation is going to be more and they will take more ownership for what they're doing and take it a bit more seriously and take their responsibilities more seriously.'

Constraints

While the participant teachers discussed enablers as largely philosophical in nature, they perceived the factors that limited their ability to implement the Cooperative Learning model in more structural terms. Salient to the implementation of the Cooperative Learning model in schools is the reality that it is a labour-intensive process, which takes time and energy. 'This is not business as usual' (field notes). Time needs to be allocated to planning and organizing the lessons as well as time in the unit to allow students the time to process the work. This is similar to findings from other Cooperative Learning model research projects (Dyson, 2001, 2002; Dyson and Strachan 2004; Dyson *et al.*, 2010). Jemma talked about the lack of time available in the unit of work to concentrate on how students understood their work. She complained:

> [T]ime being a factor, for example the length of the unit, to be able to stop and unpack particular things. But also we're obviously all busy people, and trying to give credit, you know the right amount of time for something like this.

At the end of her third unit Sally commented that she felt her time management had become more efficient: 'It will decrease as it becomes more instinctive because it's a new model ... it will get easier. It will be become more instinctive.' Kay could see the benefits to her students in the long run.

A second limiting factor was the teachers' knowledge of Cooperative Learning. As they experimented with and proceeded through their units of work, they began to want more information and examples of how to implement the Cooperative Learning model, and resources. While they had been to the initial workshops and were able to discuss issues with the visiting researchers who acted as critical friends, they often felt limited by their lack of knowledge of Cooperative Learning. Jemma felt this in the sense that she needed lots of ideas to draw upon, because in her view, 'I'm not a very creative person. I find the creativity, like in thinking outside the square of how it can be implemented in different ways or different activities, just in my teaching in general, that's generally a weak area of mine.' In a similar way, Michelle stated:

> I would have liked to have seen more of what people were doing in a PE context. And seen it in different contexts in PE, to see how people could do it, what worked. With me as well, my lack of understanding or confusion there seemed to be lots of ideas in there. Particularly around what was needed for Cooperative Learning. Were all five elements needed?

Michelle's comment reflected some of the uncertainty she had as she experimented with the model – certainly a typical response in the first year of implementing the Cooperative Learning model (Dyson, 2001, 2002; Dyson *et al.*, 2004). While the initial workshops were important to establish the conceptual and philosophical basis for cooperative learning, there was also an ongoing need to support the teachers.

In addition, the lack of stability of the learning context was a limiting factor. Issues such as student absences, interruptions to lessons or poor learning environment all impacted on the teachers' ability to implement the model. Student absences frustrated teachers in their attempt to shift significant responsibility to the students and undermined the structuring of positive interdependence. Jackson commented that, if students 'don't turn up, like today when we had a few missing I had to change the groups, which changes the dynamics a little bit so that also hinders me and often disorganized [sic] obviously happens'. Interruptions to lessons were caused by a variety of things, including school assemblies, interschool sport or bad weather. Sally talks about how the various things happening in the school life at one point of the year severely limited her attempts to keep implementing Cooperative Learning. She lamented, 'And it just never started going again. And I guess I did elements of it within lessons, but it just, it didn't work, we had no space, and we had the school production and we had no hall.' Sally's comment is a valuable reminder of the way pedagogy is enabled by context and is an emergent phenomenon from complex situations teachers often find themselves situated within (Fullan, 1999; Hodkinson and Hodkinson, 2005).

Not all the elements of the Cooperative Learning model were used in all lessons and in some cases group processing was not seen in a positive light by students.

> Quite interesting though with that, the feedback from my girls was that the group processing, some of them didn't like it. ...They felt it was wasted a little bit because the unit was so rushed. They would have liked to practise.
>
> (Jemma)

One constraint that has been shown in other studies to have an impact is teacher subject matter knowledge (Casey *et al.*, 2009). While it was not readily evident in the data from our participants, we feel it was one of the reasons why our participants chose to remain with or withdraw from the project. This is most easily observed in the comments from Jo, one of the teachers who withdrew from the study. As a primary-school classroom teacher, Jo felt that one of the key contributors to her withdrawal from the project was her lack of physical education content knowledge. As she said, 'In my case I had to make up quite a few things like that so in my case it did take more time and more planning ... but then when it comes to the lesson, you know you're a facilitator.' In addition she explained that the priorities of her senior school management were not physical education.

> [An academic focus] that comes from senior management, but that doesn't happen in PE. ... So for someone like me who doesn't have that experience

in teaching PE, it's a tricky thing to just sort of go out there and do it. Yeah, like for maths, I know that this term I need to be teaching time, temperature, addition and subtraction. But for PE, apart from being told that I need to do ball skills, that's it, yeah. And for someone who's not an experienced PE teacher, I don't know how to go out there and teach ball skills.

Conclusions

Teachers' perspectives are not static, but constantly evolving in response to their ongoing experiences as they teach and reflect upon their teaching and the contexts in which they teach. The reality for teachers often means that in addition to having to teach on a daily basis, they also have to adapt to educational reform, make sense of new and sometimes competing educational ideas promoted through professional development and continue to ensure quality educational outcomes for their students. In other words, while researchers may promote the value of a particular pedagogical model, teachers enact those models within the complex settings of contemporary schooling (Casey *et al.*, 2009; Dyson *et al.*, 2010).

The project demonstrated a positive way in which professionals working in the field of physical education can work collaboratively to enhance the quality of teaching in physical education. By working with teachers, university researchers could provide a supportive framework to help teachers reflect on their teaching and align with the goal of promoting lifelong physical activity (Ministry of Education, 2007).

> Both primary and secondary teacher unions have given feedback to the Iterative BES Programme that student groupwork is a weakness in practice and have advocated for the provision of professional development to support an evidence-based approach to cooperative groupwork in New Zealand.
>
> (Alton-Lee, 2011, p. 17)

Our research suggested that:

1   The Cooperative Learning model can be a feasible pedagogy for New Zealand teachers implementing the revised national curriculum (Ministry of Education, 2007).
2   A number of factors enable and limit implementing the Cooperative Learning model in school settings, but key to this is the necessity of philosophical alignment. Philosophical alignment appears to provide teachers with a resilience to work through the various constraints present in their work situations and use the model in a generative sense to guide their teaching.
3   This change in pedagogical practice takes time, support, guidance and critical reflection.
4   Teachers in this study reported a shift towards an inclusive, student-centred pedagogy and a move away from a teacher-directed and a competitive model of teaching.

To support current reform efforts in schools, where teachers might infuse the Cooperative Learning model to inform their pedagogical decision-making, we propose:

- University faculty work with teachers on continuing professional development to facilitate the Cooperative Learning model in schools with teachers and students.
- Facilitators of ongoing professional development must be aware of the need for philosophical alignment between the teacher's beliefs and the ideas being promoted.
- Initial teacher education programmes must provide a sound professional knowledge base of different pedagogical models (Cooperative Learning, Sport Education, Teaching Games for Understanding, Adventure-based Learning, Personal and Social Responsibility models, etc.).
- Professional development programmes must provide ongoing training and collaborative support in a variety of pedagogical models and innovative pedagogical practices *with* teachers and with students.

Slavin (2010) has stated 'In the learning environments of the 21st century, co-operative learning should play a central role' (p. 174).

References

Alton-Lee, A. (2003). *Quality teaching for diverse students in schooling: best evidence synthesis*. Wellington: Learning Media.

Alton-Lee, A. (2011). (Using) evidence for educational improvement. *Cambridge Journal of Education* 41,(3), 303–29.

Casey, A. (2010). Practitioner research in physical education: teacher transformation through pedagogical and curricular change. Unpublished PhD dissertation, Leeds Metropolitan University.

Casey, A., Dyson, B. and Campbell, A. (2009). Action research in physical education: focusing beyond myself through Cooperative Learning. *Educational Action Research* 17: 407–23.

Cohen, E.G. (1994). Restructuring in the classroom: conditions for productive small groups. *Review of Educational Research* 64: 1–35.

Denzin, N. and Lincoln, Y. (2005). *The handbook of qualitative research*, 3rd edn. Thousand Oaks, CA: Sage Publications.

Dyson, B. (2001). Cooperative Learning in an elementary school physical education program. *Journal of Teaching in Physical Education* 20: 264–81.

Dyson, B. (2002). The implementation of Cooperative Learning in an elementary school physical education program. *Journal of Teaching in Physical Education* 22: 69–85.

Dyson, B., Griffin, L. and Hastie, P. (2004). Sport education, tactical games, and Cooperative Learning: theoretical and pedagogical considerations. *Quest* 56: 226–40.

Dyson, B., Linehan, R.N. and Hastie, P. (2010). The ecology of Cooperative Learning in elementary school physical education classes. *Journal of Teaching in Physical Education* 29: 113–30.

Dyson, B. and Strachan, K. (2004). The ecology of Cooperative Learning in a high school physical education program. *Waikato Journal of Education* 10: 117–40.

Elliot, J. (1991). *Action research for educational change*. Buckingham: Open University Press.

Fullan, M. (1999). *Change forces: the sequel*. London: Falmer Press.

Fullan, M. (2005). *Leadership and sustainability systems: thinkers in action*. Thousand Oaks, CA: Corwin Press.

Groundwater-Smith, S. and Mockler, N. (2005). Practitioner research in education: beyond celebration. Paper presented to the Australian Association for Research in Education, Cairns, Australia, 4–6 July.

Hodkinson, H. and Hodkinson, P. (2005). Improving school teachers' workplace learning. *Research Papers in Education* 20: 109–31.

Johnson, D.W. and Johnson, R.T. (2009). An educational psychology success story: social interdependence theory and Cooperative Learning. *Educational Researcher* 38: 365–79.

Kemmis, S. and Grootenboer, P. (2008). Situating praxis in practice: practice architectures and the cultural, social and material conditions for practice. In S. Kemmis and T. J. Smith (eds), *Enabling praxis: challenges for education*, 37–62. Rotterdam: Sense.

Lincoln, Y.S. and Guba, E. (1985). *Naturalistic inquiry*. Newbury Park, CA: Sage.

Ministry of Education (2007). *The New Zealand curriculum*. Wellington: Learning Media Limited.

Ovens, A. (2010). The New Zealand curriculum: emergent insights and complex renderings. *Asia-Pacific Journal of Health, Sport and Physical Education* 1(1): 27–32.

Patton, M.Q. (2002). *Qualitative research and evaluation methods*, 3rd edn. London: Sage.

Sinnema, C., Sewell, A. and Milligan, A. (2011). Evidence-informed collaborative inquiry for improving teaching and learning. *Asia-Pacific Journal of Teacher Education* 39: 247–61.

Slavin, R.E. (1996). Research on Cooperative Learning and achievement: what we know, what we need to know. *Contemporary Educational Psychology* 21: 43–69.

Slavin, R. (2010). Cooperative Learning: what makes group-work work? In H. Dumont, D. Instance and F. Benavides (eds), *The nature of learning: using research to inspire practice*. Paris: OECD.

Stenhouse, L. (1975). *An introduction to curriculum research and development*. London: Heinemann.

Tousignant, M. and Siedentop, D. (1983). A qualitative analysis of task structure in required secondary physical education classes. *Journal of Teaching in Physical Education* 3: 47–57.

2 Teacher action in the Cooperative Learning model in the physical education classroom

Ingrid Bähr and Jonas Wibowo

Key terms: *erziehender Sportunterricht*, educational philosophy, teacher action, student performance

---

Introduction

Over the last 10 years, in sports pedagogy in Germany there has been a call for an *erziehender Sportunterricht*, which when translated means that physical education should give priority to the educational aspects of its remit. This type of education would incorporate movement-oriented and personality-oriented learning, such as achieving social competences or self-determination, an objective reflected in what has been called the 'dual contract' of physical education in German schools. That is, education 'in' and 'through' physical education. This claim is also made for school sports, since physical education and sports are not separated in the German sport curriculum. These claims call for a review of the contents, structures and teaching methods used in physical education (PE) as well as the role of the PE teacher. The subsequent debate exposed an 'instructional gap' or *Vermittlungslücke* (Prohl, 2004), which implies a discrepancy between scholarly and educational policy claims on one hand and classroom reality or rather established teaching methods on the other hand (Casey and Dyson, 2009).

Today, the Cooperative Learning model is considered an example of *erziehender Sportunterricht* that would allow for closing this instructional gap. In Germany the Cooperative Learning model in general can be defined in terms of Slavin (1989), where students work in small groups in order to help each other to learn a subject. In the German PE perspective, all the five elements of the Cooperative Learning model mentioned in the Introduction to this book are regarded as essential. But there is an emphasis on the students' accountability and responsibility for their group work process and result in a special way, affected by the tradition of educational philosophy, which is quite popular in the academic discussion of German sport didactics (Meinberg, 2010). Therefore, a short rationale for the Cooperative Learning model from this perspective will be given in this chapter. Our third section focuses on the question, 'what kind of teacher action in the setting of Cooperative Learning is necessary to provoke students' accountability and responsibility in their learning processes?'. It will be shown that giving some leeway to the students in their cooperative tasks seems to be a central feature of Cooperative Learning. Subsequently, in the fourth section we will present a quasi-experimental field study that analyses and contemplates teacher action in three different class settings: two cooperative classes ('Jigsaw' and 'Group Tournament', as experimental groups) and a traditional, 'teacher-centred' approach (as a control group). The results of the study will be presented and discussed in the final section.

Educational philosophy-oriented reasons for the Cooperative Learning model in PE

Educational philosophical approaches attribute a central significance to the active experience of the learner (Prohl, 2010). Moreover, they emphasize that education must be understood as a self-activity of the subject. Self-activity must not be understood as an individualist activity but always as an interaction with 'the other' in a double sense: on one hand, 'the other' in the sense of our material world, for instance the environment in which we perform a movement; and on the other hand, 'the other' in the sense of our social environment (Meinberg, 1994). Thus, during a gymnastics class, movement relationships are established both with the gym equipment and the person providing assistance. From the perspective of educational philosophy (Prohl, 2010), the central moment in PE is the entering and designing of these movement relationships in a 'self-active' way, which is described by the German term *Bildung*. Following a long academic tradition, there are two different words, *Bildung* and *Erziehung*, in the German language: *Bildung* can be done only by the student him- or herself, whereas education (*Erziehung*) is the job of the teacher: in the sense that the teacher creates with his or her pedagogical inputs the environment for the students' *Bildung*.

If we take this argumentation seriously, we deduce a paradox:

- On the one hand, *Bildung* cannot be created directly (by the teacher). Only the student him- or herself can act in a self-active way, the teacher cannot act on the learner's behalf. For example the teacher may force the student to play basketball in a team; but an active and gainful involvement in the game, a feeling for the game and the team-mates, becoming part of the team – all these things can neither be commanded nor enforced. They originate only through the voluntary self-activity of the student, called *Bildung*.
- On the other hand, we do know that being involved with a team, becoming a part of it, does not happen automatically just by playing the game, and neither does learning how to shoot accurate lay-ups or other sportive skills. All of which means that social and movement-oriented learning do not happen automatically – at least not systematically.

The paradox in this is that the teacher can't create *Bildung* (on the student's behalf) directly, but neither does students' *Bildung* systematically take place without any action of the teacher. From the German perspective of educational philosophy, a gainful handling of this paradox is seen in creating the 'conditions for the possibility of *Bildung*', of which the students can subsequently take advantage. The teachers' action (education) is, then, first and foremost an initiation of self-activity *(Bildung)*. For example, as a teacher, I can systematically use the Cooperative Learning model to create conditions that will motivate the students to enter constructive movement relationships with each other by their own acts. The pedagogue Benner calls this type of educational influence a 'summons to self-activity' (Benner, 2001, p. 80).

From the perspective of the theoretical assumptions described hitherto, the educational potential of PE to integrate movement- and personality-oriented learning lies in creating specific situations in terms of a summons, an invitation. In other words, this summons by the teacher during teaching will help the students initiate gainful movement relationships in a self-active way (not only on the movement level but also on the social level), while they also perceive these relationships as successful. As a result, the *process* of collaboration while developing movement tasks becomes the central carrier of the educational potential – at least as central as the learning result of that process. In this perspective both the process and the result of learning in PE are of equal importance. This is because the process of learning needs orientation towards an aim, which in PE is generally the individual growth of movement competence. In that sense, the educational potential can be unfolded in an ideal-typical way through Cooperative Learning, for instance.

As a consequence of these theoretical considerations, the following question regarding the teacher's action arises: how should the teacher act in the Cooperative Learning model during PE so as to allow the educational potentials described above to be best unveiled? In other words, how should the teacher act to make sure the students learn in a 'self-active' way, in the sense of *Bildung*?

Consequences of the perspective of educational philosophy for teacher action in the Cooperative Learning model

The following considerations of teacher action in the Cooperative Learning model focus on the monitoring phase undertaken by the teacher during the autonomous work of students in small groups. Of course, the phases of lesson planning (especially task formulation for small groups), grouping, the organization of general conditions and the reflection on group work are crucial for the success of the Cooperative Learning model. However, research literature already contains well-developed information on those topics (e.g. Dyson *et al.*, 2010; Green and Green, 2007; Bähr, 2005; Konrad and Traub, 2001; Grineski, 1996). Nevertheless, teacher action during the phase when groups work autonomously has not been described as thoroughly in the literature: indeed the only 'advice' it does offer is that the teacher should slip into the role of a counsellor and monitor the students' learning process. But it does not explain, in detail, *how* concretely this role should be played and what the teacher as a counsellor should do or avoid doing (the latter is the focus of the following elaboration and the empirical study presented in the fourth section). Concurrently, the optimal teacher action will be depicted alongside the educational philosophy-related considerations about *Bildung* discussed in the previous section.

An examination of the literature suggests that the teacher is expected, having first made sure that all students have understood the organizational form of the group work and their respective tasks, to step out of his or her role as 'direct imparter' of optimal movement execution sequences and social norms. He or she then becomes a monitor of the learning processes. This means that ideally, the teacher becomes active only when the students ask for help. In this way the teacher functions as the expert for the respective movement task, but also as a socially competent counsellor who ultimately offers 'self-help assistance'.

But what are the guidelines for this sort of teacher action? From the perspective of educational philosophy, there is a feature of the Cooperative Learning model that should be highlighted, a feature that is closely related to students' accountability and responsibility for their working process and results. Various authors mention this characteristic only implicitly but, for example, Huber emphasizes that 'the task formulation in the Cooperative Learning model should always give *leeway for decision making*' (Huber, 2001, p. 223). This means that the students should be allowed and *must* be able to make decisions as to how the specific movement task or problem is to be solved. Huber argues that this feature, which is typical in cooperative teaching and learning settings, is needed in order to make the students learn how to 'find the critical questions and tasks and acquire new knowledge and new skills' (p. 223). In order to ensure that the students really work self-actively, it is the duty of the teacher not only to afford them leeway in their cooperative task, but he or she should expect and allow them to make use of that flexibility. As a consequence, the teacher must accept and admit that the students may try to solve the problem in their own ways, that is to say, they might take wrong turns or move in circles. Studies show that most teachers have a hard time dealing with that requirement (Haag *et al.*, 2000). Many teachers intervene much too often and too invasively into the students' group work. According to the studies mentioned earlier, the basic conflict in the mind of the teachers is the following: should they allow students to do things their own way (and therefore maybe also make mistakes, engage in conflicts or explore unexpected solutions) or should they monitor or guide the students' learning processes closely (in order to avoid mistakes, conflicts and taking the wrong turn)? Educational philosophy considers it of central significance that the students' self-activity is not disturbed or disrupted through invasive teacher action; otherwise, there is no room left for pedagogically valuable self-responsible and self-active learning.

One consequence of these considerations is that while planning units using the Cooperative Learning model – especially while selecting the cooperative script and the task formulation – it is important to make a mental note of how much leeway should be given (or conceded) to the target group. The educational philosophy pleads for as much leeway as possible but also as much structure as necessary. Out of the conceptions of the Cooperative Learning model that have been pre-structured to different extents, the teacher selects the one appropriate for the learning group. For instance, the 'Jigsaw classroom' might be a more appropriate task for a learning group who are less experienced in autonomous working than a Group Tournament because in a Jigsaw, the phases of group autonomous work are more pre-structured as a result of the use of the expert roles. In summary, we can assert that the teacher should try his or her best to confine themselves to being responsive (that is, when the students request it) when intervening in a group's work.

Consequently, 'invasive' interventions (which means that the teacher interferes in group work without being asked to do so by the students) should be reserved for situations presenting a risk for the students, where the students have stopped dealing with the task (either lapsing into sideline activities or not doing anything at all) or situations where the group work gets paralysed over a certain time by disputes or by the lack of constructive suggestions. However, both 'invasive' interventions as well as 'responsive' interventions (teacher interferes only when he or she is asked for help by the students) are 'teaching moments', as Metzler (2011) described them, and they are important and non-negotiable aspects of the teacher's job. Nonetheless, the Cooperative Learning model does not advocate that teachers should adopt a role of 'competent bystander' (Tousignant and Siedentop, 1983). However, if the students ask the teacher to help or if one of the situations mentioned above arises requiring an invasive intervention, then the question arises as to how the teacher should behave during this intervention. A study conducted by Dann *et al.* (1999) in the context of geography and language instruction offers a first indication. The researchers identified the following features as positive specifics of the teacher action:

- High *orientation* as the teacher's attitude while gathering information: the teacher observes the situation within the group thoroughly and listens carefully to the group's discussions before intervening. Likewise during the teacher–student intervention, the teacher catches up on the prevailing situation of the group work, for instance by asking relevant questions over and over.
- High score for *task orientation* is given when the teacher estimates the intragroup process correctly, when he or she understands the students' thoughts and concerns and addresses the students' problems in an appropriate manner.
- High *quality of contact*: the teacher acts in a friendly and respectful manner towards the students, he or she encourages them to carry on with the work and does not behave in an offensive way but in a comforting way wherever necessary.
- Very little *guidance:* in the first instance, the teacher tries his or her best to keep their knowledge to themselves and he or she constructively monitors the problem-solving process by asking questions and encouraging targeted suggestions (p. 128).

The latter implied procedure is in accordance with what is called 'the Socratic conversation' (according to Heckmann, 1993) and which some authors consider a recommended action for teacher intervention (Bähr, 2005; Landau, 2005). The central moment of the Socratic conversation consists of *questions* that the teacher asks and through which he or she tries to steer the conversation with regard to the topical issue or learning problem, ideally in the characteristic style of a reciprocal communication structure between the teacher and the student. A similar thought can also be found in Green and Green (2007), who identify the question as the 'basic pattern of instruction's interaction structure' (p. 114). The published literature on the Cooperative Learning model in PE hardly addresses the quality and the application context of questions in general and of the Socratic conversation in particular.

The explanations above show that both on the theoretical and the empirical level, there is still need for clarification on the way the Cooperative Learning model should be implemented in PE, especially as far as the teacher action with regard to groups' autonomous work is concerned. This fact gives cause to focus more profoundly on teacher action. Hereafter we shall present a field study evaluating the Cooperative Learning model in PE and which deals with the matters discussed in the previous section. In that process, we shall determine the conformity of teacher action with the concept – that is, find an answer to the question as to whether the teachers who participated in the field study have applied the Cooperative Learning model the way it is described in the technical literature.

Field study evaluating the Cooperative Learning model in PE with regard to teacher action

Lesson-setting

The reported study observed the instruction of nine Form 5 classes (N = 238; 10–12 years old) over six 90-minute lessons in regular PE with the learning goals 'handstand' and 'dive-forward roll'. The instruction was carried out according to three different methodological-didactic concepts, using two of the Cooperative Learning model structures: six classes were instructed according to the Cooperative Learning model, three by means of the 'Jigsaw' script (Aronson and Patnoe, 1997) and the other three by means of the Group Tournament script (Slavin, 1994). Three further classes received traditional PE instruction on the same content. In these classes, the exercise sequences consisted of working under tight guidance at stations and generally a rather directive teacher style as a methodological framework (the 'teacher-centred instruction style'). The students were instructed by their respective subject teachers (two female; four male: average age 39 years). The teachers involved were trained in the application of the different concepts. As outlined previously, the teachers were instructed to assume the role of counsellors with regard to the autonomous group-work phases. In order to ensure comparability between the six classes, the teachers were given detailed guidelines for the organization and content framework of all six 90-minute lessons as well as various teaching materials (i.e. pre-printed cards with work assignments, illustrations and reflection sheets).

Based on the results of the motor skills entry test carried out prior to the lesson series, the students were assigned to small groups within the individual classes according to their motor performance. Taking into account the respective teaching method's requirements, the individual small groups of the Group Tournament classes were composed heterogeneously with regard to ability. However, across the small groups, the grouping was homogeneous with regard to ability, so the tournament between groups was fair. As to the Jigsaw classes, they were homogeneous ability groups. Based on the entry test method mentioned above, each class was composed of five to six mixed-gender groups of four to five students each. The Group Tournament classes were informed that at the end of the lessons series, there would be a gymnastics Olympiad in the form of a group contest. In the Jigsaw classes, all groups were required to contribute to a part of a gymnastic performance, which would be presented to a parallel class as a show at the close of the lesson series. Well informed about these settings, the students had time until the fifth 90-minute class to learn the elements 'handstand' and 'dive-forward roll'. In order to ensure that the motivational conditions were similar for the teacher-centred classes, these classes as a whole practised a gymnastics show/performance developed by the teacher and which was to be performed in front of another class.

Analysis of teacher action with regard to a typical application of the Cooperative Learning model in PE

In what follows, we present an analysis of teacher action in the Cooperative Learning model in comparison to teacher action in teacher-centred instruction. This analysis attempts to examine how and to what extent Cooperative Learning methods clearly differ from teacher-centred instruction. Therefore, we highlighted four evaluation criteria following Dane and Schneider (1998):

1   adherence – compliance with the programme guidelines (= integrity of execution);
2   exposure – implementation frequency (= programme range);
3   programme delivery (= quality of programme transfer);
4   participant responsiveness (= participants' involvement).

These criteria were originally developed within the psychology discourse and seem to be adequate for an application in a pedagogical context as they focus on both the teacher's action and on the student's action. A unilateral evaluation of teacher action (as is especially the case with the first two criteria) would be problematical from the perspective of educational philosophy since the subject's self-activity, which is interpreted as the central mechanism of education, would not be depicted directly in teacher action. The last two components of the Dane and Schneider criteria transcend the teacher's action: by considering the teacher–student interaction, the third criterion, 'quality of programme transfer', implicates at least potentially an analysis of student action as well. And finally, the fourth criterion, 'involvement of the participants' with a focus on the students, deals explicitly with the moment of the students' self-activity.

In the following subsections each of the Dane and Schneider criteria will be explained in terms of how data were collected and which of the emerging relate to the criteria. In fact, there are two research questions for each criterion: (1) whether teachers are able to implement Cooperative Learning in the classroom typical to the concept (which means high transfer quality to the Cooperative Learning model); and (2) whether any difference can be seen in comparison with teacher-centred instruction. The thesis is that if there is a high transfer quality of the Cooperative Learning model then there should be a clear difference from the teacher-centred approach.

Integrity of execution

1   Is the essential phase structure of the Cooperative Learning model recognizable in the classroom (giving work assignments to the groups phase; group work phase; reflection/presentation of learning result in the whole class phase)?
2   To what extent does this phase structure differ from a teacher-centred instructional approach?

In order to ensure that the concept guidelines were observed, we started by creating outline plans (in the sense of transcripts) that were to control the phase structure of the lesson. The relevant phases of the lesson were defined according to a model by Dann *et al.* (1999). The outline plans stated that in all the classes, scheduled work assignments (Cooperative Learning model) or proper instructions on what was to be learned (teacher-centred class) were given to the students. They also revealed that in all subsequent classes, phases of group work (Cooperative Learning model) or phases of supervised exercises (teacher-centred class) took place in their respective setting. Finally, the outline plans also revealed that the scheduled evaluation of the respective class work results had been carried out in the form of a reflection phase and/or a final presentation. In the classes instructed cooperatively, there were one or two phases of autonomous group work per class hour. In the teacher-centred classes instead, there were three or four rather short exercise and execution phases per class hour, alternating with phases determined by teachers' action.

Programme range

1   Do the teachers manage to secure enough activity time in the Cooperative Learning model classes?
2   What are the differences between the Cooperative Learning model and the teacher-centred instruction?

To verify the phases of autonomous group work (Cooperative Learning model) and the phases of practice (teacher-centred instruction) the teachers' activities (group dialogue; assisting; observing; organization; demonstrating; announcement; class dialogue) as well as the students' activities were categorized in a number of typical actions (italicized below). The categories were drawn from the video documentation of the classes. The categorization was not only done with regard to their frequency per class hour but also with regard to the length as expected in the respective concepts. The video data were divided into two-minute sequences over the total class time. Activity time in this setting refers to the students 'trying to handstand; trying to make a high flight roll', that is, trying to improve their performance for gymnastics.

For each of those sequences two trained observers scored the activity that was undertaken in the main course in the respective sequence. This procedure provided the evidence that the share of students' exercise time (i.e. self-motivated exercise within small-group work) in the total class time was 52 per cent in the Jigsaw and 50 per cent in the Group Tournament and, by contrast, 32 per cent in the teacher-centred class (i.e. self-motivated exercise upon teacher's instructions; see Figure 2.1). In the case of the latter method the students spent more time *listening/watching* or participating in channelled *group dialogues*. In these classes the teacher accordingly uttered *explanations/announcements* frequently or for a longer time and led *group dialogues*. Alternatively the teacher *demonstrated* an exercise or let students demonstrate an exercise. This result must be interpreted in terms of the respective lesson design using the specific concepts: in the Cooperative Learning model, the share of a student's self-directed exercise time is supposed to be as high as possible, while by comparison, the teaching phases framed by the teacher make up a larger share of the teacher-centred instruction.

In summary, for the last two subsections it can be stated that the teachers abided by the lesson plans. It was also shown that the phase structure inherent in the concepts of the Cooperative Learning model and the teacher-centred approach respectively was recognizable, and the last subsection showed that the self-directed exercise time prevailed to the extent allowed by the respective concepts.

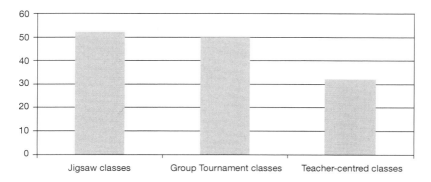

Figure 2.1 Share of students' activity time (i.e. self-motivated exercise within small-group work) in total class time.

Quality of programme transfer

1   Do the teachers manage to let the students work autonomously in the Cooperative Learning model?
2   Does their practice differ from that of the teachers in the teacher-centred instruction in that regard?

One of the aspects relevant when controlling the transfer quality of the lesson concepts is the teacher's invasiveness (as explained previously). It would be typical in a Cooperative Learning model classroom for the teacher to place his or her expert knowledge and his or her pedagogical competence at the students' disposal only when they require him or her to do so (= responsive intervention). The contrary applies for an instructional set-up such as teacher-centred instruction: the teacher interferes in the group work or any exercising process at his or her own discretion, that means when he or she has not been asked by the students to do so (= invasive intervention). For that purpose, data were collected from two perspectives, the teacher's lesson diary and observation of the video documents. The teacher's personal view was established by means of a lesson-diary item after each class hour: 'Today, I did not at all/often intervene unless the students requested me to do so' (bipolar survey scale developed by the authors with the poles 'not at all' = 1 and 'often' = 4; for details concerning the psychometric properties refer to Bähr, 2009). The Jigsaw classes scored an average of 1.6 scale points for the six 90-minute lessons, the lowest of all. The Group Tournament classes had a slightly higher average result of 2.3, while the highest result was found in the teacher-centred classes (2.7). Furthermore, in the course of the video data analysis, each intervention by the teachers was appraised from an observer perspective by trained observers as to whether they were to be considered 'invasive' or 'responsive' according to the above definition. The invasive interventions made up 32 per cent of the total amount of intervention for the Jigsaw, 38 per cent for the Group Tournament and 71 per cent for teacher-centred instruction.

The results show that both in the teachers' personal view and from the observer perspective, invasive interventions by the teacher occurred considerably more often in teacher-centred instruction than in the Cooperative Learning model. A key quotation from the interviews with the teachers of the Group Tournament classes in the Cooperative Learning model concepts supports this finding: 'To begin with, I did take it seriously … your instructions, I mean, that if possible, I should not intervene, and only when it gets dangerous and only if it is the only option.'

With reference to Haag *et al.* (2000), the degree of steering of the learning process by the teacher in the case of an intervention into autonomous group work represents another analysis criterion, which was taken into account in defining the quality of concept transfer.

Therefore, in the course of the video data analysis, each teacher intervention was evaluated by observer on a bipolar scale with the poles 1 = 'directive' and 4 = 'Socratic' (see Figure 2.2). This showed that within the Cooperative Learning model methods, there is a slightly stronger tendency to adopt the Socratic scheme for the teacher–student interaction as explained previously (the right-hand side of

Directive instructions, proposal of solutions for movement problems		Undecided	Non-directive instructions, questions, Socratic scheme, indirect instructions			
The teacher gives direct instructions aimed at solving the movement problem concerned; 'it works this way'; 'you have to do it like this'; teacher never asks a question back, instead transfers immediately (and without being requested to do so) and directly expert knowledge/skills.			The teacher relinquishes the learning process to the student; encourages the students to search for and find own solutions for movement problems; avoids giving direct instructions to the students during interventions; tries to solve any problems arising through a 'Socratic' conversation during which the teacher keeps her own ideas to herself and keeps returning questions by the students to them, but in a different form.			
1	1.5	2	2.5	3	3.5	4

Figure 2.2 Rating scale for the variable 'Steering of the learning process by the teacher in case of intervention into autonomous group work'.

Figure 2.2 can be seen as a typical Socratic scheme): Jigsaw, with a 1.6 scale points average, and Group Tournament, average 1.9; in comparison teacher-centred instruction average was 1.3. However, the results turn out very low in general: one would have expected high scores in this survey scale for the Cooperative Learning model classes. But within the scope of the Cooperative Learning model concepts, the interaction between the teacher and the student scarcely manifests pronounced features of a 'Socratic scheme' or at least does not manifest them distinctly. In the course of the present study, the reciprocal interaction between the teacher and the students in autonomous group work barely got underway or did not begin at all.

Participants' involvement

1   Do the students make use of the Cooperative Learning model as a means of practising for themselves?
2   What are the differences in frequency of exercising in the teacher-centred class compared to the student-centred Cooperative Learning model classes?

The present study also examined whether the exercise phases offered by the teachers are used by the students as a means through which to learn movement. What might provide a relatively concise criterion is how often the students executed the handstand or the dive roll. In an ideal-typical case, one would expect that in all three concepts mentioned, the gymnastic elements would be performed with sufficient frequency or at least that there would be sufficient attempts to perform or execute the preliminary exercise. Yet, how much is 'enough' to enable students to learn how to perform these actions? How many times would we expect a student to perform a handstand (or attempt to do so) in a lesson with the aim of learning to handstand? Since it can be assumed that in the teacher-centred class, with its tight guidance, movements are actually performed by the students just about as often as the teacher deemed to be reasonable when planning the lesson, one can consider these frequencies as initial value or baseline in terms of a traditional instruction. However, exercising in the Cooperative Learning model-oriented groups should not be allowed to fall behind this baseline. Quite the contrary, by virtue of the lower percentage of teaching time taken up by teacher comments, instructions and so on, the Cooperative Learning model-oriented groups should have more opportunity for exercise. Counting the movements performed by the students (including related attempts and preliminary exercises) with the help of the video material revealed that in the 'Jigsaw' classes, each child practised 35 times per class hour and 25 times in the Group Tournament and in the teacher-centred classes. When appraising these figures, one must bear in mind that within the Jigsaw method, the student action is pre-structured quite clearly: the respective group experts act as 'teachers' for the rest of group, as in other studies (Casey, 2010; Dyson *et al.*, 2010). Obviously, this setting leads to a vivid bustling exercise activity within the groups. Within the less pre-structured Group Tournament setting, there is less motor activity, but only deeper analyses of the student action would provide an insight into what happens in these groups in lieu of frequency of exercise. Anyway, even the children in this self-organized exercise situation exercise as often as children in the teacher-centred classroom with explicit guidelines. At this point, one can establish that the use of the proposed exercise time by the students may be interpreted as acceptable in terms of the concept.

Conclusion

In this chapter, the Cooperative Learning model is presented as an opportunity to integrate movement and personality-oriented learning. This was grounded in educational philosophy in the theoretical part of this chapter. On the basis of this theory, giving leeway and the reticent quality of teacher action in the phases of autonomous group work within the Cooperative Learning model were highlighted as important pivotal points of this teaching method's pedagogical potential. Hence, on one hand, in the group work, it must be ensured that all students can experience successful movement relationships to guarantee that group and learning processes take place constructively. On the other hand, group work must pave the way for the students as they search for this success in the most self-active way possible – that is, not to have teachers intervene too often and too profoundly into the group's processes. In the light of this outline of the problem, the study consisted of an analysis of selected aspects of the application of the Cooperative Learning model method in teacher action and, to some extent, in student action, with reference to the meaningfulness of students' self-activity in the learning process.

In summary, it can be said that there are a number of aspects of the implementation of the Cooperative Learning model by the teacher (and students) that can be classified at the level of the lesson's 'surface structure' (programme range). The results of this research favour the assumption that the implementation of the teaching method was successful in this study. It shows that the teachers in the Cooperative Learning model classes were able to shape the lesson organization (structure of the lesson with all essential elements of the Cooperative Learning model phase; sufficient time for self-directed exercise – integrity of execution) and the degree of invasiveness in accordance with the concept. Through comparison with a 'control group', the findings indicated that with identical learning goals (handstand and dive-forward roll) and identical duration of the lesson series (six 90-minute lessons), there is, as expected, a difference between the action of teachers working cooperatively and that of their colleagues in the teacher-centred classes. Furthermore the study showed that the students were able to get involved in the exercise (self-directed in cooperative groups) in the phases designated for that purpose (participants' involvement).

Uncertainties in the interaction between teachers and students appeared clearly in the analysis of the quality of programme transfer, which attempt to capture the 'deep structure' of the lesson. The 'centrepiece' of the Cooperative Learning model, the sensitive and constructive mentoring by the teacher during the autonomous group work phase, seems to more or less ask too much of the teacher systematically. The findings suggested that the teachers acted only partly or even seldom in accordance with the 'Socratic' methods of teaching as advocated by the concept of the Cooperative Learning model, presented here as a German perspective on educational philosophy. Instead, the teachers fell back into a rather directive teacher action. These research results reveal a need for optimization in the implementation in the practice of physical education.

On the basis of the described results, one must conclude that the potentials of the Cooperative Learning model could not be realized entirely within the scope of the present study. With regard to content, this result indicates significant consequences for teacher education at university level: the teachers involved indeed mastered the 'static' structured phases of the lesson but they were insufficiently prepared for the 'flowing' phases of autonomous group work. This symptom probably reflects a systematic deficiency in current 'teaching methodology' education in the context of the education and training of future teachers in German universities and reveals results that could transfer to other countries. The empirical evidence presented in this chapter indicates that it seems necessary and promising to design a targeted education for future PE teachers so as to prepare them for the implementation of the Cooperative Learning model structures (this concept is discussed by Zach and Cohen, Chapter 6 of the present volume). This purposeful education should also involve continuing professional development and the training of teachers who are already on the job. In doing so, the emphasis should be put on competences, which are necessary to help the group work become autonomous, that is, in the sense of 'self-help assistance'. Relevant university curricula are yet to be developed, at least for the German-speaking universities.

References

Aronson, E. and Patnoe, S. (1997). *The jigsaw classroom: building cooperation in the classroom.* New York: Longman.

Bähr, I. (2005). Kooperatives Lernen. *Sportpädagogik* 29(6): 4–9.

Bähr, I. (2009). Lehrer- und Schülerhandeln als methodologisches Problem bei der Implementierung von Unterrichtskonzepten. In P. Brandl-Bredenbeck and M. Stefani (eds), *Schulen in Bewegung – Schulsport in Bewegung*, 179–84. Hamburg: Czwalina.

Benner, D. (2001). *Allgemeine Pädagogik. Eine systematisch-problemgeschichtliche Einführung in die Grundstruktur pädagogischen Denkens und Handelns.* Weinheim: Juventa-Verl.

Casey, A. (2010). Practitioner research in physical education: teacher transformation through pedagogical and curricular change. Unpublished PhD thesis, Leeds Metropolitan University.

Casey, A. and Dyson, B. (2009). The implementation of models-based practice in physical education through action research. *European Physical Education Review* 15: 175–99.

Dane, A.V. and Schneider, B.H. (1998). Program integrity in primary and early secondary prevention: are implementation effects out of control? *Clinical Psychology Review* 18: 23–45.

Dann, H.-D., Diegritz, T. and Rosenbusch, H.S. (1999). *Gruppenunterricht im Schulalltag. Realität und Chancen.* Erlangen: Univ.-Bund Erlangen-Nürnberg.

Dyson, B., Linehan, N. and Hastie P.A. (2010). The ecology of Cooperative Learning in elementary physical education classes. *Journal of Teaching in Physical Education* 29: 113–30.

Green, N. and Green, K. (2007). *Kooperatives Lernen im Klassenraum und im Kollegium. Das Trainingsbuch.* Seelze-Velber: Klett/Kallmeyer.

Grineski, S. (1996). *Cooperative Learning in physical education.* Champaign, IL: Human Kinetics.

Haag, L., Fürst, C. and Dann, H.D. (2000). Lehrervariablen erfolgreichen Gruppenunterrichts. *Psychologie in Erziehung und Unterricht* 4: 266–79.

Heckmann, G. (1993). *Das sokratische Gespräch. Erfahrungen in philosophischen Hochschulseminaren.* Frankfurt am Main: dipa-Verlag.

Huber, G.L. (2001). Kooperatives Lernen im Kontext der Lehr/Lernformen. In C. Finkbeiner and G.W. Schnaitmann (eds), *Lehren und Lernen im Kontext empirischer Forschung und Fachdidaktik – Innovation und Konzeption*, 222–45. Donauwörth: Auer.

Konrad, K. and Traub, S. (2001). *Kooperatives Lernen. Theorie und Praxis in Schule Hochschule und Erwachsenenbildung.* Baltmannsweiler: Schneider.

Landau, G. (2005). Lehrkunst im Bewegungsunterricht – WAGENSCHEIN in bildungs-theoretischer Absicht ausgelegt. In J. Bietz, R. Laging and M. Roscher (eds), *Bildungstheoretische Grundlagen der Bewegungs- und Sportpädagogik*, 309–19. Baltmannsweiler: Schneider.

Meinberg, E. (1994). Sozialverhalten im Sport – bildungstheoretische Akzentuierungen. In U. Pühse and D. Alfermann (eds), *Soziales Handeln im Sport und Sportunterricht*, 58–72. Schorndorf: Hofmann.

Meinberg, E. (2010). Schulsport und Bildungsforschung: Ansätze. In N. Fessler, A. Hummel and G. Stibbe (eds), *Handbuch Schulsport*, 77–90. Schorndorf: Hofmann.

Metzler, M.W. (2011). *Instructional models for physical education*, 3rd edn. Scottsdale, AZ: Holcomb Hathaway.

Prohl, R. (2004). Vermittlungsmethoden – eine erziehungswissenschaftliche Lücke in der Bildungstheorie des Sportunterrichts. In M. Schierz (ed.), *Sportpädagogisches Wissen. Spezifik – Transfer – Transformationen*, 117–27. Hamburg: Czwalina.

Prohl, R. (2010). *Grundriss der Sportpädagogik*. Wiebelsheim: Limpert.

Slavin, R.E. (1994). Student teams-achievement divisions. In S. Sharan (ed.), *Handbook of Cooperative Learning methods*, 3–19. Westport, CT: Greenwood.

Slavin, R.E. (1989). Cooperative Learning and student achievement. In R.E. Slavin (ed.), *School and classroom organisation*, 129–56. Hillsdale, NJ: Erlbaum.

Tousignant, M. and Siedentop, D. (1983). A qualitative analysis of task structure in required secondary physical education classes. *Journal of Teaching in Physical Education* 3: 47–57.

3 Innovative practice through the use of self-made materials

The Cooperative Learning model in Spain

Javier Fernández-Río and Antonio Méndez-Giménez

> I realized that physical education is more than just running and vaulting.
> Pedro, ninth grade

Key terms: self-made equipment, homemade, creativity

Introduction

This chapter explores the use of self-made materials as a resource to enhance the possibilities of the Cooperative Learning model. The process of constructing and sharing equipment fosters the five critical elements of Cooperative Learning in physical education (see Dyson and Casey's Introduction). When students are asked to build a piece of equipment in small groups (in this case, a cardboard 'ringo'), they are guided into a face-to-face interaction process. Consequently, interpersonal skills are developed through group processing in order to solve possible contingencies. The challenge of the task implies individual accountability, because students must create low-cost, efficient equipment for the group. In addition, this context helps develop positive interdependence among students when they play different roles (such as builder, presenter or assessor). Once built, these self-made materials can be integrated in physical education sessions like conventional equipment, with all the advantages that the process of construction has generated (e.g. creativity, active learning, student-centred learning, social learning).

Physical education and equipment

In today's sustainability-oriented curriculum the mantra is 'reduce, reuse and recycle' in every aspect of our life, but these terms have been around for a long time. Over the past 40 years, different authors have worked on the idea of employing 'used or old' materials to create equipment for physical education or recreation. Pearson (1973) called it 'inexpensive and innovative'. Others have described it as 'improvised' (Bradtke, 1979) or 'low-cost' or 'inexpensive'

(Jackson and Bowerman, 2009; Werner and Simmons, 1990), but most refer to it as 'homemade equipment' (Davis, 1979; Walkwitz, 2005). All these authors were talking about 'found' (Davis, 1979), 'thrown away' (Corbin and Corbin, 1983), 'non-traditional' (Maeda and Burt, 2003) or 'recycled' materials (Grigg, 2009) that are not difficult to adapt and use in physical education (Moss, 2004).

With this in mind, the first pillar of this 'homemade' approach to physical education equipment is the idea of raising ecological awareness in the school's community (i.e. students, teachers and parents) through the recycling of materials and their use in class. As Marston (1994, p. 46) has clearly pointed out, 'if children learn to make a connection between improvised equipment and their enjoyment of movement, they may become more sensitive, and responsible, to environmental concerns'. Thus, the goal would be to increase the students' consciousness of the physical environment, so they could become sustainability-oriented (Grigg, 2009). Nevertheless, this is not the only reason for developing materials of this type.

The second pillar of this approach is the search, by many educators, for resources that could fit the needs of many learners with disabilities (Cowart, 1973). As Jackson and Bowerman (2009, p. 8) have recently written, 'many times, all that is needed to motivate an individual with a disability to become involved ... is the use of an adapted piece of equipment designed for his/her individual needs'. Certainly, when physical education materials are constructed with the needs of individual students firmly in mind, then they can expand their movement possibilities. Moreover, all students can benefit from these types of materials, since they can be manufactured to fit the real needs of any student in physical education. Authors such as Bradtke (1979, p. 4) believe that 'having proper equipment can make the difference between successful and enjoyable ... experiences, and frustration and fear at not being able to perform certain skills'. Undoubtedly, many young students have difficulties using traditional resources, since commercially produced equipment is not always as adaptable or as developmentally appropriate as children need. Instead, homemade materials allow for changes in aspects like size, weight, shape and grasp, which, in turn, make them more usable by children and, therefore, expand their movement possibilities within the physical education class.

The third pillar of this approach was the scarcity of materials available in physical education as a result of limited budgets. Unfortunately, this level of deprivation is found in many areas of the world today. Hardman (2008) has reported that 50 per cent of the teachers evaluated worldwide considered that the amount of their physical education materials was 'limited' or 'insufficient'. In Africa (66 per cent), Asia (53 per cent), Central/Latin America (87 per cent) and the Middle East (57 per cent), the majority of teachers regarded their equipment as deficient. Sadly, authors such as Robinson and Melnychuk (2006, p. 8) consider that 'activities are often inequitably chosen due to the absence of material resources', which, in turn, affects students and their movement experiences. Therefore, the quantity and quality of a school's equipment can detrimentally influence the excellence of its physical education curriculum. Moreover, O'Reilly *et al.* (2010, p. 219) have observed that 'for these teachers, the restrictions imposed by ... insufficient equipment … were constant sources of frustration'. In many cases, large classes and/or the lack of enough equipment prevent children from having time to practise and improve their psychomotor skills. Furthermore, discipline and behavioural problems often appear when students have to wait for long periods of time because of limited resources (Werner and Simmons, 1990). Nevertheless, as Maeda and Burt (2003, p. 32) have stated, 'costly equipment is not a prerequisite to elicit purposeful movement in children, nor is it a prerequisite for an effective movement program'. Homemade equipment will allow each student to have his/ her own piece of equipment, thereby maximizing involvement and participation, since they will all have many opportunities to explore a wide variety of movement patterns and experience many different physical activities in and out of school.

Finally, the fourth pillar of this perspective refers to the individual who builds the materials. Many authors believe that homemade equipment should be constructed by those teachers who feel that they need extra materials to enhance their physical education programmes (Bradtke, 1979; Cowart, 1973; Davis, 1979; Jackson and Bowerman, 2009; Kozub, 2008; Maeda and Burt, 2003; Moss, 2004; Spire *et al.*, 1995; Walkwitz, 2005). Other authors believe that these materials could be constructed by teachers or students alike, depending on how difficult the construction process seems to be (Corbin and Corbin, 1983; Grigg, 2009; Marston, 1994; Pearson, 1973; Werner and Simmons, 1990). Our proposal goes beyond these two perspectives, and moves from homemade to self-made materials. The rationale behind this change relies on the conviction that students, with the help of their peers or their family, should construct at least some pieces of their physical education equipment. Why? Because this approach actively involves all students in the process of construction of the equipment that they are going to use. Furthermore, it develops their social as well as academic learning (a key aim in the cooperative framework) as they negotiate the construction of their equipment with their peers. Such involvement, as we will explain in the next two sections, is in keeping with both the Cooperative Learning model and the constructivist theory of learning.

Self-made materials and Cooperative Learning

Research has shown that the process of constructing, using and sharing self-made materials can foster the five critical elements of Cooperative Learning in physical education (Méndez-Giménez and Fernández-Río, 2010b). The following subsections list these elements.

Promotive face-to-face interaction

When students are challenged to build their own equipment in small groups (two to four members), they are encouraged to engage in a face-to-face interaction process that promotes communication and the development of social skills at three different times: during the construction process, during the assessment of the materials and while using them. The aim is to give all group members ample opportunities to get involved in the construction process (supporting each other) to overcome the different challenges offered by the task. Nevertheless, where, when and how to build self-made materials count among the most common worries expressed by physical educators (Davis, 1979). Developing the construction process itself in class can be an effective way to enhance promotive interaction. However, from an interdisciplinary perspective, involving teachers from other subjects (e.g. arts, technology, mathematics or science) could also be very rewarding. Unfortunately, collaboration among teachers is not always possible or likely in schools. Consequently, investing a few minutes of the physical education class to develop simple resources may be needed. However, if the students have enough autonomy and the requirements of the construction allow it, working on homework tasks in groups outside school could be an appropriate alternative. This option is preferred by teachers who feel that time in physical education is too limited and should be devoted solely to keeping the students physically active (Méndez-Giménez and Fernández-Río, 2010a). Additionally, parents are also encouraged to help their children complete the task started in class. Similarly, the cooperative interaction continues during the peer-assessment process of the finished materials by the group that constructed the material, as well as other groups. The goal is to monitor the self-made objects' characteristics, and check that those objects meet the requirements for their use. Particular emphasis should be placed on assessing the materials' safety, consistency and efficiency, as well as their aesthetic and creative assets (Méndez-Giménez and Fernández-Río, 2009). Finally, the interaction process occurs when students use the self-constructed material in the physical education class, during recess or in their leisure time outside the school. In these different settings, they tend to share with other youngsters the equipment developed in class or at home, increasing the promotive interaction process.

Positive interdependence

The essence of the Cooperative Learning model lies in the necessity of linking personal success with the success of partners, either through common goals, shared resources or complementary roles (e.g. player, coach, equipment manager and encourager). Some of the roles that students can perform when constructing self-made equipment are:

- *Information searcher*: this student tries to gather as much information as possible on how to build the material through written resources provided by the teacher, web pages or other sources.
- *Equipment manager*: this student tries to find the raw material and the tools needed to build it. Positive interdependence stems from the need to share the materials (e.g. cardboard, plastic bags, newspapers, masking tape) and/or tools (e.g. scissors, rulers, pens, cutter). Prior to starting work, the student collects only what is needed and takes care of this at the end of the process.
- *Builder*: this student transforms the raw material into physical education equipment ready to be used in class. It requires basic craft skills such as

drawing, cutting, pasting or taping, but these skills can be improved through the construction process.

- *Presenter*: this student explains to other groups how his group has built the equipment and the materials that they have used. It is very important to show other people the ideas that the group managed through the construction process.
- *Reviewer*: this student applies the criteria established by the teacher to evaluate the equipment constructed (see Figure 3.1). This is crucial, since each student's safety while using the self-made materials lies in the hands of the person that performs this role. Nonetheless, the teacher must also check for safety.

In addition, roles such as photographer or journalist (to take pictures or write a report of the building process) could be added to enrich the possibilities and scope of these students' roles. Nevertheless, all group members should perform all the different roles at some stage during the construction process. Furthermore, any role could be shared between several group members in order to increase positive interdependence (i.e. every student brings four or five plastic bags to put them together and build a volleyball or football).

Individual accountability

Physical educators have frequently claimed to work on the development of children's moral and social values, such as personal and social responsibility, yet many feel that they have failed in this endeavour (Metzler, 2005). The process of constructing equipment allows the teacher to work on those skills. For example, for the group to succeed, each member must be aware of his or her commitment to the group, take responsibility for it and perform his or her part of the task. Without this personal contribution, group cohesion could be harmed and the equipment may not be accurately constructed. Strategies such as 'learning cues in an observation sheet for the reviewer' emphasize this student role, and helps students feel accountable for their actions. The challenge of cooperating to construct equipment develops each student's individual accountability, because they have to create low-cost, efficient equipment for their group. As mentioned earlier, teachers can hand out to their students guidelines for building the materials or upload them onto a web page in an effort to hold the students and their parents responsible for the task at home. At the same time, the fact that one member of the group must introduce the material to the rest of the class helps to make him or her feel accountable for a presentation describing how it was built. Finally, teachers can use peer assessment as an evaluation tool that promotes students' individual responsibility (see Figure 3.1).

Interpersonal and small-group skills

Social skills, such as learning to transmit information, listening carefully, making eye contact with the speaker, sharing ideas and decisions, working together or

Assessment Sheet

Material: _____
Builders: _____
Evaluator: _____

Check and use the material with your peers. After a few minutes, evaluate it using this scale:

(1)   (2)   (3)   (4)   (5)

⎯⎯⎯⎯⎯⎯⎯⎯⎯⎯⎯⎯⎯⎯⎯⎯⎯⎯⎯⎯⎯⎯⎯⟶

NONE   FEW   SOME   MANY   MOST

1. **Safety.** It is not dangerous. I trust it.	1	2	3	4	5
2. **Robustness.** It is hard. It does not break easily.	1	2	3	4	5
3. **Utility.** It works well. It is useful.	1	2	3	4	5
4. **Adequacy.** It is developmentally appropriate.	1	2	3	4	5
5. **Aesthetics.** Design and finishing are attractive.	1	2	3	4	5

Total score: _____
Observations: _____
_____
_____

Figure 3.1 Self-made material peer-assessment sheet.

giving and receiving feedback can be taught to students and practised through the construction or the evaluation process. Children should be told to emphasize the positive aspects of each piece of equipment they evaluate, stressing the things that have been done well, and politely showing which aspects could be improved. No derogatory comments should be allowed. All the ideas should be referred to materials, but not to individuals (for instance, 'this paper bat is very light and manageable, but it is too small'; or 'this cardboard ring is beautiful, but, in our opinion, it needs to be made safer to be able to play with it').

Group processing

Groups should systematically reflect on the quality of the equipment they have developed, and teachers must create opportunities for this to happen. Teachers should also decide if the material has been worn out during the sessions, and decide if students must repair it *in situ* or after the session. *In situ* repair requires that some basic raw materials and tools (e.g. scissors, masking tape, cardboard) should be available in class. Similarly, if the damage is too heavy, teachers must have extra equipment ready in order not to lose time from the physical education session. Likewise, students may hold discussions on how to improve the functionality and/or durability of the equipment after they have used it. Again, teachers should allocate time for this task. Finally, students could be challenged to invent games using the new resources available. As Pearson (1973, p. 2) aptly suggested, 'there is no limitation or restriction on ingenuity, invention, creativity, and innovation', and the process of developing one's own equipment allows for all these.

Nevertheless, it is advisable for teachers to start with only a few of the elements and roles described above, and gradually increase the complexity of the overall class structure in order to empower students' autonomy, and obtain full advantage of the blending of the process of equipment construction and Cooperative Learning. In the next section, we will show how the construction and use of self-made material from a Cooperative Learning perspective is in keeping with the wider notion of constructivism. We introduce findings from several studies to illustrate how self-made materials, Cooperative Learning and constructivism provide rich contexts for learning in and through physical education.

Self-made equipment and constructivism

Benjamin Franklin claimed: 'Tell me and I forget. Teach me and I remember. Involve me and I learn.' This statement succinctly summarizes the idea behind the constructivist theory of learning. Within this framework, Perkins (1999) proposes that the three tenets of constructivism are the active learner, the social learner and the creative learner. To become active learners, students should be involved in tasks that stimulate decision-making, critical thinking and problem-solving skills. The process of self-constructing equipment allows the students to develop these skills since they must decide where to find the materials needed, and they must debate how to best use them to construct their assigned piece of equipment. With enough materials in class, there is an increase in the students' active learning time (Méndez-Giménez *et al.*, 2010). Therefore, they have more opportunities to practise the skills and the games (in lessons as well as in extra-curricular time), and develop as active learners. To grow as social learners, students must build knowledge through social interaction with their peers. While constructing materials and assessing their effectiveness, students interact with others (i.e. peers and relatives) in and out of the school setting, and, consequently, become social learners. Finally, in order for the students to be creative learners, they should be guided to discover knowledge by themselves, and to create their own understanding of the subject matter. When students are asked to build a piece of equipment, they must find a good functional design, they must negotiate rules and they must share information to develop a 'useable' end product. Moreover, the construction and the usage of self-made materials can help students develop responsibility for their own and their peers' equipment. This is directly related to each student's personal and social responsibility.

The constructivist paradigm emphasizes the need to involve students in their own learning process. Research shows that this active participation leads students to a greater retention, a deeper understanding and a more active usage of knowledge (Dyson, 2002; Dyson *et al.*, 2010). Indeed, the fact of building their own equipment for physical education, as well as the search for the elements needed to carry out this task, activates the students mentally, positively predisposes them toward its use and also motivates them to become more active in and out of the school setting.

Our research shows that the use of self-made materials can contribute to extending the three tenets of constructivism using the Cooperative Learning model. In a recently published study (Méndez-Giménez *et al.*, 2010) the effects of self-made materials on sixth-grade (11 years old) students' interest, enjoyment and motivation were analysed. Within a multidisciplinary Cooperative Learning framework, a physical education teacher involved his students in the construction of their own cardboard paddles from recycled materials (see Figure 3.2). With this equipment, he implemented a learning unit using a game called *paladós*. In this game, students wear a hand-paddle made out of cardboard on each hand that they must use to hit the ball across a net in a court similar to the one used in badminton. At the end of the eight sessions, students evaluated the experience positively. They also thought that working with self-made materials was fun, useful, attractive and motivating. It was very interesting and relevant to discover that they had extended the use of those materials during recess, and into their leisure time. The study showed that constructing and using their own equipment had motivated the students to play with it 'beyond the gates of the school'. They also felt that the experience of constructing their own equipment had allowed them to develop their creativity, and to connect the contents of several school subjects (e.g. history, maths and art).

Finally, we would like to highlight that the girls involved in the study rated the whole experience significantly higher than the boys. Perhaps girls identified themselves more than boys with the aesthetic element of constructing materials and, therefore, valued it more. Or perhaps they valued working together with a shared aim more than their previous experiences of physical education. Whatever the reason, it was very surprising, but also very rewarding, to observe the high level of girls' participation in free play during recess with the materials that they had built, as well as their level of engagement in their lessons. Unfortunately, as widely reported, physical education holds a long tradition of reinforcing gender stereotypes (Scratton, 1986; Flintoff and Scratton, 2006; Evans, 1988). Indeed, Williams (1993, p. 128) has clearly denounced the structure of physical education, stating that it is plagued by a 'sort of games-dominated curriculum which … is particularly disadvantageous to girls'. Self-made materials, such as the cardboard paddles, used in the correct settings seem to attract the interest of girls in physical activity, which adds value to physical education for them.

Figure 3.2 A group of students showing the self-made paddles

Future investigations should study the influence of these materials, as well as unconventional sport activities, in promoting coeducation in both classroom and extra-curricular settings. Finally, it would also be worth examining whether the involvement of girls in building their own materials could stimulate their participation in sport.

The construction process of self-made equipment seemed to have positive psychological effects on students, such as increased self-worth or improved motivation (Méndez-Giménez *et al.*, 2010). Furthermore, converting, transforming or building new elements, which will be used in the physical education classes, can generate feelings of usefulness among students. It can also help develop a special sense of pleasure similar to that of carpenters, craftsmen or potters when they transform raw materials into artworks. Furthermore, we believe that involving the students in constructing and sharing materials with their peers can also increase their respect for their partners' objects.

In another study, Méndez-Giménez and Fernández-Río (2010a), using the Cooperative Learning model, studied the impact of self-made materials in physical education teacher education (PETE) students' motivation, and their beliefs as future teachers (see Figure 3.3). Students were systematically involved in the construction of their own resources using discarded or recycled materials. This strategy was used to address the subject's contents (traditional and popular games), but also as a formative assessment tool. At the end of the whole experience, students commented that they felt that the use of self-made materials was a very positive experience that allowed them to learn the contents of the subject from a more 'hands-on' perspective. The students enjoyed the experience, and felt that they had developed a better appreciation of the potentialities of self-made materials: 'It is rewarding to see what you can produce' (Sofía, third-year university student). They also thought that they would use them in the future as teachers: 'It is a great way of engaging students in physical education' (David, third-year university student). They considered that this approach actively engages the learner, and helps in the inclusion of students with special needs: 'These materials really fit each student's needs' (Juan, third-year university student). Finally, they highlighted the potential of self-made materials to extend physical activity out of the school, to teach values such as coeducation and respect for objects and to develop the students' creativity: 'They help children think about the class equipment, be conscious about recycling and be creative' (Ana, third-year university student).

In a third study carried out in a group of special education teacher education students, we recorded a significant increase in the students' view of self-made materials as a teaching tool that could include students with special needs, help curricular individualization and act as a coeducational instrument (Méndez-Giménez and Fernández Río, 2011). Subjects also reported that the act of constructing materials make them feel proud of what they had made, and helped them to value the equipment that they and others had built more. Students also saw self-made materials as a valuable teaching tool in their professional career.

Figure 3.3 PETE students showing bats and balls made of paper.

Finally, Perkins (2006) considered that the social dimension of learning, sometimes called cooperative or collaborative learning, helps strengthen this process,
since it requires the students to discover and rediscover knowledge through
social interaction with their classmates. Moreover, Dyson *et al.* (2004) have
established theoretical connections between the Cooperative Learning model
and the constructivist theory. Through this instructional model, the teacher can
facilitate learning, while he or she shifts responsibility to the students through
activities specifically designed to hold them accountable (e.g. fixed teams, roles,
peer assessment). Méndez-Giménez and Fernández-Río (2010b) extended this
idea by connecting the hybridization of several instructional models (including
Cooperative Learning) and the use of self-made materials. They showed how
these resources can fortify the connection between instructional models, and
enhance their effects on students' learning. Authors such as Kirk (2005) also
considered that modifying the equipment (and other elements such as rules or
playing area) was basic to understanding instructional models such as tactical
games, and, certainly, self-made materials modify the equipment to fit each individual's needs and maximize their possibilities. The basic link in the hybridization of instructional models is, in the words of Casey and Dyson (2009, p. 192),
'to produce intelligent performers', and including the construction of equipment
at home in this hybridization adds on to this goal, even before the students reach
the school.

Advantages and disadvantages of self-made equipment

As we have remarked throughout this chapter, an increasing number of articles refer to the construction of materials as a valuable tool in primary and secondary physical education (Corbin and Corbin, 1983; Davison, 1998; Hynes-Dusel, 2004; Lichtman, 1999; Marston, 1994; Méndez-Giménez, 2003; Moss, 2004; Pearson, 1973; Stillwell, 1980; Werner and Simmons, 1990). They all show that, to some extent, these materials offer many advantages:

- They can increase students' active participation time: the idea is to build enough resources to avoid having children waiting for one piece of equipment, and maximizing their activity time.
- They can be adapted to fit each student's needs: commercialized equipment has a standard use. Self-made equipment is constructed by teachers and/or students according to the specific characteristics, and therefore needs, of each student.
- They are low-cost: they use very cheap resources, so they can be produced in great numbers, for minimum sums of money.
- They promote students' inventiveness: 'creativity and innovative use of yet safe equipment can be endless' (Maeda and Burt, 2003, p. 34), and this happens not only during the construction process, but also while using the resources created. Certainly, self-made equipment can enhance the possibilities of game-invention by the students (Hastie, 2010).
- They allow for multidisciplinary projects: school subjects such as maths (calculating the size of the parts needed to create a specific resource) or arts (decorating and painting the material) can contribute to the process of developing and constructing these materials.

Nevertheless, these self-made resources also present some difficulties that teachers must be aware of to be able to overcome them:

- *Safety*: this is always a major issue. Teachers should carefully monitor all constructed equipment to minimize possible risks on users (students). They must be sure that it is non-toxic, sturdy and clean, 'and discard it properly when it can no longer be safely repaired' (Pearson, 1973, p. 3).
- *Extra time for construction*: teachers must be aware that if they want their students to build their materials in class, they should allocate specific time for that task.
- *Extra space for storage*: having more materials for the students means that teachers must have enough room to store them, and sometimes this can be a problem. Nevertheless, it is a minor difficulty when you see all your students actively participating in class with their materials.

Conclusion

The rationale behind the self-made materials approach in physical education is to actively involve all students in the process of construction of the equipment that they are going to use in class. More importantly, such involvement allows for the development of the key element of the constructivist theory of learning: achieving the transformation of our students into active learners, social learners and creative learners. The search for the elements needed to carry out the construction process activates the students mentally, positively predisposes them toward the use of the materials that they have built with their classmates and also motivates them to become more active (i.e. using that equipment) in and out of the school's setting. Research has shown that the use of self-made materials can contribute to extending these three tenets of constructivism using the Cooperative Learning framework.

Certainly, the five critical elements of Cooperative Learning in physical education can be developed through the use of self-made equipment.

1   *Promotive face-to-face interaction:* when students are challenged to build their own equipment in small groups, they are encouraged to engage in a face-to-face interaction process that promotes communication and the development of social skills at three different times – during the construction process, during the assessment of the materials and while using them.
2   *Positive interdependence*: the essence of Cooperative Learning lies in the necessity of linking personal success with the success of partners, through common goals, shared resources or complementary roles. Regarding this last issue, students can perform many different roles while constructing self-made equipment (e.g. information searcher, equipment manager, builder, presenter or reviewer), and all of them lead to positive interdependence among group members.
3   *Individual accountability:* the challenge of cooperating to construct equipment develops each student's individual accountability, because they have to create low-cost, efficient equipment for their group. If the final product is ineffective, the group will be penalized, and no one wants to hurt his or her group.
4   *Interpersonal skills*: social skills such as learning to transmit information, listening carefully, making eye contact with the speaker, sharing ideas and decisions, working together or giving and receiving feedback can be taught to students and practised through the construction or the evaluation process.
5   *Group processing:* students should systematically reflect on the quality of the equipment they have developed, and teachers must create opportunities for this to happen. It is important that students have the opportunity to share ideas, to discuss possible solutions or to brainstorm problems that the group has faced while constructing and/or using the materials that they have made. Finally, those teachers who have used self-made equipment in their physical education classes highlight the potential of these materials to extend physical activity 'beyond the gates of the school'. Certainly, this is very important if we want our school subject to survive in this digital age.

Beyond these five critical elements, self-made materials give Cooperative Learning in physical education four distinctive factors: (a) they mean not only sharing ideas, but also physical resources among group members, which reinforces their connections; (b) they actively promote students' invention, creativity and innovation, which is the basis of student improvement; (c) they allow for an increase in girls' active participation, particularly in physical activity, which is an extremely important goal in today's sedentary society; and (d) they have the potential to actively involve parents in their children's learning process at home through homework assignments. These unique elements, which self-made materials bring to the overall teaching–learning process, give Cooperative Learning in physical education an edge over the use of this methodology in any other school subject.

Topics for reflection and small-group discussion

*   What are the different rationales behind constructing equipment?
*   Reflect on how self-made equipment can help students become active learners, social learners and creative learners.
*   What are the links between Cooperative Learning and self-made materials?
*   How can self-made materials foster the five critical elements of Cooperative Learning?
*   Discuss the potential of self-made equipment to promote students' involvement in physical education.
*   Find suitable examples of how to design developmentally appropriate activities through adaptation/modification of material/equipment's features (size, weight, colour, texture, etc.)
*   Discuss the potential of self-made equipment to enhance the possibilities of students to create and/or invent games and activities.
*   How do you think that Cooperative Learning and self-made equipment can help in the inclusion of students with special needs?

Accessible websites

1   New materials for physical education and recreation http://www.youtube.com/watch?v=TcrihUz6ks4&feature=related
2   Constructing new materials for physical education http://youtube.com/watch?v=2X7eV66ita0
3   Recycling materials http://youtube.com/watch?v=wHISLiUvyYQ&feature=related
4   Constructing cardboard paddles http://youtube.com/watch?v=Y-roSqECG1I
5   Building balls http://www.youtube.com/watch?v=6K1A-tIh4k8
6   Making a paddle ball http://www.youtube.com/watch?v=aTn68oKDTBk
7   Creating a pompon http://www.youtube.com/watch?v=MlXVbDEkamo&feature=related

References

Bradtke, J.S. (1979). Adaptive devices for aquatic activities. *Practical Pointers* 3(1): 1–17.
Casey, A. and Dyson, B. (2009). The implementation of models-based practice in physical education through action research. *European Physical Education Review* 15(2): 175–99.

Corbin, E.C. and Corbin, C.B. (1983). Homemade play equipment for use in physical education class. *Journal of Physical Education, Recreation and Dance* 54(6): 35–36, 38.

Cowart, J.F. (1973). *Instructional aids for adaptive physical education.* Hayward, CA: Alameda County School Department.

Davis, K.R. (1979). Homemade equipment that can be used in teaching physical education classes. Unpublished manual.

Davison, B. (1998). *Creative physical activities and equipment: building a quality program on a shoestring budget.* Champaign, IL: Human Kinetics.

Dyson, B. (2002). The implementation of Cooperative Learning in an elementary school physical education program. *Journal of Teaching in Physical Education* 22: 69–85.

Dyson, B., Griffin, L. and Hastie, P. (2004). Sport education, tactical games, and Cooperative Learning: theoretical and pedagogical considerations. *Quest* 56: 226–40.

Dyson, B., Linehan, R.N. and Hastie, P. (2010). The ecology of Cooperative Learning in elementary school physical education classes. *Journal of Teaching in Physical Education* 29: 113–30.

Evans, J. (1988). *Teachers, teaching and control in physical education.* Lewes: Falmer Press.

Flintoff, A. and Scratton, S. (2006). Girls and physical education. In D. Kirk, D. Macdonald and M. O'Sullivan (eds), *The handbook of physical education*, 767–83. London: Sage Publications.

Grigg, A. (2009). Trash balls. *Physical & Health Education Journal* Autumn: 24–6.

Hardman, K. (2008). Physical education in schools: a global perspective. *Kinesiology* 40(1): 5–28.

Hastie, P. (2010). *Student-designed games.* Champaign, IL: Human Kinetics.

Hynes-Dusel, J. (2004). Creating homemade equipment. In R.L. Clements and L. Fiorentino (eds), *The child's right to play: a global approach*, 191–6. Westport, CT: Praeger.

Jackson, D.J. and Bowerman, S.J. (2009). Development of low cost functional adaptive aquatic equipment. *TAHPERD Journal* Fall: 8–10.

Kirk, D. (2005) Future prospects for teaching games for understanding. In L.L. Griffin and J.I. Butler (eds), *Teaching games for understanding: theory, research, and practice*, 213–27. Leeds: Human Kinetics.

Kozub, F.M. (2008). Goal-directed physical education for learners with disabilities. *Palaestra* 21(2): 19–27.

Lichtman, B. (1999). *More innovative games.* Champaign, IL: Human Kinetics.

Maeda, J.K. and Burt, T. (2003). Inexpensive equipment preschool movement activities. *Teaching Elementary Physical Education* March: 32–4.

Marston, R. (1994). Constructing equipment from recycled materials. *Journal of Physical Education, Recreation and Dance* 65(8): 44–6.

Méndez-Giménez, A. (2003). *Nuevas propuestas lúdicas para el desarrollo curricular de Educación Física. Juegos con material alternativo, juegos predeportivos y juegos multiculturales.* Barcelona: Paidotribo.

Méndez-Giménez, A. and Fernández-Río, J. (2009). La construcción y exposición de materiales como elemento de evaluación formativa. Paper presented at the IV Congreso Internacional de Evaluación Formativa en Docencia Universitaria. La evaluación formativa en el proceso de convergencia hacia el EEE. Segovia, 17–18 September.

Méndez-Giménez, A. and Fernández-Río, J. (2010a). Efectos del uso de materiales auto-construidos sobre la satisfacción, el aprendizaje, las actitudes y las expectativas del alumnado de magisterio de la asignatura Juegos Tradicionales. Paper presented at the Association Internationale des Ecoles Supérieures d'Education Physique

(International Association for Physical Education in Higher Education) conference, A Coruña, 26–29 October.

Méndez-Giménez, A. and Fernández-Río, J. (2010b). The use of homemade materials to enhance constructivist learning within the Sport Education-Tactical Games Model: the case of an ultimate learning unit. Paper presented at the Association Internationale des Ecoles Supérieures d'Education Physique (International Association for Physical Education in Higher Education) conference, A Coruña, 26–29 October.

Méndez-Giménez, A. and Fernández-Río, J. (2011). Homemade equipment as an educational tool in a group of students enrolled in a physical education teacher education program. In *Book of proceedings, International Congress AIESEP 2011, Limerick, 22–25 June*, 270–8. Limerick: University of Limerick.

Méndez-Giménez, A., Martínez-Maseda, J. and Fernández-Río, J. (2010). Impacto de los materiales autoconstruidos sobre la diversión, aprendizaje, satisfacción, motivación y expectativas del alumnado de primaria en la enseñanza del paladós. Paper presented at the Association Internationale des Ecoles Supérieures d'Education Physique (International Association for Physical Education in Higher Education) conference, A Coruña, 26–29 October.

Metzler, M.W. (2005). *Instructional models for physical education*, 2nd edn. Scottsdale, AZ: Holcomb Hathaway.

Moss, D. (2004). *Sports and physical education equipment you can make yourself.* Ontario: Physical Education Digest.

O'Reilly, E., Tompkins, J. and Gallant, M. (2001). They ought to enjoy physical activity, you know? Struggling with fun in physical education. *Sport, Education and Society* 6(2): 211–21.

Pearson, L.R. (1973). *Guide for homemade innovative play equipment for activities in physical education and recreation for impaired, disabled, and handicapped participants.* Washington, DC: American Association for Health, Physical Education, and Recreation.

Perkins, D. (1999). The many faces of constructivism. *Educational Leadership* 57(3): 6–11.

Perkins, D. (2006). Constructivism and troublesome knowledge. In Jan Meyer and Ray Land (eds), *Overcoming barriers to student understanding: threshold concepts and troublesome knowledge*, 33–47. London: Routledge.

Robinson, M. and Melnychuk, S. (2006). A call for physical education consultants and specialists: let's get serious about implementing quality physical education. *Physical & Health Education* Autumn: 6–11.

Scratton, S. (1986). Images of femininity and the teaching of girls' physical education. In John Evans (ed.), *Physical education, sport and schooling*, 127–46. Lewes: Falmer Press.

Spire, R., Boggan, J., Rowen-Disedare, R. and Kelley, D.R. (1995). Need equipment? Organize a make-it/take-it workshop. *Journal of Physical Education, Recreation and Dance* 66(7): 10–13.

Stillwell, J. (1980). *Making and using creative play equipment*. Champaign, IL: Human Kinetics.

Walkwitz, E. (2005). High energy rainy day physical education cheapskates. *Teaching Elementary Physical Education* July: 13–14.

Werner, P. and Simmons, R. (1990). *Homemade play equipment.* Reston, VA: American Alliance for Health, Physical Education Recreation and Dance.

Williams, A. (1993). Who cares about girls? Equality, physical education and the primary school child. In John Evans (ed.), *Equality, education and physical education*, 125–38. London: Falmer Press.

Part 2

Cooperative Learning in the curriculum

4 Putting Cooperative Learning and physical activity into practice with primary students

Carlos Velázquez-Callado

Key terms: cooperative games, Cooperative Learning, primary physical education, structures, assessment, learning strategies

Cooperative Learning is a pedagogical model where students work together in small, structured and generally heterogeneous groups to maximize their own and each other's learning (Johnson and Johnson, 1999; Slavin, 1999), solve a problem, complete a task or accomplish a common goal (Artz and Newman, 1990). Therefore students are not only responsible for learning the material but also for helping their group-mates learn (Dyson, 2001, 2002; Putnam, 1997), which in turn serves to promote both academic and social goals.

Although the concept of Cooperative Learning is well known in Spain, physical education teachers associate it with different pedagogical strategies such as working groups, cooperative games, team-building activities or highly structured processes of group learning. Indeed, there is a wealth of research, in different subjects and different contexts, which has gone a long way to proving the advantages of the Cooperative Learning Model over such traditional methods as individualized instruction or competitive interaction among students. This work has led to the improvement of student academic achievement while also allowing the same students to transfer their knowledge from one situation to another (Slavin and Lake, 2008). Furthermore, Cooperative Learning has been effective in achieving social goals (Marín and Blázquez, 2003; Slavin, 1999), mainly in inter-ethnic contexts (Cohen, 1999; Slavin and Cooper, 1999), or with pupils at the risk of social exclusion (Díaz-Aguado, 2004), and in the inclusion of pupils with special educational needs (Dugan, *et al.*, 1995; also see Wendy Dowler's chapter in this book (Chapter 10)). Studies of the relationship between the Cooperative Learning model and affective variables such as self-concept (Poveda, 2007), learning motivation (Pérez-Sánchez and Poveda-Serra, 2008) or human values (Vinuesa, 2002) have also been conducted.

In physical education, different research has reported similar conclusions to those developed in conceptual areas (such as language, sciences or mathematics)

thus, emphasizing the advantages of Cooperative Learning to promote the development of motor skills (Barrett, 2005; Dyson, 2001, 2002), social skills (Dyson, 2001, 2002; Fernández-Río, 2003; Goudas and Magotsiou, 2009), inclusion of students with disabilities (Cervantes *et al.*, 2007; Dowler, this volume; Velázquez, 2010b) and students' self-esteem and motivation towards physical activity (Fernández-Río, 2003). Nevertheless, contrary to what might be concluded from the results of this research, the use of Cooperative Learning in physical education can occasionally be misinterpreted, especially when students are involved in group work.

It is important to underline that creating an authentic Cooperative Learning experience is not simply about creating groups with our students and telling them that they must help each other in order to reach a certain goal. Johnson and Johnson (1999) studied the different negative behaviours generated during group activities, relating them to the presence or absence of a set of conditions. They concluded that the occurrence of a number of mediating conditions is necessary to avoid negative situations arising in group work. These conditions constitute the essential components of the Cooperative Learning model: positive interdependence, promotive face-to-face interaction, individual accountability, interpersonal and small-group skills and group processing (for a complete overview of these elements the reader can review the Introduction to this book).

A first step: cooperative games

According to social interdependence theory (Deutsch, 1949; Johnson and Johnson, 2009) the way in which individuals perceive how goals are structured in a situation determines the ways they interact. In this sense, we can distinguish between 'two types of social interdependence: positive (when the actions of individuals promote the achievement of joint goals) and negative (when the actions of individuals obstruct the achievement of each other's goals)' (Johnson and Johnson, 2009, p. 366). We can apply the principles of social interdependence theory to create a classification of the different activities and games used in physical education lessons (Velázquez, 2004). In this way, the first criterion of differentiation is determined by the existence of an interrelation between the actions of the participants. Consequently we can distinguish between individual activities (where this interrelation does not exist) and collective or group activities (where we can find those interrelations in the actions of the participants). Therefore, there are two types of interaction:

- Opposition: the actions of some tend to obstruct those of others, for example in the traditional game of tag, where someone tries to touch the rest of the participants, who, in turn, try to avoid being tagged.
- Cooperation: the actions of some are made in an effort to benefit the others, for example in the game of human knot, where a group of people join their hands randomly and then try to untangle the formed knot without letting go of each other's hands.

In competitive activities opposition is always present but another element is added: the incompatibility of the goal. That is, when somebody reaches the goal it necessarily means that one or more people cannot. On the contrary, in cooperative activities if somebody reaches the goal then everybody else reaches it too. In other words, in competitive activities, if somebody wins then unavoidably somebody has also lost, while in cooperative ones if somebody wins, everybody can feel that they contributed to this.

However, there are also activities that, without being competitive, involve opposition. An example is the aforementioned game of tag. In these types of activities there are no winners or losers, but a change of role is produced during the game. In other words, the goal of the activity is not the same for all participants, as it depends on the role that they play at a given moment. This change of role can be reversible (again the game of tag serves as an example) or irreversible as in a chain tag game, where the tagged people link hands to form a human chain that tries to catch everyone else and the game ends when all participants have been touched.

Figure 4.1 outlines the information of the previous paragraphs. The taxonomy presented in the table lets us situate any activity based on its logical structure, according to the variables listed, and can classify it into a single category. This represents a big step towards understanding the internal logic of any individual or collective activity. There is another element that needs to be outlined: the distinction between opposition and competition. Opposition refers to a type of interrelation between the actions of the participants. At the same time, competition involves an incompatibility of goals between opponents. All competitive activities involve relations of opposition, but the existence of opposition does not always mean competition.

Cooperative games are therefore group activities in which there is no opposition between the actions of the participants, who all combine their efforts, give

Interrelation between the actions of the participants			
No	Yes		
Individual activities	**Group activities**		
	Type of interrelation		
	With opposition	Without opposition	**Goal incompatibility**
	Competitive activities	**Competitive activities**	Yes
	Non-competitive activities with opposition	**Cooperative activities**	No

Figure 4.1 Taxonomy of physical activities.

and ask for help and contribute to reach the same goal or several complementary goals. They may thus become an important resource in physical education classes to promote social skills and teamwork (Garaigordobil, 2002; Grineski, 1996; Street *et al.*, 2004), to facilitate the inclusion of all students in class group (Omeñaca *et al.*, 2001), improve the classroom climate (Rossetti, 2001) and to reduce students' aggressive behaviours (Bay-Hinitz *et al.*, 1994).

We can see that cooperative games have some features in common with Cooperative Learning, in that they can both facilitate the achievement of social aims, but these approaches should not be confused, as they have several differences (Velázquez, 2010a). The first is related to the objective pursued. In cooperative play the fundamental goal is the fun of the participants. Conversely, in the Cooperative Learning model the principal goal is to learn motor and social skills and this necessarily involves assessment. The second difference is that cooperative games are activities for specific moments (i.e. teaching episodes or lessons), while Cooperative Learning is a pedagogy that could be extended over time. Moreover, while the presence of positive interdependence, promotive face-to-face interaction, individual accountability, interpersonal and small-group skills and group processing are indispensable in the Cooperative Learning model, in cooperative play one or more of these components may not be present. For example, individual responsibility is often missing from cooperative games, which in turn means that some participants can have a passive role and/or attitude in the game, without influencing its outcome. Finally, in cooperative play there is no opposition between the actions of participants and, therefore, no competition. However, some structures of Cooperative Learning, such as team-games tournaments, can lead to a phase of intergroup competition.

The differences between cooperative play and the Cooperative Learning model are summarized in Figure 4.2.

Cooperative play	Cooperative Learning
Occasional activity	Pedagogical practice. Extended over time
Main objective: fun	Main objective: learning
Assessment not necessary	Assessment indispensable
Presence of all five elements, especially individual accountability, not necessary (only group accountability)	Typically involves: positive interdependence, promotive face-to-face interaction, personal and individual accountability, interpersonal and small-group skills and group processing
No opposition at any time between the actions of participants	Intergroup competition can be present

Figure 4.2 Differences between cooperative play and Cooperative Learning.

Summing up, the incorporation of cooperative activities and games in physical education classes in primary education can promote a positive group climate and the achievement of social goals. Furthermore, such provision allows students to understand the logical structure of cooperation and helps them to develop basic social skills and the social relationship abilities needed to engage them in more complex learning situations. However, it is important to highlight that cooperative play is only a first step towards Cooperative Learning and should not be mistaken for it. The use of cooperative play can be complemented by designing and incorporating basic Cooperative Learning structures into physical education classes. According to the structural approach (Kagan, 2000), this would ensure the presence of the five essential components, while at same time promoting simultaneous interaction and equal participation in each of the groups.

From cooperative games to basic Cooperative Learning structures

'The structural approach to Cooperative Learning is based on the creation, analysis, and systematic application of structures, or content-free ways of organizing social interaction in the classroom' (Kagan, 1990, p. 12). A structure involves a series of steps that can be duplicated within different contents to develop lesson plans, which allows the teacher to reach academic goals and, at the same time, to reinforce social, communicative and team-building skills. Some structures designed for other classroom subjects such as Jigsaw (Aronson *et al.*, 1978) can be adapted for use in physical education, but it is also possible to create new structures to be implemented specifically in physical education classrooms (e.g. 'I do – We do' (Velázquez, 2004) and 'Think–share–perform' (Grineski, 1996)).

'I do – We do' is a variation of Jigsaw that can be introduced from the first grade of primary education, and follows this process:

1   Students are divided in small heterogeneous groups (from four to six).
2   Teacher presents an open motor task, with different potential for a successful performance. For example, how to throw a ball up and to catch it without it bouncing on the floor; what to do while the ball is up.
3   Each group member practises individually and tries to find different motor answers to successfully complete the task and then chooses two possible solutions that he/she is able to perform. Therefore, for a while students are free to look for different ways to solve the problem before getting together in their respective groups.
4   Each student shows the group one of their two answers. He/she is responsible for teaching the rest of the group the chosen answer and making sure that every student can successfully perform it.
5   The teacher can randomly choose a student from each group to demonstrate the different answers to their group and then assess the group response to that student's ideas. Another possibility is that the teacher asks all members of the group to perform together or one by one.

6   Rewards may be given based on the quality of work, based on predefined parameters known by students.

'I do – We do' has two differences from the original Jigsaw. First, the starting point is not a set of contents selected by the teacher that students have to learn but a motor problem that each student tries to solve individually. Second, in 'I do – We do' there are no expert groups to discuss the main points of the work. Thus, this structure allows for the improvement of motor skills from the initial level of students and there is no possibility of success without every student contributing to the process, which in turn ensures that equal participation is inherent in the process (i.e. positive interdependence).

In 'Think–share–perform', students are divided into small, heterogeneous groups to resolve different cooperative challenges. The main problem is how to organize a class in which several groups are simultaneously working at these challenges. When we consider that groups do not need the same amount of time to resolve a challenge, and that the selection of a Cooperative Learning structure seeks to promote both motor and social goals, it is better not to give the groups a set time for each problem but instead allow them all the time needed to try different solutions until they can overcome the challenge. In this way, students can decide what to do and how to do it, depending on the results of their endeavours. Subsequently, the teacher can organize the gym with five or six different cooperative physical challenges that could be introduced through task cards like that presented in Figure 4.3.

CIRCLE OF FIRE

Purpose:
All group members must go through the circle of fire from top to bottom.

Rules and penalties:
1 No one may touch the circle of fire.
2 The circle of fire must be traversed from top to bottom.
3 If any rule is broken, the person making the mistake has to start again and a mistake is scored against the group.
4 If the group makes seven mistakes, everyone has to start the challenge again.

THINK–SHARE–PERFORM

Figure 4.3 Think–share–perform task card.

Depending on the number of students in a class, three or four heterogeneous groups could be formed, so that there are always two (or three) free challenges. Groups can choose the challenge they wish to try, read the task card and follow the steps of 'Think–share–perform'. Each group has a different coloured sticker that they put on the back of the task card when they overcome a challenge, before moving on to another one. In this way, the teacher would know which challenges have been overcome by each different group and can change the challenges achieved for all groups in the next class.

Cooperative Learning structures involve the improvement of individual motor and social skills mainly through their application to problem-solving tasks. It means that teachers have to ensure learning assessment of both academic and social goals for students. However, while it is common for teachers to assess students' motor achievements in physical education it is not common to assess social achievements. Instead these are supposed to be developed naturally when students work in groups (Hellison, 2003). This assumption seems pedagogically unsound. Instead, by including the assessment of social skill learning within Cooperative Learning structures, students come to know that these skills are equally important. Furthermore, students learn to analyse new skills and identify which behaviours are positive and which are negative when trying to achieve their aims when they work in groups and therefore determine which behaviours should be maintained and which ones should be modified.

The problem is how, in practice, to meaningfully assess the social skills that teachers currently pay lip-service to in order to improve the learning of primary-school students through Cooperative Learning structures in physical education. In this sense, we need to promote an individual's reflective thinking at the end of each class. For this, teachers can randomly select one or two students per group and ask them to complete a simple self-assessment sheet (such as the one shown in Figure 4.4, for upper primary) while the teacher and the rest of students comment on the behaviours and achievements shown during the class in an oral group reflection process.

Teachers can compare what students say in their self-assessment question-naires with his or her notes to determine the social skills that should be rein-forced in different groups. He or she can also address the needs of individual students by giving them feedback that hopefully aids their learning. With this assessment process teachers will have useful information by the end of a learning unit on which to make judgments about the progress of different students and groups regarding social skills learning. Teachers can even complete the assess-ment using an individual self-assessment sheet at the end of the learning unit where each student gives opinions about themselves and his or her group-mates with respect to social behaviours during the lesson (see Figure 4.5). This assess-ment could be useful at the upper-primary, middle-school and high-school levels.

Using the Cooperative Learning model involves significant development from cooperative play in order to promote both academic and social learning. However, this is not enough. Structures imply a fixed sequence of teaching actions that are important for the completion of the task. On one hand this allows in experienced teachers in Cooperative Learning a way to control the new learning context.

SELF-ASSESSMENT SHEET				
Name:		**Date:**		

We are learning and one of the first steps is to identify what we still have to improve. So, read the next sentences about your work today and mark your answer. Remember to be honest: there is no right or wrong answer to the question, your opinion is valuable.

Today in physical education class ...	Always	Often	Rarely	Never
I have listened carefully while others were speaking				
I have presented my ideas to my group				
I have encouraged my group mates				
I have helped my group mates				
I have asked for help when I needed it				
I have criticized someone				
I have been distracted from the task				
I have accepted the group decisions				
I have made positive comments to my group mates				
I have been rude to someone				
I have shared and taken turns when appropriate				
I have helped to solve conflicts in a constructive way				

According to your answers, indicate what is the main factor you should improve and what you will do to achieve it.

....
....
....
....

Indicate the factors you have improved from the first class with your group so far.

....
....
....
....

Would you like to add any suggestion or comment about today's class?

....
....
....
....

Figure 4.4 Example of social skills self-assessment sheet.

INDIVIDUAL GROUP-ASSESSMENT SHEET	
Name:	**Date:**

We are learning and one of the first steps is to identify what we still have to improve. So, read the next sentences about your work today and mark your answer. Remember to be honest: there is no right or wrong answer to the question, your opinion is valuable.

Disagree ⟵⟶ Agree

1   2   3   4   5   6

Your Name:	1	2	3	4	5	6
Assumes his/her responsibilities						
Helps group mates with difficulties						
Disturbs the others						
Refuses to participate						
Encourages the others when things do not go as expected						
Criticizes the others						
Is distracted from what he/she has to do						
Accepts group decisions without necessarily agreeing						

Mate 1 Name:	1	2	3	4	5	6
Assumes his/her responsibilities						
Helps group mates with difficulties						
Disturbs the others						
Refuses to participate						
Encourages the others when things do not go as expected						
Criticizes the others						
Is distracted from what he/she has to do						
Accepts group decisions without necessarily agreeing						

Mate 2 Name:	1	2	3	4	5	6
Assumes his/her responsibilities						
Helps group mates with difficulties						
Disturbs the others						
Refuses to participate						
Encourages the others when things do not go as expected						
Criticizes the others						
Is distracted from what he/she has to do						
Accepts group decisions without necessarily agreeing						

Figure 4.5 Social skills individual group-assessment sheet for a group of three members.

On the other hand, it allows the class group to reinforce social behaviours when students do not have enough experience of working in groups. Therefore, if we wish to develop students' self-directed learning then it is necessary to advance this process in a way that students are able to put motor and social skills into practice in any situation.

From a basic Cooperative Learning based in structures to a successful Cooperative Learning based in concepts

The development of basic teacher knowledge, understanding and specific classroom practices about Cooperative Learning as a pedagogical approach is important when using it with primary students or with students with no prior knowledge of the model. Nonetheless, it is important to note that the main objective must be to help students to cooperate without the help of the teacher. In moving toward this pedagogical objective, the conceptual approach (Johnson and Johnson, 1999) can be useful to help teachers apply general principles to the development of Cooperative Learning activities, lessons and strategies in physical education. Once the principles are understood, teachers then have the flexibility to design cooperative lessons that develop different physical education content and achieve course goals. The advantage of conceptual principles is that they can be used with students of different ages, ability levels and/or background with only small adaptations.

A higher level of student autonomy in Cooperative Learning requires that teachers have in mind a set of decisions before, during and after the group's interaction: the specific resources needed, how the groups will be formed, what roles will be established, when to intervene, how to promote group processing and how to provide feedback to the students. Therefore, before group interaction occurs it is important to create specific resources that can be used by students during Cooperative Learning lessons to reach the planned instructional objectives. Teachers have to decide the key concepts to include in these learning sheets while taking into account the students' level of understanding. The main objective of these sheets is to promote students' ability to correct mistakes and to ensure the effectiveness of motor performance, which includes learning skills and then applying what students learn to real game situations. Another objective of the learning sheets is to guarantee (as much as possible) that students are on-task. Furthermore, as a form of accountability, if a teacher observes a student who is distracted from the task he or she could simply ask for written evidence on the learning sheet of what the student has been doing. Such a mechanism supports the cooperative nature of the task while ensuring that all students contribute to the aims of their group. An example of a learning sheet for the initial movement that a student has to master in order to juggle is shown in Figure 4.6. In this case one student is the juggler and the other is the coach.

The second teacher decision is about the formation of groups. The size and duration of groups will depend on the instructional objectives, the complexity of the task and the existing level of the students' cooperative skills. However,

First step: Basic movement with a ball

Start at the base position: your arms slightly away from your stomach and parallel to it, your forearms parallel to the floor. Your forearm and upper arm form an angle of 90 degrees. Then:

1   Put a ball in your right hand and throw it through your left hand in an arc about eye level.
2   Repeat the movement but throwing the ball from your left hand to your right hand.
3   Throw the ball from hand to hand several times until you master the movement.
4   Bear in mind the feedback of your coach. He/she will help you to correct your mistakes.

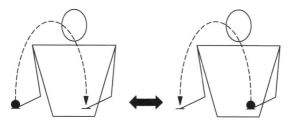

First step: Basic movement with a ball

Check:
• Juggler takes the correct basic position before starting work.
• Ball goes up, more or less, at his/her eyes level.
• Juggler doesn't move his/her feet to catch the ball.
• When juggler throws and catches the ball, his/her forearms move up and down just a little and his/her arms barely move.

Most common mistakes:
• Ball is thrown correctly with the right hand (left hand if your juggler is left-handed) but when juggler throws the ball with his/her other hand, the ball barely rises.

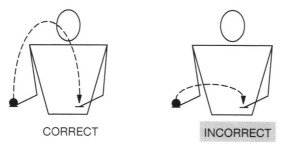

CORRECT   INCORRECT

Figure 4.6 Reciprocal task sheets for Cooperative Learning. (*Continued overleaf*)

- Ball is thrown without precision, which requires the juggler to move to catch it.
- Ball is caught but very high, juggler moves his/her arms far away from the body.

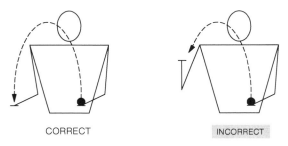

CORRECT   INCORRECT

Figure 4.6 Reciprocal task sheets for Cooperative Learning.

the teacher must also decide how the heterogeneous groups will be formed. To achieve this, the teacher can assign students to groups, allow students to self-select or choose another system such as a random assignment. Although teacher assignment is preferred by researchers (Cohen, 1999; Johnson and Johnson, 1999), some physical education teachers prefer to allow the students the freedom to choose their own group partners (Pérez-Pueyo, 2010) to promote a higher level of group cohesiveness. In this sense, Velázquez (2010b) concluded that there are no significant differences between groups formed by the teacher according to criteria of heterogeneity and groups freely formed by students. In both cases when students focused on the task, regulated their conflicts, attended to teacher feedback, corrected mistakes themselves and reached partial aims, their groups were successful regardless of how they were formed.

To promote individual accountability, that teacher can decide to introduce different roles or specific functions that a student assumes at a given time. Some examples of roles for a learning unit in physical education are: recorder (writes down every day's outcomes), encourager (avoids discouragement when difficulties appear, invites shy members to participate and reinforces good performance), keeper (takes care of all equipment used and ensures its correct use) or organizer (takes care that everybody is focused on the assignment). Each student should assume each of the selected roles for at least one session during the learning unit in order to understand what is involved and its importance for optimal group working.

Once the Cooperative Learning model is running efficiently, the teacher can walk among the groups taking notes about what is happening for later analysis. Cooperative Learning allows teachers the chance to write a diary of the class in real time instead of doing it after the session. Subsequently, the teacher can register the most significant activities of the different groups and then make decisions to help groups in their learning process.

During the group interaction element, the teacher can also take part but he or she has to decide when and how to participate. His or her participation should be considered alongside one of the most useful learning outcomes of the Cooperative Learning model, that is, students are able to correct their own mistakes, learn from them and regulate their own conflicts using their social skills. It requires students to make decisions in groups by assessing the consequences of their practices and therefore changing their decisions when necessary. However, students do not always work in groups efficiently or diligently. Teachers need to learn when to intervene if they observe that students have not understood what they have to do, if they are not on-task or if there is a destructive conflict in a group. Individual accountability can be achieved through the use of brief questions or comments to focus the students on the problem before the teacher allows the students the opportunity to discuss and to solve the problem on their own (Cohen, 1999). Sometimes specific problems in a group can prompt the introduction of a new role in the group that had not initially been considered. In any case, the teacher's intervention in Cooperative Learning should not be to correct errors or give a valid solution to the task but to orientate the students in the search process in a way that helps them find a response or solution on their own.

During class the teacher can also promote brief 'time outs' if needed where the task is stopped to facilitate group processing. This can be used to determine why uncooperative behaviours are occurring and to define a set of promises to eliminate such inappropriate behaviours and set out the consequences for students who do not behave properly.

At the end of the session, groups finish by completing their documents and giving them to the teacher. This exercise facilitates a group processing session about the students' performance and behaviours during the work and a reflection about the relationship between behaviours and the completion of tasks. It is important to end the class with a debriefing process, which is student-centred and guided by the teacher, and in which groups reflect about their work, explaining their motor and social achievements, their difficulties and their improvement goals for the next session. Moreover, the teacher could reinforce the knowledge of achievements or the perception of inadequate behaviours in the groups through individual processing that each student undertakes at home. The teacher can ask students to answer an open question, to complete a short questionnaire or any reflective exercise that focuses on the different situations that occurred in class.

The work of a teacher does not finish when students finish the physical education session. He or she has to analyse all the information recorded during the session from their notes and the students' documents. The teacher should write a set of observations for each group, which students could read before starting work on the next session. This feedback refers to ideas to be considered in the student groups and can also help in reinforcing group achievements so that students are motivated to continue learning in cooperative teams.

Cooperative Learning is a pedagogical model that can be used in physical education, even with junior primary children, to allow teachers and their students to reach a set of specific objectives of learning. The Cooperative Learning model can assist group-mates in their learning and help group members to look for solutions to motor and tactical problems through different approaches and plans. Students in Cooperative Learning structures are able to work in groups, distributing tasks, roles and responsibilities and developing interpersonal skill and social abilities. In addition, students can learn to regulate their conflicts in a constructive way and increase affective skills, democratic attitudes and motivation for learning.

Nonetheless, the implementation of the Cooperative Learning model in physical education in primary education is not easy and requires that teachers recognize its essential characteristics and development learning strategies that help their students understand the logical structure of cooperation and apply it in different learning tasks and situations (Dyson *et al.*, 2010). This can occur initially in a playful way, through cooperative games, and later through the use of a basic Cooperative Learning pedagogy that involve a series of steps that can be duplicated within different contents to develop the lesson plans, and progress to working in 'automatic Cooperative Learning' teams to reach not only motor aims but also a set of competencies needed for life in democratic societies.

Conclusion

Cooperative Learning in physical education is a student-centred pedagogical model in which motor skills and social goals are the explicit learning outcomes. The interdependence of all students and the ways in which they work together in small heterogeneous groups encourage students to make decisions together in order to reach the group goals, which is the key way to complete the task. In this approach the teacher acts as a facilitator of learning who provides resources for the students to help enhance their learning, orientate their work and aid their self and co-assessment. Cooperative Learning structures can develop students' ability to verbalize and to apply what they have learned to other contexts and activities.

References

Aronson, E., Blaney, N., Stephan, C., Sikes, J. and Snapp, M. (1978). *The jigsaw classroom*. Beverly Hills, CA: Sage.

Artz, A.F. and Newman, C.M. (1990). Equivalence: implementing the standards: Cooperative Learning. *Mathematics Teacher* 83: 448–52.

Barrett, T. (2005). Effects of Cooperative Learning on the performance of sixth-grade physical education students. *Journal of Teaching in Physical Education* 24(1): 88–102.

Bay-Hinitz, A.K., Peterson, R.F. and Quilitch, H.R. (1994). Cooperative games: a way to modify aggressive and cooperative behaviors in young children. *Journal of Applied Behavior Analysis* 27(3): 435–46.

Cervantes, C.M., Cohen, R., Hersman, B.L. and Barrett, T. (2007). Incorporating PACER into an inclusive basketball unit: all students can succeed and gain confidence in Cooperative Learning settings. *Journal of Physical Education, Recreation and Dance* 78(7): 45–9.

Cohen, E.G. (1999). *Organizzare i gruppi cooperativi. Ruoli, funzioni, attività*. Trento: Erickson.

Deutsch, M. (1949). A theory of co-operation and competition. *Human Relations* 2: 129–52.

Díaz-Aguado, M.J. (2004). *Prevención de la violencia y lucha contra le exclusión desde la adolescencia. La violencia entre iguales en la escuela y en el ocio. Programa de intervención y estudio experimental*. Madrid: Instituto de la Juventud.

Dugan, E., Kamps, D., Leonard, B., Watkins, N., Rheinberger, A. and Stackhaus, J. (1995). Effects of Cooperative Learning groups during social studies for students with autism and fourth-grade peers. *Journal of Applied Behavior Analysis* 28(2): 175–88.

Dyson, B. (2001). Cooperative Learning in an elementary physical education program. *Journal of Teaching in Physical Education* 20(3): 264–81.

Dyson, B. (2002). The implementation of Cooperative Learning physical education program. *Journal of Teaching in Physical Education* 22(1): 69–85.

Dyson, B.P., Linehan, R.N. and Hastie, P.A. (2010). The ecology of Cooperative Learning in elementary school physical education classes. *Journal of Teaching in Physical Education* 29: 113–30.

Fernández-Río, J. (2003). *El aprendizaje cooperativo en el aula de educación física para la integración en el medio social: análisis comparativo con otros sistemas de enseñanza y aprendizaje* [CD-ROM]. Valladolid: La Peonza.

Garaigordobil, M. (2002). *Intervención psicológica para desarrollar la personalidad infantil. Juego, conducta prosocial y creatividad*. Madrid: Pirámide.

Goudas, M. and Magotsiou, E. (2009). The effects of a cooperative physical education program on students' social skills. *Journal of Applied Sport Psychology* 21: 356–64.

Grineski, S. (1996). *Cooperative Learning in physical education*. Champaign, IL: Human Kinetics.

Hellison, D. (2003). *Teaching personal and social responsibility through physical activity*. Leeds: Human Kinetics.

Johnson, D.W. and Johnson, R.T. (1999). *Aprender juntos y solos. Aprendizaje cooperativo, competitivo e individualista*. Buenos Aires: Aique.

Johnson, D.W. and Johnson, R.T. (2009). An educational psychology success story: social interdependence theory and Cooperative Learning. *Educational Researcher* 38(5): 365–79.

Kagan, S. (1990).The structural approach to Cooperative Learning. *Educational Leadership* 47: 12–16.

Kagan, S. (2000). *L'apprendimento cooperativo: l'approccio strutturale*. Rome: Edizioni Lavoro.

Marín, S. and Blázquez, F. (2003). *Aprender cooperando: el aprendizaje cooperativo en el aula*. Mérida: Dirección General de Ordenación, Renovación y Centros.

Omeñaca, R., Puyuelo, E. and Ruiz, J.V. (2001). *Explorar, jugar, cooperar*. Barcelona: Paidotribo.

Pérez-Pueyo, A. (2010). *El estilo actitudinal. Una propuesta metodológica basada en las actitudes*. León: ALPE.

Pérez-Sánchez, A. and Poveda-Serra, P. (2008). Efectos del aprendizaje cooperativo en la adaptación escolar. *Revista de Investigación Educativa* 26(1): 73–94.

Poveda, P. (2007). Implicaciones del aprendizaje de tipo cooperativo en las relaciones interpersonales y en el rendimiento académico. Unpublished PhD thesis, Universidad de Alicante.

Putnam, J. (1997). *Cooperative Learning in diverse classrooms*. Upper Saddle River, NJ: Prentice-Hall.

Rossetti, E. (2001). Se a criança aprende a competir, porque nâo ensiná-la a cooperar. Unpublished master's dissertation, Unimonte – Centro Universitario Monte Serrat, Brazil.

Slavin, R.E. (1999). *Aprendizaje cooperativo. Teoría, investigación y práctica.* Buenos Aires: Aique.

Slavin, R.E. and Cooper, R. (1999). Improving intergroup relations: lessons learned from Cooperative Learning programs. *Journal of Social Issues* 55: 647–63.

Slavin, R.E. and Lake, C. (2008). Effective programs in elementary mathematics: a best-evidence synthesis. *Review of Educational Research* 78(3): 427–515.

Street, H., Hoppe, D., Kingsbury, D. and Ma, T. (2004). The game factory: using cooperative games to promote pro-social behaviour among children. *Australian Journal of Educational and Developmental Psychology* 4: 97–109.

Velázquez, C. (2004). *Las actividades físicas cooperativas. Una propuesta para la formación en valores a través de la educación física en las escuelas de educación básica.* México, DF: Secretaría de Educación Pública.

Velázquez, C. (coord.) (2010a). *Aprendizaje cooperativo en Educación Física. Fundamentos y aplicaciones prácticas.* Barcelona: Inde.

Velázquez, C. (2010b). Influencia de los agrupamientos en la eficacia del aprendizaje cooperativo en Educación Física en Educación Primaria. In *Actas del VII Congreso Internacional de Actividades Físicas Cooperativas. Valladolid: 30 de junio 3 de julio* [CD-ROM]. Valladolid: La Peonza.

Vinuesa, M.P. (2002). *Construir los valores. Currículum con aprendizaje cooperativo.* Bilbao: Desclée de Brouwer.

5 Cooperative Learning through the eyes of a teacher-researcher and his students

Ashley Casey

Key terms: professional learning, teacher-as-learner, participant interaction, teacher-as-facilitator, teacher-as-researcher

Changing education paradigms

> We're getting children through education by anaesthetising them. And I think we should be doing the exact opposite. We shouldn't be putting them to sleep, we should be waking them up to what they have inside them.
>
> (Robinson, 2010)

In his address to the Royal Society of Arts, Robinson (2010) described an educational malaise that is worryingly a little too familiar. That is not to say that I subscribe to a notion of an anaesthetizing education system but instead that some aspects of it may have been attributable to me, through my teaching, a decade or so ago. As a young teacher I now believe that was I was guilty of putting the content (the sport) and the teacher (myself) before the learning and the learner. For some pupils – those who shared my passion for all things rugby and cricket – it was a chance to enjoy the very same physical education that had inspired me at the age of 15 to become a physical education teacher, that is, team games and inter-school fixtures. Yet for others, in hindsight, it was dull, boring and year-on-year repetitive (in other words anaesthetizing) and in all retrospective probability the antithesis of everything they were likely to enjoy about physical activity and school. In many ways I am doing my younger self an injustice – things were not so black and white – but for the sake of this argument, that is how I now look back on those years of instruction.

In 2002 I started a self-selected programme of professional development that ultimately saw me complete a master's degree and a PhD and then leave secondary education for a job in a university. However, this journey took seven years and involved a seismic shift in my personal philosophy about teaching and learning from teacher-led instruction to student-centred learning. It is beyond the scope of this chapter to explore this paradigm shift in any detail, but it is enough to say that I deliberately moved away from a pedagogy that sent some of my students to sleep and tried to adopt one that woke all of them up – especially those who had previously slumbered.

I used a number of pedagogical approaches (including Sport Education and Teaching Games for Understanding) in this 'awakening' process, but most significant for this chapter was my use of Cooperative Learning in the teaching of games, swimming, athletics and gymnastics. To this end I will examine the personal, pedagogical and curricular changes I engendered as a teacher/researcher (Stenhouse, 1977). I will use my voice alongside the voices of my students to show how we co-created a Cooperative Learning approach that engaged both teacher and students in new ways of learning through its five elements: individual accountability, positive interdependence, promotive face-to-face interaction, group processing and interpersonal and small-group skills. By doing this I acknowledge that teaching is a socially-contracted space where the interactions between a teacher and her students are constantly under negotiation and renegotiation. As Michelle Grenier and Pat Yeaton later suggest in Chapter 8, Cooperative Learning is contingent on the successful interactions, both verbal and non-verbal, of all group members allowing them to work together with classmates of varying abilities. What I argue here is that the interactions between the teacher and the students are congruent in the successful implementation of the Cooperative Learning model.

In asking teachers to consider their practices within broader social and educational practice, Kirk (1995) wanted them to be reflective in their choice of pedagogy. My decision to use Cooperative Learning emerged from my engagement in that very process and was derived directly from adjustments I wished to make in my practice. Prior to 2002, I had been guilty of 'teaching innocently' and foolishly believing that the meaning and significance that I placed on my actions were the ones that my students took from my lessons (Brookfield, 1995). Yet the more I delved and peeled back the layers of traditionalism (Sparkes, 1991) the more I came to understand that many of the practices that I held as central needed changing. Furthermore, and as the chapter will now begin to show, through the use of pedagogical models such as Cooperative Learning my teacher-centredness began to erode.

Individual accountability

My first encounter with Cooperative Learning occurred in September 2003 as a consequence of my efforts to be a reflective practitioner. Originally it was envisioned as a way to explore a change in personal pedagogy in my teaching of gymnastics and was undertaken as a comparative study between two units of work: the first was a traditional curriculum, familiar to the students involved, in which the teacher occupied the central role. The second was a new Cooperative Learning environment in which the students, through a highly structured curriculum framework, took a greatly increased responsibly for their lessons and the direction of their learning.

The traditional curriculum ran for six weeks. During this time the students undertook skill development practices, partner work and sequence creation, and were assessed on their gymnastic ability in preparation for this project. The Cooperative Learning structure used was Jigsaw (Aronson *et al.*, 1978) and ran for seven weeks. During this time data were gathered through participant questionnaires, teacher field notes and focus-group interviews.

It had been my hope that my role in the Jigsaw classroom would be on the periphery, as a problem-solver (Aronson *et al.*, 1978) and a facilitator, rather than at the heart of everything. Yet the learning process was as marked for me as it was for the students. I had to learn about the Cooperative Learning model and then I had to translate that into a single lesson and then into a unit of work. Furthermore, I had to reconsider and then change my role as a teacher and what that meant within a Cooperative Learning classroom. Simultaneously the students had to learn to learn in a new way (Casey *et al.*, 2009). All the while I was learning a new role for myself, one in which I would try to engender, rather than force, learning. This dual change in responsibility made both teacher and students accountable, as individuals, for their actions and/or inactions. I had to begin to trust my students to take on increased responsibility. Equally they had to trust me that putting them in 'the spotlight' was good for their development as learners. I was ultimately responsible for their education, and this meant that every action I took had to be weighed against the educative gains that were made as a result.

One of the most difficult tasks for me was not interfering when the activities of the students were 'none of my business' (Hammersley, 1977):

> Steve was unable to do a forward roll on the box – Harry went across to help him, having overcome his own fear in previous weeks – poor judgement and intervention from me sent him back to his group. Upon realizing my mistake, I apologized and asked him to demonstrate again ... which he did. ... I then worked on his cues and helped Steve to perform the skill ... five minutes later and he is quite happy and comfortable doing the forward roll on the box top.
>
> (Field notes)

Previously, teaching Steve was my responsibility. Yet in deciding to teach the students through Cooperative Learning I had made a decision to trust them to take on part of my role (the face-to-face positioning, at least). The roles for which I had previously been responsible, such as leader, recorder, encourager and checker (Johnson *et al.*, 1994) had been passed on to the students. Consequently, for my teaching to be successful I now needed to help them to undertake these roles.

Yet despite my early trepidation the Jigsaw classroom became an authentic learning experience for the students involved and it became 'increasingly obvious that, despite my concerns that my teaching may be compromised by a change of role (through peer-teaching and listening), students were having to attempt things that they could not or would not do previously' (field notes):

Steve and Theo were adamant that they couldn't do a headstand. Using question-and-answer and the knowledge of Martin and Len I was able to get the experts to teach the performers through their answers.

(Field notes)

Yet despite the observations made above, I also forgot that Cooperative Learning was as new to my students as it was to me and that they needed constant help finding their role within these lessons. Indeed, as Theo points out, not everything went to plan, and as teacher I am accountable for this slip:

I found it quite a hard six weeks but also I find things like forward rolls, backward rolls etc. … quite difficult so in that respect I didn't really enjoy much of it … 'cause it was just hard and the people that were teaching it, not when you showed me it but when other people were showing me then they just expected me to just be able to pick it up and 'cause I couldn't I found it quite difficult.

(Pupil interview)

The frustration experienced by Theo's group-mates or 'teachers' is a familiar one. Brookfield (1998) called this 'the Nike school of pedagogy', for when the student cries at last 'I just don't get it', the teacher cries in equal frustration, 'Just do it' (p. 22). Brookfield was talking about experienced teachers, so it is not surprising that some of the participants in this project experienced both sides of this scenario. It is important to remember that the students are learners first and foremost, and I am culpable in this situation (and any others that were experienced by the other 55 students in the study). Learning to teach through Cooperative Learning takes practice and planning to ensure that no participant (myself included) is placed in Theo's position. I was responsible for delivering the unit of work, and for this I was ultimately held accountable by the students.

Positive interdependence

My second use of the Cooperative Learning model occurred in the summer of 2004 as the scaffolding pedagogy for a hybrid Cooperative Learning/Teaching Games for Understanding unit – this time in tennis. While this study has been reported on in detail elsewhere (see Casey and Dyson, 2009), I have used it here as I felt that it typified how my desire to change my teaching created an environment of positive interdependence between my understanding of how to teach through Cooperative Learning and the learning experienced by my students.

The initial study set out to design, implement and evaluate a combined model of Cooperative Learning and tactical games in three secondary-school Year 7 (11–12 years old) physical education classes. Data were gathered from three sources: (1) my assessments of students' decision-making, skill-execution and positioning (by having students return to a base after each shot), undertaken in the first and last week using the Games Performance Assessment Instrument

(GPAI) (Mitchell and Oslin, 1999); (2) from field notes; and (3) from group interviews undertaken at the conclusion of the unit.

In exploring the mutual interaction between teacher and students I first examined our experiences of mutual goals, joint rewards, shared resources and assigned roles. In preparing and delivering the Cooperative Learning/Teaching Games for Understanding unit curriculum, the preparatory work (i.e. the development of shared resources, the definition of roles and the allocation of mutual goals) was fundamental. This background work typified the collegiality created when teaching was focused on the students rather than centred on the teacher. Fundamentally however, as Dyson and Strachan (2004) similarly found, this pre-lesson preparation allowed me to spend considerably less time in the lessons on organization, which in turn gave many more opportunities to help students navigate the nuances of the Cooperative Learning approach and facilitate their learning.

Most particularly I was able to help them familiarize themselves and each other with the new roles they had to play in the lessons; which in turn met with a high level of success. Students were responsible to and responsible for each other, and everybody had a role to fulfil in every lesson. The primary roles were those of player and coach, and each student had the opportunity to alternate between these two responsibilities numerous times in a single lesson, with one coach always watching a single player at any one time. Through the role of coach, students gained the confidence to tell their peers what they were doing right and what they were doing wrong as performers. Lee explained, 'Like if they [the players] were doing it, something wrong we weren't afraid to tell them but we won't tell them in a really nasty way we'd try and help them which I thought was good and everyone tried to help, they weren't just nasty.' 'It was good,' Nick added, ''cause we like had coaches and when we made bad decisions or good decisions it was filled in [on a sheet] so we could see how to improve.' However, this was not purely a student role and while I had deliberately decentralized myself in the actual teaching I needed to remain on hand to facilitate student learning:

> I was able to interject when appropriate to discuss – 'Shifting the base backwards when playing against an opponent who is hitting hard to the baseline' and 'Awareness of the court boundaries' – these are high-level skills but the students seem to have a greater understanding of the game.
>
> (Field notes)

While this student–teacher interdependence went a long way to ensuring that the unit had a positive outcome, there were supplementary roles to consider. In addition to the basic roles of player and coach, the students were also required to undertake secondary roles (equipment manager, encourager, recorder and reader) within their groups, which likewise rotated but this time on a weekly basis. Stuart commented on its usefulness, 'We had different jobs and we wouldn't have had time to do it all ... everyone has been doing certain jobs', a view upon which Lee elaborated: 'We had different jobs ... each time there was an encourager and I thought it was good to have an encourager because if you do something good you want to know that you've done it good so you need to be told.'

The impact of these roles soon became important to the relative success or failure of a group within a lesson. I observed that when the roles were undertaken effectively,

> the students arrived within a few minutes of each other and got changed immediately. The first ones changed, collected their folders and clip-boards and having ascertained who was doing what role they left the changing room, collected the equipment and headed out to their usual tennis court. When I locked the changing rooms and came onto the courts all the groups were either in huddles having discussions about the first sheet or were already playing.
>
> (Field notes)

The breakdown in any of these stages, most notably the failure of the group to define their roles for the day, led to a less efficient start to the lesson. Robert's comment on the importance of the different roles to their learning was probably the most significant vindication of the model:

> It helped in the groups because if someone didn't understand it then it was most likely that someone else would and they'd explain to the group. And the way we had different jobs like equipment manager and encourager, and he was to encourage people and tell them what they were doing wrong ... so they do it right next time.
>
> (Reflective diary)

Early experiences indicated, as Putnam (1993) and Dyson (2002) found, that cooperation was not simply achieved by placing the boys into heterogeneous groups. Two of the three classes had to restart the programme when it became clear to me that things had started badly: 'Everything was in place but it seemed to ALL go wrong ... they were unfamiliar with everything and it showed. I was also unfamiliar with the actual working process and had to think about what needed to be done' (field notes). Only one class avoided a repeat of the first lesson, as 'everyone seemed happy with their roles' (field notes), but even they proceeded 'somewhat hesitantly at times' (field notes).

In hindsight it might have been easier to have kept going, but my willing-ness to take the time to start again was a significant factor in the success of the unit. In 'normal' teaching – the traditional approach to teaching as described by Metzler (2005) – this would not have occurred. Yet in this unit it was vital that the students understood Cooperative Learning and could play their interde-pendent role in every lesson. As a consequence of this change one class made a huge improvement after I spent a non-tennis lesson explaining the processes of Cooperative Learning, while another class still found things a 'bit chaotic' (field notes) and 'spent much of [a later lesson] bickering' (field notes). Dyson (2002) found something similar in his work on the implementation of Cooperative Learning in elementary physical education and concluded that students initially were not happy to be placed in groups without their friends, which may account for some of the bickering that occurred within the teams, especially in the initial weeks of the programme.

The time taken to repeat the first lesson was worthwhile and highlighted the need to teach the students to use a new and unfamiliar model correctly. The vagaries of the British weather (field notes) and inexplicably poor choices of clothing on the part of the boys played their part in the early failures, but my inadequate preparation of the groups must bear the brunt of any criticism. I failed to heed the warnings I had received through colleagues and the literature 'to introduce Cooperative Learning in Physical Education ... begin with students working in pairs and I had to expect good and bad lessons' (Dyson and Rubin, 2003, p. 14).

Face-to-face interaction

My third study of my use of Cooperative Learning occurred in the summer of 2005 as the pilot study for a PhD (Casey, 2010). Again, while this study has been reported on in greater detail (see Casey *et al.*, 2009), I have returned to the data to highlight how Cooperative Learning allowed me to truly interact with my students on a pedagogical level. Indeed the strongest conclusion I can draw from this re-examination of the data is that this unit signified the first occasion when I really asked open-ended questions instead of prompting them with simple questions to give the answers that I wanted and expected.

The focus in Cooperative Learning shifts between teacher and students, depending on the stage of learning. During the pre-unit stage I had undertaken all the preparations, but when I came to employ the model I needed to hand over responsibility to the students. This meant limiting my instructional interventions to those that facilitated the cooperative interaction of the students. What I experienced instead was a personal reluctance to take the back seat. This was not revealed intentionally but instead came out during the numerous interactions with my students.

As a direct consequence I strove hard to become less directive and I tried to give my students the chance to make meaningful decisions that I was not going to challenge or correct. Yet that is exactly what I did. My latent 'teacher-centredness' was simply more difficult to forget in the spontaneous 'teaching moments' (Metzler, 2011) inherent in the classroom, which in turn led me to direct and lead the conversation. In fairness to myself I got better but the nature of my intervention occupied much of my thoughts as I reflected on the lessons that I had taught. A month into the unit, while examining the changes that I would make to the lesson the next time I taught it, I wrote in my post-teaching reflection:

> Continue to step back from the central role of sole expert, and be more prepared to allow mistakes and then challenge the students to find ways of overcoming them. This is a gradual process, but as I evaluate I need to learn what it means to fully decentralize myself.
>
> (Reflective diary)

This improvement in my face-to-face interactions with my students continued throughout the unit. Ernie, who assisted me in every lesson, summed up the pedagogical change that I had worked for when he wrote his own reflection:

> The most significant aspect of the whole process is that a lot of the responsibility of the teaching and learning is based on the pupils themselves. ... It is a more open style of learning which gives the pupils more responsibility. The reward is that the pupils get a sense of achievement, either by completing a task they didn't believe they could or by being successful in teaching another pupil a technique or skill.
>
> (Reflective diary)

My reflections on this use of Cooperative Learning were not recorded as a complete success in which everything went according to plan and the pupils flourished under this new pedagogy. However, my reflections show that my key development as a teacher was in my ability to interact with my students and to help them learn, rather than simply telling them what to do and how to think:

> I found myself staying in the wings a little more and finding ways of facilitating inquiry amongst the pupils rather than them seeking the answers solely from me ... I was better at acting as a guide rather than a director.
>
> (Reflective diary)

Group processing

The fourth intervention study occurred in the autumn of 2005 and targeted my teaching of swimming. The focus on this aspect of my teaching occurred as a direct result of this diary entry:

> Take yesterday's lesson with 1C – poor start by me compounded by bad and unclear instructions. Yes, the boys seemed to forget everything but I really didn't help. I knew what I wanted to do but it was very mundane and, well, static really. I am still a way away from being the teacher that I want to be.
>
> (Reflective diary)

Yet I did not want to just change the way I taught swimming; I also wanted to meaningfully involve my students in the change process. I achieved this by sharing in the end-of-lesson group processing element and by responding to these conversations to modify and adapt the ways in which I used Cooperative Learning. I did this by asking the students to fill in anonymous comment cards (similar to the ones you find in restaurants) at the end of every lesson. These cards allowed the students to remark on the lesson and suggest improvements.

In doing this I came to realize that things (my teaching and their learning) were not as rosy as I thought, and more importantly, perhaps, I was able to find solutions that fitted both their needs as learners and my changing philosophy of learning and my place in the classroom. Further, by using Cooperative Learning

I deliberately placed the pupils at the centre of their learning environment and then listened to them and observed them. I made changes on a lesson-by-lesson basis and changed myself as much as I changed them. They learned to take responsibility for their own and their peers' learning and they became constructive talkers and biddable listeners within their groups.

An example of this group processing showed that the students were learning to reflect on the teaching and learning that was occurring in their swimming lessons. Their post-lesson comments were positive: 'Not as confusing and very good; Very good, helps you find out how good you are; They [the worksheets] were easier to understand; It is really good for practising arms.' Yet other students' comments were not as positive: 'I didn't find this lesson as good as the last one because we had to keep the float in-between our legs the whole time'; 'Better than last week, can be harder; it wasn't good because it wasn't a challenge'; or 'Maybe you could make swimming more challenging for experienced swimmers'. As a result I tried to address the points they made and make noticeable improvements in my teaching. As a direct consequence of these and other, similar comments, I split the groups into three groups (improver, intermediate and advanced swimmers) and set different tasks with different language for the various ability groups.

However, there were some major limitations in what could be achieved by individuals and by groups. When the more able swimmers asked if they could swim lengths, I knew that I would be unable to allow this because of the need of weaker swimmers (both in ability and confidence) to swim widths. However, I was able to increase the amount of time they spent in the water by increasing the number of widths they completed in each section of the pair–check–perform cycle (Kagan, 1993). While I feel that the lessons were made a greater success through our engagement in group processing, I am not sure that I made the most of the insights afforded by this two-way conversation, especially in the early stages of the unit. I genuinely feel that the pupils learned a lot about themselves and about swimming. The gradual introduction of pair-check and then the use of files worked well, and they were able to practise much more intensively than in previous years. The boys made a significant number of positive comments about the lessons and it was clear that they enjoyed them.

Interpersonal and small-group skills

The final study took place in the summer of 2006 with the same students involved in the previous athletics unit (Casey *et al.*, 2009). It was developed and taught in direct response to Siedentop's (2002) suggestion that physical education teachers are guilty of teaching the same introductory units again and again. Consequently, I sought to teach a developmental curriculum rather than teaching as I had for the previous seven years, that is, in the same way regardless of the age or prior learning of the students:

> The context is the same, the method of delivery is the same, and in fact nearly everything is the same except for the boys involved. Truth be told,

they may already have been taught this lesson last year, not that it matters because most of them will make the same mistakes anyway.

(Reflective vignette)

I wrote that reflection in 2005, yet it served as the antithesis to what I aspired towards. However, unbeknown to me, it was also incompatible with the students' expectations around good teaching. As the second-year study highlighted:

> I was pretty surprised that we hadn't done the same things again, normally it happens all the time but we didn't do it, which kinda helped a bit because it feels like you're being treated like a baby when you go over the same thing about 50 times.

(Pupil interview)

Indeed, this notion and aspiration of teaching that developed the learning from the previous year was built on the back of the students' ability to work together. Their interpersonal and small-group skills in turn went a long way towards ensuring that they did work together cooperatively. In fact the familiarity they showed with the roles (and associated responsibilities) that they were expected to undertake in the classroom – learned the previous year – served as the catalyst for their learning. Furthermore, the level of responsibility afforded them in Cooperative Learning increased, and this was not something that they were used to:

> At primary school … they [the teachers] didn't think you'd be able to do it all on your own and you'd always need a teacher, but now you can just, they'll just, teacher will let you do it yourself, like um, and not always be there and you just kind of do it yourself.

(Pupil interview)

My goal was to move my teaching and my students' learning forward and take both well beyond the habits I had assumed when teaching the same unit again and again. Specifically I wanted the challenges experienced by my students to be developmentally appropriate and build on their prior experience – especially since I had been responsible for the most recent of this. What was great was to see that the pupils worked together as a group and to hear that they recognized the steps that I was taking to make this a reality:

> I think it's all been built on what happened last year 'cause last year we did kind of the same thing but it was a bit basic and now it's getting more technique into it and then probably like next year and the years that go will be more and more technique put into it so we'll get better and better at each activity.

(Pupil interview)

Importantly in trusting the students to work together and in acknowledging the significance of these interpersonal and group skills I was freed up to act in the role of facilitator of learning. The 'teaching moments' described by Metzler (2005), while not a thing of the past, were certainly much less likely to be dealt with by me. The strength of the groups allowed me to develop my teaching to be much more localized in its focus. That is to say that I could concentrate on the individual and/or the group rather than concentrating on the centre ground, the so-called 'average' student. By facilitating the students to work in groups I came to see the individuals in each class and began to structure my teaching to help students on a one-to-one basis:

> You get involved and if you notice like one person is doing something wrong you'll talk to them and sort it out with them and often like follow them around and see if they get it right and then you'll go on to someone else, so that's helping more than just standing back and telling people what to do.
>
> (Pupil interview)

By sharing my learning outcomes with the students, by working with them and by being honest with them about my aims I felt that I was able to create a more accommodating and supportive learning environment. However, this was not achieved by chance. It occurred as a result of a concerted effort over a number of years to work with, for and because of my pupils. It is this openness that, for me, defines the purpose of Cooperative Learning, that is, to help students and teachers to work together in the co-construction of learning.

What is Cooperative Learning in physical education?

Currently the notion of Cooperative Learning we have in physical education has been borrowed from classroom practice and from the work of a number of diverse content areas such as mathematics, science and English. For this pedagogical approach to be truly capable of enhancing learning in a physical-activity environment it must have a number of features that are particular to our subject. I believe these to be activity-based, social and performance-based learning in the physical domain. Therefore teamwork (in the old-fashioned sense of people working towards a common goal), support of each other's learning and group and individual problem-solving must all occur within what Larsson and Quennerstedt (2010) recently termed socio-cultural human movement. In particular, Larsson and Quennerstedt were referring to a notion of movement that travels beyond the corporal body and instead starts to explore what human movements mean and what they signify. In this case I believe it suggests a notion of human movement as being undertaken within cooperative relationship with others (including students and teachers). For me this is quintessential in understanding the difference between Cooperative Learning and Cooperative Learning in Physical Education.

It is about challenging teachers to make physical education an 'aesthetic experience' for their students by thinking about human movement in different ways, and, as I have tried to show in this chapter, it is about becoming co-participants in the learning journey.

References

Aronson, E., Blaney, N., Stephan, C., Sikes, J. and Snapp, M. (1978). *The jigsaw classroom*. London: Sage.

Brookfield, S. (1995). *Becoming a critically reflective teacher*. San Francisco: Jossey-Bass.

Brookfield, S. (1998). On the certainty of public shaming: working with students 'who just don't get it'. In C. Rust (ed.), *Improving student learning: improving students as learners*, 17–31. Oxford: Oxford Centre for Staff Learning and Development.

Casey, A. (2010). Practitioner research in physical education: teacher transformation through pedagogical and curricular change. Unpublished PhD thesis, Leeds Metropolitan University.

Casey, A. and Dyson, B. (2009). The implementation of models-based practice in physical education through action research. *European Physical Education Review* 15(2): 175–99.

Casey, A., Dyson, B. and Campbell, A. (2009). Action research in physical education: focusing beyond myself through Cooperative Learning. *Educational Action Research* 17(3): 407–23.

Dyson, B. (2002). The implementation of Cooperative Learning in an elementary physical education program. *Journal of Teaching in Physical Education* 22(1): 69–85.

Dyson, B. and Rubin, A. (2003). Implementing Cooperative Learning in elementary physical education. *JOPERD: The Journal of Physical Education, Recreation and Dance* 74(1): 48–55.

Dyson, B. and Strachan, K. (2004). The ecology of Cooperative Learning in a high school physical education programme. *Waikato Journal of Education* 10: 117–39.

Hammersley, M. (1977). *Teacher perspectives*. Milton Keynes: Open University Press.

Johnson, D.W., Johnson, R.T. and Johnston-Holubec, E. (1994). *Cooperative Learning in the classroom*. Alexandria, VA: ASCD Publications.

Kagan, S. (1993). *Cooperative Learning*. San Capistrano, CA: Kagan Cooperative Learning.

Kirk, D. (1995). Action research and educational reform in physical education. *Pedagogy in Practice* 1(1): 4–21.

Larsson, H. and Quennerstedt, M. (2010). Understanding movement: a socio-cultural approach to analysing human movement. Paper presented at the Australian Association for Research in Education (AARE) Conference, Melbourne, 28 November–2 December.

Metzler, M.W. (2005). *Instructional models for physical education*, 2nd edn. Scottsdale, AZ: Holcomb Hathaway.

Metzler, M.W. (2011). *Instructional models for physical education*, 3rd edn. Scottsdale, AZ: Holcomb Hathaway.

Mitchell, S.A. and Oslin, J.L. (1999). *Authentic assessment in games teaching: the game performance assessment instrument*. NASPE Assessment Series. Reston, VA: NASPE.

Putnam, J.W. (1993). The process of Cooperative Learning. In J.W. Putnam (ed.), *Cooperative Learning and strategies for inclusion: celebrating diversity in the classroom*, 15–40. London: Paul H. Brookes Publishing.

Robinson, K. (2010). Changing education paradigms. Online. Available HTTP: <http://www.youtube.com/watch?v=zDZFcDGpL4Uandfeature=player_embedded> (accessed 3 April 2011).

Siedentop, D. (2002). Content knowledge for physical education. *Journal of Teaching in Physical Education* 21(4): 368–77.

Sparkes, A.C. (1991). Exploring the subjective dimensions of curriculum change. In N. Armstrong and A.C. Sparkes (eds), *Issues in physical education*, 1–19. London: Cassell Education.

Stenhouse, L. (1977). *An introduction to curriculum research and development*. London: Heinemann.

6 Using the Cooperative Learning model in physical education teacher education

From theory to practice

Sima Zach and Rona Cohen

Key terms: teacher education, field experience, instructional models, social behaviour, academic achievements

---

The impetus for this chapter is twofold: first, to argue for the importance of teaching pedagogical models in physical education teacher education (PETE), and second, to respond to the perceived need for practical knowledge about Cooperative Learning in physical education in general and in PETE in particular. One of the major challenges of teacher-education programmes is to help student teachers put knowledge into practice, or, as others have proposed, to close the gap between academic knowledge and practical knowledge (e.g. Cheng *et al.*, 2010; Zeichner, 2010). The first part of this chapter aims to address this challenge by describing the theoretical background and justification for using the Cooperative Learning model in teacher-education programmes. Since not all pedagogical models can be studied thoroughly during pre-service training, it is important to justify the choice of those that are included and implemented in field experience. The second part of the chapter is application-oriented. It presents an intervention study implemented in and around the field experiences of university PETE students and in which the college student teachers acted as the participants. The aim of the study was to examine the advantages and disadvantages of teaching Cooperative Learning in teacher education, and the extent to which the model can be integrated into the teacher-education process. In the study an attempt was made to create a 'third space' – a learning opportunity for student teachers that was not previously familiar to them, neither in their experience as learners nor in their teacher preparation programme. This third space, as argued by Gutiérrez (2008), can be created by bringing together academic knowledge, in our case the theory underlying pedagogical models, and field experience, as reflected by the student teachers' self-efficacy, their planning skills and their reflections on this experience. The chapter concludes with lessons to be gained from the intervention study and recommendations regarding teacher education in general and PETE in particular. It is important to note that we are deliberately using the term 'pedagogical models' rather than Metzler's (2011) idea of model-based instruction. We do this as the teaching and learning process that we are referring to is, as suggested by Kirk (2010), more than just instruction; it is also about the curriculum, the learner, the teaching and of course the instructive strategies.

The importance of teaching Cooperative Learning methods to pre-service teachers

Developing independent teacher candidates with professional educational beliefs is one of the building blocks or main goals of many teacher-education programmes (Kallestad and Olweus, 1998; Stephens *et al.*, 2004; Zach *et al.*, in press). If addressed, these beliefs facilitate a greater influence of the teacher-education programme on pre-service teachers' (PSTs) views of teaching and learning (Tsangaridou and O'Sullivan, 2003), whether they experience either major or minor changes in their personal beliefs during their teacher preparation (Kagan, 1992; Tsangaridou, 2008; Zach *et al.*, 2005). Understanding their beliefs is therefore important when trying to adopt educational approaches that best suit their philosophy (Cothran *et al.*, 2005). Insight into their belief structure is also critical in improving teacher-education programmes and teaching practices (Ennis, 1996). Richardson (1996) described three major categories of experience that influence the development of PSTs' beliefs about teaching: experience as pupils in school, life experience and/or the teacher-education professional preparation programme. It is suggested that teacher-education programmes will offer a variety of teaching approaches, in a way that PSTs will be able to choose, adopt and successfully implement the approach most appropriate for them in any given situation, as complex as it may be. We assert that PSTs' preferences will lead them to choose an approach in their 'zone of self-confidence', meaning that they will teach according to their teaching abilities and teaching efficacy (Zeichner, 2010).

Hence, each college and university with a teacher-education programme faces the challenging mission of including a variety of pedagogical approaches, each bearing a justifiable philosophical-educational-moral rationale for being included or prioritized over other approaches. In physical education, the 'physical' rationale in particular must be acknowledged and emphasized. We believe that when seeking educational approaches to be included in PETE programmes, certain objectives and principles (e.g. developing cardiovascular and muscular fitness, developing intellectual and social abilities) need to be considered as the most important and relevant ones. Identifying objectives should help in guiding the aims and purposes of a programme and in selecting the approaches to be studied, as well as in setting the content and expected learning outcomes (Metzler, 2011; Siedentop, 1998). The need for programmes to strive to meet students' needs led us to search for tools that would help to attain this end, which is why various learning styles such as peer teaching, inquiry teaching and inclusion style were extensively explored (e.g. Dunn *et al.*, 1995; Lovelace, 2005).

Dunn and Dunn (1993) defined a learning style as the way a person begins to concentrate on, process and internalize, and retain new and challenging information. According to their model, most people can learn, and each has his/her own unique ways of mastering new and challenging subject matter (Dunn, 2000; Dunn and Dunn, 1993). They presented a comprehensive model that identifies each individual's strengths and preferences across five categories (see Table 6.1).

In their model, students were described as either 'analytic' or 'global processors', or a combination of both, which Dunn and Dunn (1993) referred to as 'integrated'. In a review of 35 years of research on perceptual strength, Dunn and Dunn (2005) reported that the majority of school-age pupils were global. Perceptual strength enabled students to learn easily, with difficulty or not at all – depending on how they were taught (Dunn *et al.*, 2009). Over four decades, Dunn, Dunn and colleagues developed and experimented with a variety of instructional methods that gradually demonstrated their effectiveness with students' selected learning-style characteristics (Dunn and Griggs, 2007). It was reported that in special education (Fine, 2003), regular education (Favre, 2007) and among the gifted (Milgram *et al.*, 1995), learning-style-responsive instruction increased students' learning outcomes and achievement, and improved their attitude towards learning.

Extending this work to the physical education domain, a variety of teaching approaches, styles and instructional models (Metzler, 2011), or pedagogical models (Haerens *et al.*, 2011), were suggested. Metzler (2011) maintained that in order to teach a variety of content matter and address a variety of students' abilities effectively, physical education teachers should know and use several different pedagogical models. In addition to that, Lund *et al.* (2008) redefined Cochran *et al.*'s (1993) seven hypotheses into postulates reflecting the essential setting for the development of pedagogical content knowing for model-based instruction. They also suggested that these postulates be examined further in three stages of teaching: pre-service, induction and veteran.

Table 6.1 Dunn and Dunn (1993) learning-style model

Stimuli	Elements
Environmental	Sound, light, temperature and seating design
Emotional	Motivation, task persistence, responsibility and structure
Sociological	Learning alone, in pairs, with peers, in a team, with either an authoritative or collegial teacher, with social variety or in patterns
Physical	Perceptual strengths, such as auditory, verbal/kinaesthetic, visual text or visual picture, tactual and/or kinaesthetic; and intake, time-of-day energy levels and mobility requirements
Psychological	Analytic versus global and impulsive versus reflective characteristics, left side of the brain or right side of the brain

In the last decade a few reviews were conducted to explore the influence of these pedagogical models on various indices of student learning in PE; see, for example, Hellison and Martinek's (2006) chapter on teaching social and personal responsibility (TPSR), Wallhead and O'Sullivan's (2005) and Hastie *et al.*'s (2011) reviews of sport education, Ward and Lee's (2005) article on peer teaching and Casey (2011) on teachers' use of and feelings towards model-based practice. The focuses in all of these reviews were mainly elementary- and high-school students, with few studies of PSTs cited.

Our chapter highlights Cooperative Learning as it pertains to teacher education. Since not all pedagogical models can be studied and implemented thoroughly in teacher education, it is important to justify the rationale for those chosen to be taught (Metzler *et al.*, 2008). Our pedagogical instructors at the Zinman College of Physical Education and Sport Sciences at the Wingate Institute in Israel learned about various pedagogical models over a period of one year, and in the following year staff workshops were held for each model selected for incorporation into the curriculum. These workshops included a series of theoretical lectures from expert pedagogues in the country and from other countries, practical classes, peer assignments, lesson demonstrations and film observations. After this two-year process, we chose to teach the Cooperative Learning model as one of five pedagogical models. The others were: Sport Education, Tactical Games, Social and Personal Responsibility, and Inquiry Teaching.

The rationale for choosing the Cooperative Learning model as an important pedagogical model in the PETE programme is related to the model's main advantages for learners. First, learning in cooperating teams promotes intergroup relations and positive social development (Barrett, 2005; Johnson and Johnson, 1989, 2009); second, it improves academic achievements (Slavin, 1991); and third, it increases the level of active participation (Johnson and Johnson, 1989; 2009; Slavin, 1991). Learning in teams also enhances the learners' knowledge repertoire and responses (Ames and Murray, 1982).

Five critical elements of Cooperative Learning as a pedagogical model have been identified: (1) positive interdependence, (2) face-to-face interaction, (3) individual and group accountability, (4) interpersonal small-group skills and (5) group processing (see Johnson *et al.*, 1993). These elements (which are explained in greater detail in the first chapter of this book) suit physical education because of the social interaction and social processes that constantly occur in physical education lessons, such as competition in ball games, imitation of performance in gymnastics, encouraging each other in outdoor training or creativity in dance.

In general, during physical education classes, children are extensively engaged in team and group activities, therefore it was suggested that teacher preparation should include Cooperative Learning as an appropriate pedagogical model for the prospective teachers. Following the decision to include Cooperative Learning in the teacher-education programme, the pedagogical staff conducted a study designated to examine the model's implementation by PSTs in their field experience. Although our study can be found elsewhere (Cohen and Zach, in press), it is described briefly in the next section.

Cooperative Learning among physical education teacher-education majors

The following intervention study was conducted with PSTs as participants who were trying to implement the knowledge they acquired in college in their field experience. The aim of the study was to understand the advantages and disadvantages of teaching Cooperative Learning in teacher education, and to what extent this approach can be internalized and used during the teacher-education process. We also discuss the implications of this study for teacher-education programmes.

More specifically, the purpose of this study was to examine whether the Cooperation Learning model contributed to the PSTs' teaching efficacy and planning skills. We chose planning skills as one of the two dependent variables following Manross and Templeton's (1997) list of characteristics of expert physical education teachers. It was agreed that improving PSTs' ability to plan thoroughly and completely is one of the major teacher preparation objectives, and therefore it should be evaluated at the end of the intervention, as well as at the end of each field experience semester in the curriculum. Bearing in mind the connection between perception and performance, physical education teaching efficacy was chosen as the second dependent variable, following Gurvitch and Metzler's (2009) suggestion that being successful in achieving challenging experiences may foster strong efficacy beliefs. This study focused on four classes of PSTs in their third year of field experience, and their two supervisors. PSTs were assigned to two groups: the Cooperative Learning group (CLG), $n = 25$, and the direct instruction group (DIG), $n = 24$. Both groups were divided into small teams of three to five students. Programme constraints meant that the PSTs remained in their college-assigned classes and the classes were randomly assigned into the intervention condition. This means that all teams in one class learned either the CL or the DI model.

During their third year in the college programme, the PSTs attended a 15-week methodology class taught by a faculty member who specialized in teaching pedagogical models in physical education. They practised their field experience once a week throughout the year. Additionally, they taught 12 consecutive days in school, supervised by mentor teachers in schools and by their faculty-supervisors.

The CLG intervention included 15 hours of content knowledge during the methodology course, emphasizing the basic principles and essence of the Cooperative Learning model. Students also gained experience in setting up Cooperative Learning teaching unit activities, and they practised this knowledge in school. Data were collected throughout two semesters. The PSTs were asked by their supervisors to plan one Cooperative Learning teaching unit and to explain why and how they chose the activities, using the criteria of the five elements of the Cooperative Learning model, namely positive interdependence, individual accountability, promoting face-to-face interaction, interpersonal and small-group skills and group processing that included student reflection and goal-setting.

The direct instruction model is characterized by teacher-centred decisions, while students mostly follow teachers' directions and respond when they are asked. In order to promote student achievement, teachers structured the learning. The essence of the model is to give students adequate supervised practice time with specific feedback (Metzler, 2011). The DIG participated in the same methodology classes taught by the supervisors-faculty members, and were asked to plan and teach their unit plan during the 12 days of field experience. This pedagogical model is traditionally the main model taught in the college. It should be noted that most of the instructors, lecturers and coaches still use this as their sole pedagogical model.

The data collected from both groups pertained to: (1) the results of a physical education self-efficacy questionnaire before and after intervention, and (2) the quality of the unit plan and lesson plan. The participants in the study were asked to complete a questionnaire examining their teaching self-efficacy in PETE. The questionnaire included 22 statements describing teaching skills for physical education teachers. Participants had to evaluate their confidence in their ability to perform these skills on a 10-point Likert scale (1 = low confidence; 10 = high confidence) (Zach *et al.*, in press). In addition, the unit and lesson plans were evaluated by faculty members using a rubric with specific criteria for evaluation. Seven unit plans were submitted by the DIG and five unit plans were submitted by the CLG. Informal conversations were conducted with four types of groups: (1) one of the researchers with ST teams; (2) one of the researchers with ST individuals; (3) one of the researchers and a cooperating teacher; and (4) one of the researchers and a cooperating teacher with the PSTs under his/her supervision. Conversations centred on the whole process of acquiring the theoretical background of Cooperative Learning and applying it in planning and in teaching. Reflections were discussed and suggestions for improving the process were made by all the participants in the study. In addition to the planning, the teaching and the discussion after each lesson, students' assignments included submission of a weekly reflection on one lesson that they had taught.

The results of the study indicated that the PSTs in the DIG reported higher self-efficacy than the CLG STs. Although disappointing, these findings were not surprising. Cooperative Learning was a new pedagogical model for the students, and when the CLG in this study needed to apply their knowledge in class they felt unsure of their teaching abilities, and therefore their PETE self-efficacy did not increase. In contrast, the DIG implemented the traditional teaching approach they had been learning for the previous two years in the college, and therefore they felt comfortable using it during the field experience. As suggested by others, supportive environments allow learners to acquire knowledge and practise their teaching skills in a better way (Hadar and Brody, 2010). PSTs in the CLG needed more time to practise the new teaching model progressively in field experience.

As the PSTs in the current study had little teaching experience, they had to deal with a variety of obstacles, such as class management, monitoring students' participation and observing and evaluating the effectiveness of their own planning. Taking all this into consideration, the PSTs in the CLG probably felt overwhelmed. Both groups (CLG and DIG) had to face other issues during their field experience, such as developing content knowledge and challenging students to participate, and evidently they had not completely mastered the teaching skills.

Informal conversations with the students, as well as their reflection assignments, revealed that in the limited time available the CLG felt insecure teaching the CL model. For example:

> Sometimes I found myself going from one group of students to the other, teaching them as if they were a small class and not instructing them to effectively cooperate.
>
> (Dana's reflection assignment no. 2)

> The first lesson in the unit went very well. It was also the easiest to plan. Being introduced and getting to know each other is always fun. But, then I had to think how I was going to proceed with my orienteering unit plan while keeping them active and not just thinking or talking with each other.
>
> (Liron's reflection assignment no. 2)

> After five lessons in the CL model, I felt that it was difficult for me to apply the benchmarks of the model, such as monitoring and processing for social learning outcomes, even selecting an appropriate CL strategy while teaching was quite difficult. My cooperating teacher said that I was so busy trying to teach what I had planned that I could not even attend to students' improvement or students' need for my advice.
>
> (Tal's reflection assignment no. 5)

Cooperating teachers positioned themselves in-between. On one hand, they received detailed instructions about the Cooperative Learning pedagogical model. On the other, PSTs demonstrated a lack of self-confidence, and as Ariela said:

> I felt her lack of confidence and tried to convince her to teach in a way she feels comfortable ... then I realized that I am doing the wrong thing ... she must cope with her difficulties. However, it was also difficult for me to find ways to help her.

A major concern that arose from informal conversations with cooperating teachers and PSTs was the need to bring together the triad pedagogical instructor–cooperating teacher–student teacher more thoroughly and more comprehensively. Both the cooperating teachers and the PSTs needed more guidance and support while implementing the new teaching processes in the Cooperative Learning model. After completion of the study and presenting the results to the staff of the pedagogical instructors, it was decided to include the Cooperative Learning pedagogical model in the programme. Further information regarding this research can be found elsewhere (Cohen and Zach, in press).

Closing remarks

Addressing a whole range of learners' needs is an important challenge facing physical educators. To facilitate this, teacher-education programmes should provide PSTs with the knowledge and understanding that will enable them to select the appropriate pedagogical models for use in their teaching, planning units and lessons according to the selected model, and to implement each model in their schools. For example, when the target learning domain is social, teachers planning to achieve social objectives to promote social outcomes might choose Cooperative Learning as the preferred and most effective model.

An important component required by teachers in order to embed professional behaviour is the ability to use a circle-structured core reflection (see Korthagen and Vasalos, 2005). Therefore, it is recommended that PSTs first acquire the fundamentals necessary for theoretical knowledge and understanding of the model concept, and that they should understand the characteristics, advantages and disadvantages of the model. Micro-teaching is thus recommended, so that PSTs will learn what the difficulties and problems are, and in which circumstances it is best to apply the model in schools during their field experience. Lastly, they need to evaluate the process and its outcomes so as to improve their future teaching experience (Korthagen and Kessels, 1999; Korthagen *et al.*, 2001). This circle, if continued more than once during teacher preparation, increases the likelihood of understanding and implementing the model in the future. This essential process entails a considerable amount of time, and perhaps warrants the allocation of a special course in addition to the existing methods course within the programme, so that PSTs can learn the model thoroughly. Integrating the model into a sport or movement class is a necessary applied method of teaching. We claim that otherwise the PSTs will face difficulties implementing a pedagogical model such as Cooperating Learning during field experience.

Fostering the social domain is a major purpose of the mandatory physical education curriculum designed by the Ministry of Education in Israel. Nevertheless, Cooperative Learning as a pedagogical model in physical education in Israel is very rare. It is much more common to see physical education teachers using cooperative-oriented teaching styles such as inclusion, reciprocal learning or problem-solving to promote social behaviour among learners, or trying to promote the social domain using collaborative activities. Some of our participants acknowledged the importance of the social domain, but had difficulties in setting attainable objectives or planning relevant tasks in order to achieve these objectives. Ball games were considered the easiest way to relate to the social domain. However, developing social skills, and being accountable for obtaining this objective among the learners, required a creative way of thinking. To our way of thinking, physical education is one of the most appropriate and relevant fields to be taught in school through the Cooperative Learning model. In this field, cooperation is inherent in the subject matter. The following are examples from different content areas within physical education that exemplify this assertion:

1   Gymnastics – in this area content knowledge comprises four elements: basic skills, complicated-advanced skills, composition and choreography and assisting while acquiring and practising new skills. In addition to these, while coping with difficulties within the learning process in gymnastics, students often experience emotions such as fear, stress, lack of self-confidence, disappointment or frustration.

2   Orienteering – content knowledge comprises the following main elements: knowledge of topography, orienteering techniques that include reading and understanding maps, knowing how to identify features from the map in open areas, knowledge of how to improve endurance and knowledge of how to plot a route in an open area. In addition, while experiencing orienteering, students working in teams are often drawn into competition to improve their own individual record, to compete against others or participate as part of a team against other teams. They often have to cope with emotional issues such as persistence and the ability to overcome obstacles and challenges.

3   Basketball – in order to be successful in a basketball game, or even teaching the passing game, the team must apply all five elements of CL. Missing one of these can be an obstacle to the team's efforts to achieve an effective game. The group is expected to behave as more than just five individual players. Each player has to demonstrate the best of his or her ability and talent in order that their contribution to the team will be significant and effective. The social aspect in basketball is realized in an endless combination of a variety of moves, such as passing game, double-up and fast break. Personal interdependence and the interaction between the players are the most influential elements on the team and its chances of winning. In addition, while playing basketball, players often experience emotions such as the fear of disappointing others, fear of embarrassing themselves or the team, stress from hostile spectators, pride in successfully completing a difficult move and satisfaction from a successful assist.

In these three examples, learning in small teams enables students to contribute to the team according to their abilities in the physical, cognitive, emotional and social domains, and to receive the support needed to accomplish their personal and the team's goals and success. These examples demonstrate that, unlike learning in the classroom, all four domains – physical, cognitive, emotional and social – can be addressed in physical education classes while being taught in the CL pedagogical model. Moreover, in these examples we demonstrated that without the team, both the individual and the group will probably achieve, acquire and improve to a lesser extent than with the team, or even not at all.

Hence, while collaborative activities are necessary for the CL model, they are not sufficient for promoting and or achieving this model's objectives. We can see a variety of collaborative activities in physical education classes, such as assisting or coordinating defence in basketball, coordinating an attack in team handball, rising for spiking in volleyball, measuring achievement in track and field, preparing a show in dance and more. In these activities students collaborate in order to achieve a short-term goal. Nevertheless, unlike collaborative activities, in order to be considered as cohering with the Cooperative Learning model, integration of three concepts – team rewards, individual accountability and equal opportunities for success – should be implemented (Slavin, 1991), in addition to the five critical elements described by Johnson and colleagues (Johnson *et al.*, 1993).

In the last decade interest in the field of Cooperative Learning in physical education has substantially increased among researchers. Research was previously conducted mainly in elementary schools (e.g. Dyson *et al.*, 2010) and high schools (e.g. Casey *et al.*, 2009; Dyson and Strachan, 2004), and in PETE research is almost non-existent (e.g. O'Leary and Griggs, 2010). In order to make Cooperative Learning a distinct model for pedagogical development in physical education, more research is needed in teacher-education settings. It is recommended that pedagogical models be taught until mastery, so that PSTs will be able to intelligently choose among existing models that best fit their beliefs, attitudes, situation, goals, the learners and other parameters that comprise their specific setting.

References

Ames, G.J. and Murray, F.B. (1982). When two wrongs make a right: promoting cognitive change by social conflict. *Developmental Psychology* 18: 894–7.

Barrett, T. (2005). Effects of Cooperative Learning on the performance of sixth-grade physical education students. *Journal of Teaching in Physical Education* 24: 88–102.

Casey, A. (2011). A review of literature of teachers' use of models-based practice: 1996 to the present. Paper presented at the Association Internationale des Ecoles Supérieures d'Education Physique (International Association for Physical Education in Higher Education) conference, University of Limerick, Ireland, June.

Casey, A., Dyson, B. and Campbell, A. (2009). Action research in physical education: focusing beyond myself through Cooperative Learning. *Educational Action Research* 17: 407–23.

Cheng, M.M.H., Cheng, A.Y.A. and Tang, S.Y.F (2010). Closing the gap between the theory and practice of teaching: implications for teacher education programmes in Hong Kong. *Journal of Education for Teaching* 36(1): 91–104.

Cochran, K.F., DeRuiter, J.A. and King, R.A. (1993). Pedagogical content knowing: an integrative model for teacher preparation. *Journal of Teacher Education* 44: 263–72.

Cohen, R. and Zach, S. (in press). The effect of Cooperative Learning experience of pre-service teachers on their planning and teaching self-efficacy. *Physical Education and Sport Pedagogy*.

Cothran, D.J., Kulinna, P., Banville, D., Choi, E., Amade-Escot, C., MacPhail, A. and Kirk, D. (2005). A cross-cultural investigation of the use of teaching styles. *Research Quarterly for Exercise and Sport* 76(2): 193–201.

Dunn, R. (2000). Learning styles: theory, research, and practice. *National Forum of Applied Educational Research Journal* 13(1): 3–22.

Dunn, R. and Dunn, K. (1993). *Teaching secondary students through their individual learning styles: practical approaches for grades 7–12*. Boston: Allyn and Bacon.

Dunn, R. and Dunn, K. (2005). Thirty-five years of research on perceptual strengths. *Clearing House* 78(6): 273–6.

Dunn, R. and Griggs, S. A. (2007). *Synthesis of the Dunn and Dunn learning-style model research: who, what, when, where, and so what?* Jamaica, NY: St. John's University's Center for the Study of Learning and Teaching Styles.

Dunn, R., Griggs, S.A., Olson, J., Gorman, B. and Beasley, M. (1995). A meta-analytic validation of the Dunn and Dunn model of learning-style preferences. *Journal of Educational Research* 88: 353–61.

Dunn, R., Honigsfeld, A., Shea Doolan, L., Bostrom, L., Russo, K., Schiering, M.S. and Tenedero, H. (2009). Impact of learning-style instructional strategies on students' achievement and attitudes: perceptions of educators in diverse institutions. *Clearing House* 82: 135–40.

Dyson, B.P., Linehan, N.R. and Hastie, P.A. (2010). The ecology of Cooperative Learning in elementary school physical education classes. *Journal of Teaching in Physical Education* 29: 113–30.

Dyson, B. and Strachan, K. (2004). The ecology of Cooperative Learning in a high school physical education programme. *Waikato Journal of Education* 10: 117–39.

Ennis, C. (1996). A model describing the influence of values and context on student learning. In S. Silverman and C. Ennis (eds), *Student learning in physical education: applying research to enhance instruction*, 127–47. Champaign, IL: Human Kinetics.

Favre, L. (2007). Analysis of the transition of a low socioeconomic status African-American New Orleans elementary school into a demonstration learning-style school of excellence. *Journal of Urban Education* 4: 79–90.

Fine, D. (2003). A sense of learning style. *Principal Leadership* 4: 55–9.

Gurvitch, R. and Metzler, M.W. (2009). The effects of laboratory-based and field-based practicum experience on pre-service teachers' self-efficacy. *Teaching and Teacher Education* 25: 437–43.

Gutiérrez, K. (2008). Developing sociocultural literacy in the third space. *Reading Research Quarterly* 43: 148–64.

Hadar, L. and Brody, D. (2010). From isolation to symphonic harmony: building a professional development community among teacher educators. *Teaching and Teacher Education* 26(8): 1641–51.

Haerens, L., Kirk, D., Cardon, G. and De Bourdeauhuij, I. (2011). The development of a pedagogical model for health-based physical education. *Quest* 63: 321–38.

Hastie, P.A., de Ojeda, D.M. and Luquin, A.C. (2011). A review of research on Sport Education: 2004 to the present. *Physical Education and Sport Pedagogy* 16(2): 103–32.

Hellison, D. and Martinek, T. (2006). Social and individual responsibility programmes. In D. Kirk, D. Macdonald and M. O'Sullivan (eds), *The handbook of physical education*, 610–26. London: Sage.

Johnson, D.W. and Johnson, R.T. (1989). *Cooperation and competition: theory and research*. Edina, MN: Interaction Book Co.

Johnson, D.W. and Johnson, R.T. (2009). An educational psychology success story: social interdependence theory and Cooperative Learning. *Educational Researcher* 38: 365–79.

Johnson, D.W., Johnson, R.T. and Holubec, E.J. (1993). *Circles of learning: cooperation in the classroom*, 4th edn. Edina, MN: Interaction Book Co.

Kagan, D.M. (1992). Professional growth among preservice and beginning teachers. *Review of Educational Research* 62(2): 129–69.

Kallestad, J.H. and Olweus, D. (1998). Teachers' emphases on general educational goals: a study of Norwegian teachers. *Scandinavian Journal of Educational Research* 42: 257–79.

Kirk, D. (2010). *Physical education futures*. London: Routledge.

Korthagen, F. and Kessels, J. (1999). Linking theory and practice: changing the pedagogy of teacher education. *Educational Researcher* 28: 4–12.

Korthagen, F., Kessels, J., Koster, B., Lagerwerf, B. and Wubbels, T. (2001). *Linking practice and theory: the pedagogy of realistic teacher education*. Mahwah, NJ: Lawrence Erlbaum Associates.

Korthagen, F. and Vasalos, A. (2005). Levels in reflection: core reflection as a means to enhance professional growth. *Teachers and Teaching: Theory and Practice* 11: 47–71.

Lovelace, M.K. (2005). A meta-analysis of experimental research based on the Dunn and Dunn learning-style model, 1980–2000. *Journal of Educational Research* 98(3): 176–83.

Lund, L.J., Metzler, W.M. and Gurvitch, R. (2008). Pedagogical content knowing for model-based instruction in physical education and future directions for research. *Journal of Teaching in Physical Education* 27: 580–9.

Manross, D. and Templeton, C. (1997). Expertise in teaching physical education. *Journal of Physical Education, Recreation and Dance* 68(3): 29–35.

Metzler, W.M. (2011). *Instructional models for physical education*, 3rd edn. Scottsdale, AZ: Holcomb Hathaway.

Metzler, W.M., Lund, L.J. and Gurvitch, R. (2008). Adoption of instructional innovation across teachers' career stages. *Journal of Teaching in Physical Education* 27(4): 457–65.

Milgram, R.M., Price, G.E. and Dunn. R. (1995). Learning styles of highly creative Israeli adolescents. *National Forum of Special Education Journal* 5: 3–11.

O'Leary, N. and Griggs, G. (2010). Researching the pieces of a puzzle: the use of a jigsaw learning approach in the delivery of undergraduate gymnastics. *Journal of Further and Higher Education* 34(1): 73–81.

Richardson, V. (1996). The role of attitudes and beliefs in learning to teach. In J. Sikula, T. Buttery and E. Guyton (eds), *Handbook of research on teacher education*, 102–19. New York: Macmillan

Siedentop, D. (1998). *Introduction to physical education, fitness, and sport*, 3rd edn. Mountain View, CA: Mayfield.

Slavin, R.E. (1991). Cooperative Learning and group contingencies. *Journal of Behavioral Education* 1: 105–15.

Stephens, P., Tønnessen, F. and Kyriacou, C. (2004). Teacher training and teacher education in England and Norway: a comparative study of policy goals. *Comparative Education* 40(1): 109–30.

Tsangaridou, N. (2008). Trainee primary teachers' beliefs and practices about physical education during student teaching. *Physical Education and Sport Pedagogy* 13(2): 131–52.

Tsangaridou, N.N. and O'Sullivan, M.M. (2003). Physical education teachers' theories of action and theories-in-use. *Journal of Teaching in Physical Education* 22(2) 132–52.

Wallhead, T. and O'Sullivan, M. (2005). Sport education: physical education for the new millennium? *Physical Education and Sport Pedagogy* 10: 181–210.

Ward, P. and Lee, M. (2005). Peer-assisted learning in physical education: a review of theory and research. *Journal of Teaching in Physical Education* 24: 205–25.

Zach, S., Galmor, H. and Zeev, A. (2005). Educational beliefs of student teachers and physical education teachers. *Dapim* 40: 59–89. (In Hebrew.)

Zach, S., Harari, I. and Harari, N. (in press). Changes in teaching efficacy of pre-service teachers in physical education. *Physical Education and Sport Pedagogy.*

Zeichner, K. (2010). Rethinking the connections between campus courses and field experiences in college- and university-based teacher education. *Journal of Teacher Education* 61(1–2): 89–99.

Part 3

Key aspects of Cooperative Learning

7 Borrowing strategies from adventure-based learning to enhance group processing in Cooperative Learning

Sue Sutherland

Debriefing [group processing] is like painting a wall. Rather than the teacher painting the whole wall themselves you could have the whole classroom of students involved in painting the wall by sharing their opinions and ideas.

Stuhr *et al.*, 2010

> Key terms: 'I' statements, put-downs, five-finger contract, full-value contract, isomorphically framing

Cooperative Learning is a pedagogical model in physical education that uses 'small groups so students work together to maximize their own and each other's learning' (Johnson *et al.*, 1993, p.6). This is followed by a purposeful group-processing session, which addresses both academic and social goals. Johnson and Johnson (1989) found that Cooperative Learning produced increased student achievement, more positive relationships and greater psychological health than competitive or individualistic learning. In addition, Cooperative Learning involves face-to-face interaction between group members (Strahm, 2007) and to be carried out effectively requires the development of interpersonal and small-group skills (Cohen, 1994; Johnson and Johnson, 1994; Kagan, 1994). These interpersonal skills need to be taught within Cooperative Learning in a structured way that allows group members to reflect on the level of group interactions. Indeed, an important goal of the Cooperative Learning model is to facilitate students' awareness of and to help them improve how they behave in group situations (Villa *et al.*, 2010). For an explicit definition of the elements of Cooperative Learning please refer to Dyson and Casey's Introduction in this book.

What is group processing?

Group processing is one of the five principles of the Cooperative Learning model. Johnson and Johnson (1999) defined group processing as 'reflecting on a group session to (a) describe what member actions were helpful and unhelpful and (b) make decisions about what actions to continue or change' (p. 85) and can take place in small-group or whole-class situations. Villa *et al.* (2010, p. 33) described group processing as:

> [A] reflective technique that promotes students' sense of self determination and empowerment, because they learn to recognize how they have worked through conflicts in ideas and opinions, overcome their struggles in learning new content, and gained new understandings of complex or difficult material.

Within group processing students will discuss which behaviours are helpful or unhelpful in achieving their goals and which behaviours they will continue to use or change. An important aspect of group processing is to analyse how well a group or individual is performing based on the task and group goals. Johnson *et al.* (1993) provided steps for achieving a successful process: (a) allowing sufficient time; (b) providing a structure for the process; (c) positive feedback; (d) specificity rather than vagueness in the process; (e) keeping students engaged; (f) reminding students to use their cooperative social skills; and (g) stating clear expectations for the purpose of the process. When conducted effectively group processing enhances group maintenance, promotes social skills, provides feedback to group members and facilitates collaborative skills (Johnson and Johnson, 1999). Villa *et al.* (2010) advised that group processing first requires the teacher to actively monitor students during the group work by observing and analysing the strengths and challenges of both students and group, and supporting each group when needed. The teacher then shares this information with the groups during the processing time and helps students to identify their strengths and areas for improvement.

Johnson and Johnson (2009a) have identified four components of group processing. The first component is that each student, group and class gives and receives *feedback* on how effectively they worked together and achieved the task/goal. The feedback should be descriptive and specific. Having received feedback on their performance, the students then *analyse and reflect* on this feedback. During this stage of the process, it is important to use questions that promote discussion rather than 'yes' or 'no' answers. The third component of the process requires students to analyse and describe group members' actions that contributed to or inhibited the group completing the task effectively. The group will then set *improvement goals* to enhance the quality of their work. The last component of the process is to provide an opportunity for the group to *celebrate* their hard work and success.

A variety of tools are available to teachers to help facilitate group processing (see Table 7.1 for examples). These tools can range from those that are more teacher-directed to those that are more student-centred. When using group processing in each lesson, it is critical to use different methods to keep the process interesting and engaging for students. Changing the tool for group processing can also assist the teacher in structuring the processing to focus on a particular aspect of each group's performance or social skills, avoid monotony for the students and reduce the risk of receiving the same answers each lesson.

Table 7.1 Group processing tools

Tool	Application
Group share	Group members discuss with each other what they did well during the lesson.
My contributions or accomplishment	Group members state what specifically he or she did to help the group to be successful.
Checklist	Individual group members score themselves on a 5 to 10-item checklist of behaviours important to functioning as a group. The group then discusses these checklists relative to enhancing group success.
Incomplete statement	Group members complete statements to describe their performance during the lesson. These skills can focus on academic and/or social skills.
Turn to your neighbour	Each group member takes a turn complimenting another group member on his or her performance on a task or social skill used in the lesson.
Oral statement bombardment	One student is selected and each group member tells him or her how they helped the group during the lesson.
Yearbook	Each student has a note card with his or her name on that is passed around for other group members to write one thing about how this person helped the group during the lesson.
Processing questions	Each group member answers a series of questions on their performance during the lesson. These questions usually focus on how well they did with reference to: interpersonal skills; areas for improvement; and goal setting.

Research has shown that group processing has a positive effect on group achievement (Johnson *et al.*, 1990; Yager *et al.*, 1986), positive student relationships (Putnam *et al.*, 1989) and students' perceptions of self-worth and belonging (Strahm, 2007). Archer-Kath *et al.* (1994) found that group processing was more effective when combined with individual rather than whole-group feedback. Reflecting on individual group members' actions has also resulted in a reduction in social loafing, clarification of the importance of group goals and the involvement of group effort (Johnson and Johnson, 2009a). Group processing can also foster: increased self-esteem, enhanced group-member efforts to achieve group goals, commitment to the group and collective identification (Johnson and Johnson, 2009b). Despite the stated benefits of group processing, it is often one of the elements of the Cooperative Learning model that is least used by teachers (Villa *et al.*, 2010). In a study of teachers from six elementary schools Antil *et al.* (1998) found that only one third used group processing when implementing Cooperative Learning. Within physical education, Casey *et al.* (2009) reported that group processing 'simply was not possible in such a time-poor environment' (p. 418). Consequently, in this study, the constraints of implementing Cooperative Learning within a 35–40-minute lesson resulted in group processing being sacrificed in favour of other elements of Cooperative Learning.

Research in physical education (Casey and Dyson, 2009; Dyson 2001, 2002; Dyson *et al.*, 2010) has reported that group processing was used as part of Cooperative Learning with elementary and secondary students. Dyson (2001, 2002) stated that the teachers in his studies conducted both small-group and whole-class processing sessions during Cooperative Learning. In one study (Dyson, 2002) the group processing presented in the data was related to conflict resolution regarding student roles and communication within the groups. Dyson *et al.* (2010) found that utilizing group processing in every lesson provided the opportunity for students to engage in cognitive tasks. Both small-group and whole-class processing was observed in physical education lessons.

Group processing is akin to the reflection process that occurs in adventure-based learning. While the two processes are similar, different strategies and models that have been used in adventure-based learning can be transferred to group processing in Cooperative Learning. Incorporating some of these strategies and models may provide a framework for teachers to utilize group processing more consistently and effectively within Cooperative Learning.

What is adventure-based learning?

Adventure-based learning is concerned with the interpersonal and intrapersonal relationships of participants (Priest, 1990). The premise of participation in adventure-based learning is that an increased level of self-awareness is brought about by positive change experienced through participation. More specifically, adventure-based learning has been described as a deliberate sequence of activities (communication, cooperation, trust and problem solving) focusing on the personal and social development of the students (Cosgriff, 2000).

Adventure-based learning is based on the theory of experiential learning. In contrast to the traditional behavioural and cognitive theories of learning, experiential learning is seen as being more holistic, combining cognition and behaviour with conscious perceptions and reflection (Priest and Gass, 1997). Experience permeates all forms of learning (Beard and Wilson, 2002) and is the process through which individuals make sense of a situation. Experiential learning occurs when individuals participate in an activity, then critically reflect on the activity, gain insight from the reflection and this results in a change of understanding and/or behaviour (Luckner and Nadler, 1997). Although there are many different experiential models (e.g. Joplin, 1995; Kolb, 1984; Pfeiffer and Jones, 1980) most consist of four phases: experiencing, reflecting, generalizing and applying (Figure 7.1). These models are often cyclical and involve complex interrelationships within and between each phase (Luckner and Nadler, 1997).

Once an individual engages in an activity, whether it is one that occurs naturally or one that is designed to promote specific learning, they have entered the experiencing phase. Upon completion of the activity, an individual engages in guided reflection related to what occurred during the activity. Reflection is central to human learning (Dewey, 1938). Indeed, without reflection, any learning that may result from an experience is left purely to chance (Luckner and Nadler,

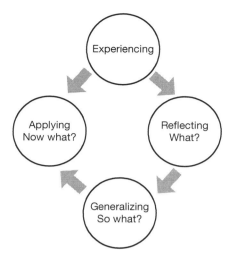

Figure 7.1 Experiential learning cycle.

1997). There are many different forms of reflection, ranging from an individual activity to a group discussion. The reflection phase answers the question 'what happened?' in the activity. Generalizing occurs when deductions can be made from the specific experience to other facets of the individual's life. To facilitate generalization, it is important to understand what happened in the activity and how that can help to inform other situations. The generalizing phase answers the question 'so what?' relative to what happened in the activity. Applying occurs when an individual puts into action the lessons learned from the generalization phase. The question of importance here is 'now what?' and involves taking what was learned from the experience and applying it to other areas of life. For experiential learning to truly take place, it is important that all phases of the model are accomplished, and that sufficient time is given for the process to be completed (Luckner and Nadler).

Gass and Stevens (2007) identified eight generations of facilitating the adventure process:

1 letting the experience speak for itself without guidance from the facilitator;
2 speaking on behalf of the experience, where the facilitator as the expert tells the participants what they learned;
3 debriefing the experience, with the facilitator guiding the participants' learning;
4 directly frontloading the experience, where the facilitator highlights the learning that will take place before the activity;
5 isomorphically framing the experience, with the facilitator using metaphors to connect the learning from the adventure experience to participants' lives;

6   indirectly frontloading the experience to address participants' issues, primarily used in therapeutic programmes;
7   flagging the experience, where the facilitator reinforces the desired behaviour changes for participants;
8   empowering self-facilitation, where the participants facilitate their own experience; used with motivated and mature learners.

The first three generations are used after an experience, the next four can be used before, during and after an experience and the last generation has the individual rather than the facilitator taking on the responsibility for processing the experience. In education programmes debriefing and self-facilitation are the most commonly used methods (Gass and Stevens, 2007). The following discussion will focus on debriefing, as this is the method I use within the adventure-based learning course in the physical education teacher education (PETE) programme at the Ohio State University.

The purpose of the course is to introduce the pre-service physical education teachers to adventure-based learning. More specifically, it deals with how adventure-based learning can be used to build community among K-12 students and foster interpersonal and intrapersonal growth, and shows how students can demonstrate responsible personal and social behaviours in physical activity settings (National Association of Sport and Physical Education, 2004, standard 5). The course focuses on the following aspects of adventure-based learning:

*   the theory underlying adventure-based learning and experiential learning;
*   the importance of sequence and flow of activities in adventure-based learning;
*   the concepts of interpersonal and intrapersonal skills;
*   the role of the facilitator and how that differs from teaching physical education;
*   the importance of processing (brief and debrief, including how to transfer learning) within adventure-based learning;
*   direct experience of activities;
*   opportunities for facilitation of activities.

A key element of the course is providing a structure for leading a student-centred debriefing session to enhance learning from the experience. Debriefing is a technique used in adventure-based learning to conduct a reflection session and is similar to group processing in the Cooperative Learning model.

Debriefing

Debriefing is arguably one of the most important aspects of experiential learning. It is the process through which the group members understand and construct meaning from the experience, and is based on the experiential learning cycle (see Figure 7.1). Debriefing is achieved through guided reflection and should result in learning being transferred to other areas of the group members' life (Sugarman *et al.*, 2000; Joplin, 1995). Debriefing should be student-centred and guided rather than driven by the facilitator (Chapman, 1995). However, this is often not what occurs in practice, where teacher-directed debriefing is more common (Estes, 2004; Brown, 2004). In this type of debrief, the students' reflection is directed by the teacher, and students are told what they have learned rather than discover what they have learned for themselves through a reflective process. A teacher-directed debrief creates a situation where the student does not learn how to learn from their own experience, but rather is told what (s)he learned (Estes and Tomb, 1995). The teacher-directed debrief process includes the following characteristics: students are allocated turns to speak, topic of discussion is determined by the teacher, the teacher paraphrases the students' response, often changing or fixing what the student said, and the talk is directed to the teacher rather than between students (Brown, 2003, 2004). In stark contrast, in the student-centred approach the teacher asks questions and encourages students to take ownership about what they learned through their participation in the activities. This demands that the teacher and student work together, that the teacher is aware of the effect of their actions on the students' response and learning and should provide students with opportunities to facilitate their own learning (Estes, 2004), and that the teacher encourages students to talk to one another and not just at the teacher. Recent research has indicated that facilitating an effective student-centred debrief session is not an easy process for pre-service physical education teachers to learn (Sutherland *et al.*, 2009a,b).

Strategies to improve reflection during debriefing

The literature in adventure-based learning proposes a number of different strategies that can be used to enhance the quality of the reflection during the debriefing sessions (Frank, 2004; Gass and Stevens, 2007; Luckner and Nadler, 1997; Panicucci, 2007). The following list is based on strategies from the literature and my own experience in facilitating and teaching adventure-based learning. I feel that these strategies are the most appropriate for use in Cooperative Learning to promote a physical and emotional environment conducive to introspective discussion.

- Provide adequate time in the lesson to conduct a processing session. As the literature has shown, group processing is often forsaken for other components of Cooperative Learning.
- Use a group structure that promotes face-to-face interaction where all students can see and hear everything. A large circle with the teacher as part of the circle can be an effective structure for whole-class processing.
- Show respect for all viewpoints by implementing only one person speaking at a time. Use student names and thank them for their contribution to the discussion.
- Give students the right to pass on participation in parts of the discussion to create an emotionally safe environment for all students. Students still actively listen to the discussion.

- Encourage the use of 'I' statements rather than placing blame through 'You' statements. 'I' statements avoid the negative messages associated with 'You' messages and are more effective in promoting change without negative confrontation. Luckner and Nadler (1997) proposed three steps in creating 'I' statements that might be useful in teaching students to acquire this skill. The first step is to describe the behaviour, for instance, 'When people laugh at someone's suggestion ...'. This is followed by the person stating how they feel about the possible consequences of the behaviour, for example, 'When people laugh at someone's suggestion I am concerned ...'. Finally the consequences of the behaviour are stated, for example, 'When people laugh at someone's suggestion I am concerned that person will have their feelings hurt and not want to help the group complete the task.'
- Promote personal responsibility by having students take responsibility for their actions and not place blame on others. Do not allow the use of 'put-downs'.
- Follow the conversation that the students feel is important. Listen to what they are saying and use follow-up questions to explore this further. Avoid moving down a sequence of pre-prepared questions without listening to what the students are saying. Use the 'in-the-moment events' to drive the debrief process.
- Do not finish students' sentences or rephrase their response to meet your needs or agenda. Listen to what they are saying, as it is clearly very important to them.
- Realize there is not only one correct answer. Do not steer students to 'the answer' that you are looking for. Rather, be open to different possibilities and explore these further as they arise.
- Use silence to give less vocal students a chance to enter the conversation.
- If an issue is not dealt with it will come back with a vengeance. Avoiding or ignoring issues may be the path of least resistance at the time, but the issue(s) will continue to fester and will be more powerful when they resurface.
- Operate within the time constraints of a class period. It is advisable for groups or teachers to work on one issue at a time and move on to a subsequent issue if time allows. Addressing more than one issue could result in sacrificing the last phase of the experiential learning cycle because of time constraints. Applying is arguably the most important phase in debriefing, as it is here that students understand how their learning can be transferred beyond the task or group.
- Provide an opportunity for ALL students to contribute to the discussion, not just those who always speak, the leaders, or those who are the loudest. If students feel that their voice is valued and respected then they are more likely to engage fully in the discussion.
- Engage in active listening when students are speaking. Modelling and teaching this skill to all students will help to create an environment that is more respectful and engaging for all.

- Establish group norms for the behaviour that is acceptable during debriefing. With elementary age students, group norms can be established using the five-finger contract. For secondary age students the full-value contract can be used to establish group norms.
- Use the funnelling technique (Priest and Gass, 1997) during debriefing. This technique guides participants through a series of steps that reproduce how individuals make cognitive connections between what happened in the experience and what it means to them. Priest and Gass identified six 'filters' or categories of questions to aid in the experiential learning process: review, recall and remember, affect and effect, summation, application and commitment (illustrated in Table 7.3).

These strategies can be employed in whole-class or small-group situations, and when used consistently will enhance the effectiveness of the reflection strategies used in both debriefing and group processing.

Table 7.2 Key terms

Term	Description
'I' statements	'I' statements allow an individual to communicate a message in a non-threatening manner.
Put-downs	Statements that are used with the intention of causing harm or pain to others.
Five-finger contract	In this contract each finger represents a group behaviour that will help to establish a safe and respectful environment as follows (Frank, 2002, p. 82): • Pinky (little) finger represents *Safety* (physical and emotional) as it is the smallest and most vulnerable • Ring finger represents *Commitment* – that is, a willingness to let things go and not hold on to grudges • Middle finger represents awareness of *Put-downs* • Pointer (index) finger represents *Taking responsibility* for actions instead of placing blame • thumb represents an agreement to *Work towards group goals.*
Full-value contract	According to Panicucci (2007, p. 42), the full-value contract asks the group: • to understand and create safe and respectful behavioural norms under which it will operate • to commit to those norms • to accept a shared responsibility for the maintenance of those norms.
Isomorphically framing	Using equivalent structures to create current and future relevance for participants. For a more detailed explanation see Priest and Gass, 2005, pp. 215–20.

Table 7.3 Stages of funnelling

Filter	Examples of questions
Review – ask the group to describe an aspect of the experience	Let's talk about communication. Using a thumbs-up, thumbs-middle, thumbs-down please show us how well you think the group communicated in today's activity.
Recall and remember – ask the individuals to identify an incident from the experience that relates to the issue/topic.	Do you remember a time where communication (or lack of communication, or miscommunication) was present in the activity?
Affect and effect – assess the influence of the event on each individual	How did this (event) make you feel? How did this emotion affect the group? What control did this event have over the group's ability to complete the task?
Summation – individuals summarize what they have learned about the issue	What did you learn from all of this? Can you summarize what you have learned from our discussion?
Application – individuals apply their new learning to real-life situations	Do you see a connection between what you have learned and your relationship with your friends or family? Can you apply this to school?
Commitment – urges individuals to look toward changing their behaviour in future situations	What will you do differently next time? How can you commit to change?

Sunday Afternoon Drive debrief model

My colleagues and I have been researching the use of adventure-based learning within physical education and physical education teacher education for the past few years (Stuhr *et al.*, 2010; Sutherland *et al.*, 2009a,b). As a result of this research, along with Paul Stuhr and James Ressler, I have conceptualized a variation on the experiential learning cycle for novice teachers in adventure-based learning who work within the time constraints of a school lesson. In our situations the novices are pre-service physical education teachers and in-service physical education teachers. Our work has focused on providing novice facilitators with specific tools and strategies to allow them to lead a meaningful debrief. The result is the Sunday Afternoon Drive debrief model (Figure 7.2). The facilitator/teacher begins the drive with ideas for the final destination based on the lesson plan, but without a set route of how to arrive there. The conversation can take many different routes to reach the final destination, and the teacher follows the various rhythms, feelings, power and aesthetics of the road (i.e., the students) as they negotiate the journey. The final destination in this model is the application (transfer) of learning to other situations in students' lives.

During the journey the *Facilitator as Co-pilot* represents the facilitator's role in the discussion. The facilitator should have some pre-planned questions for debriefing which are based on the objective(s) of the lesson or activity, the

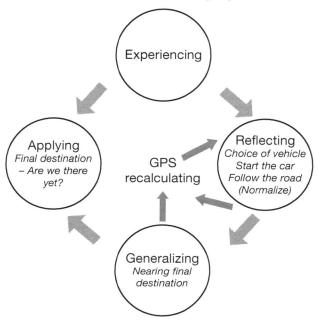

Figure 7.2 Sunday Afternoon Drive debrief model.

Source: Sutherland *et al.*, in press

specific focus of the activity, the group dynamics of the class, and what has occurred before that may need to be covered again. These questions are designed to be used merely as a back-up plan in case the conversation needs some direction or redirection.

Choice of Vehicle for the drive alludes to the difference between using a motorbike, sports car, mini-van or bus. The choice can have an impact on student participation in the discussion. Initially we recommend using a sports car or small mini-van (small groups) as the vehicle of choice, as it creates a more emotionally safe venue for students to engage in the initial conversation. Once a group or class becomes more comfortable working with each other and have established some emotional safety then different vehicles can be used based on the group dynamics and the objectives of the lesson.

To initiate the journey the teacher must *Start the Car* by providing the group with an initial debrief strategy. This is an interesting and engaging method of providing the group with a tool to initiate reflecting on the experience and is an alternative to asking the group 'what happened?' The strategies range in complexity from a 'Quick Whip' (where everyone provides one word to describe the experience) to an 'Album Playlist' (where a small group of students create an album title and song playlist that represents their experience). For additional strategies see Cain *et al.* (2008), Frank (2004) and Luckner and Nadler (1997).

Once the journey has begun the facilitator chooses a road to take based on the student responses during the initial debrief strategy. We call this part of the model *Follow the Road*. It is important for facilitators to learn to recognize which roads (comments) have the potential to lead to a powerful discussion. Having chosen a road, it is important to *normalize* the road by asking how it may relate to group members. For example during the *Start the Car* activity, a few students comment that the activity was frustrating. The facilitator recognizes the potentially powerful discussion the road of frustration could lead to and asks how many of the students were frustrated during part or all of the activity. This action helps the facilitator to see how many of the group felt frustrated and thus determine if this would be a good route for the drive. Asking this question also prompts students to think of situations in the activity that proved to be frustrating, which can enhance subsequent discussion. When a group embarks on the journey down a road that has the potential for a powerful discussion, it can be taken all the way to the final destination (i.e., through to the application phase of the experiential learning cycle).

Obviously there will be times when the group encounters a road-block in the conversation (e.g., students no longer want to talk about frustration or the responses are shallow and do not provide for further elaboration) and results in the need for a change in direction. We call this *GPS Recalculating*. If this situation arises the facilitator needs to recalculate the route for the journey, either based on other student responses during the *Start the Car*, or if that is not viable then using one of their pre-prepared questions. With this strategy it is important to understand that it is better to change routes than keep following the same road if the discussion is not productive. The key is that the new route still reaches the final destination, just in a different way.

Nearing Final Destination is the phase in the model that is related to the generalization of the experiential learning. Students gain a deeper understanding of the strategies related to the issue being discussed (i.e., the road being followed) that were used in the lesson that allowed the group to be successful. It can also allow students to see what strategies hindered their progress. To prepare for reaching the final destination, the facilitator steers the conversation to help students to think about the specific strategies that worked or didn't work and why. This phase of the model provides the road-map for the final part of the journey. For example, if we continue down the road of frustration the *Nearing Final Destination* phase would guide students to consider strategies (encouragement, rethinking the problem, better communication, enhanced cooperation and so on) that allowed them to work through their frustration to complete the activity successfully. Conversely the facilitator would also guide the students to reflect on strategies or behaviours related to frustration (checking out of the activity, taking frustration out on group members, negative comments, sabotaging the group's efforts and so on) that hindered their progress in the activity.

Final Destination – Are We There Yet? This is the question that young (and sometimes not so young) children ask on car journeys and is a wonderful analogy for the concept of transfer in experiential learning. If the *Final Destination* (the application or transfer of learning to other situations in students' lives) does not occur then we are not there yet! We believe this to be the most important phase of debriefing; without it the transfer of learning has not occurred. During this phase facilitators help the students understand how to apply their learning to other areas of their lives. When teaching this model to our pre-service physical education teachers we share a personal story of how the strategies that were discussed in the *Nearing Final Destination* phase have been used in an area of our own lives. For new facilitators this story can be pre-prepared and then shaped based on the specific strategies the students discuss. In our adventure-based learning courses, the use of this strategy during the *Final Destination* has provided the impetus for very insightful and introspective conversations about transfer that have run the gamut of sports, family relationships, military service, academics, coaching, teaching and personal relationships. Having students share how they will apply their learning to other areas of their lives during the debrief session provides the answer to the age-old question on car journeys – 'Are we there yet?' 'Yes, we have arrived!'

While the Sunday Afternoon Drive model was developed from our research to assist pre-service physical education teachers to facilitate a student-centred debrief within the time constraints of a physical education lesson, application of the model in group processing is clear. The model lends itself best to whole-class processing where the teacher is able to guide the conversation with all students to reach the final destination (transfer of learning to other situations in students' lives). However, if modelled appropriately and used consistently with students, the Sunday Afternoon Drive is a process that students can learn to use to facilitate their own small-group processing.

Conclusion

Group processing is one of the five principles of the Cooperative Learning model and when conducted well has positive benefits for both individuals and groups. However, it is the principle that is most often sacrificed as a result of time limitations. Cooperative Learning within physical education must include a structured group processing session. Without incorporating group processing the full benefit of Cooperative Learning is diminished. As with adventure-based learning and experiential learning, within Cooperative Learning the process of a critical reflection is paramount to fostering students' understanding and transfer of their learning to other areas of their lives. Drawing from adventure-based learning this chapter has provided specific strategies and a structured framework, in the form of the Sunday Afternoon Drive debrief model (Sutherland *et al.*, in press), to help teachers incorporate a meaningful group processing session in Cooperative Learning.

Websites for further resources

http://reviewing.co.uk/
http://www.pa.org/
http://wilderdom.com/
http://www.aee.org/

References

Antil, L.R., Jenkins, J.R., Wayne, S.K. and Vadasy, P.F. (1998). Cooperative Learning: prevalence, conceptualizations, and the relation between research and practice. *American Educational Research Journal* 35: 419–54.

Archer-Kath, J., Johnson, D.W. and Johnson, R. (1994). Individual versus group feedback in cooperative groups. *Journal of Social Psychology* 134: 681–94.

Beard, C. and Wilson, J. (2002). *The power of experiential learning.* London: Kogan Page.

Brown, M. (2003). Paraphrases and summaries: a means of clarification or a vehicle for articulating a preferred version of student accounts? *Australian Journal of Outdoor Education* 7(2): 25–35.

Brown, M. (2004). 'Let's go round the circle': how verbal facilitation can function as a means of direct instruction. *Journal of Experiential Education* 27(2): 161–75.

Cain, J., Cummings, M. and Stanchfield J. (2008). *A teachable moment: a facilitator's guide to activities for processing, debriefing, reviewing and reflection.* Dubuque, IA: Kendall Hunt Publishing.

Casey, A. and Dyson, B. (2009). The implementation of models-based practice in physical education through action research. *European Physical Education Review* 15: 175–99.

Casey, A., Dyson, B. and Campbell, A. (2009). Action research in physical education: focusing beyond myself through Cooperative Learning. *Educational Action Research* 17: 407–23.

Chapman, S. (1995). What is the question? In K. Warren, M. Sakofs and J. Hunt, Jr. (eds), *The theory of experiential education*, 3rd edn, 236–39. Dubuque, IA: Kendall/Hunt.

Cohen, E. (1994). *Designing groupwork: strategies for the heterogeneous classroom.* New York: Teachers College Press.

Cosgriff, M. (2000). Walking our talk: adventure based learning and physical education. *Journal of Physical Education New Zealand* 33(2): 89–98.

Dewey, J. (1938). *Experience and education.* New York: Collier Books.

Dyson, B. (2001). Cooperative Learning in an elementary physical education program. *Journal of Teaching in Physical Education* 20: 264–81.

Dyson, B. (2002). The implementation of Cooperative Learning in an elementary physical education program. *Journal of Teaching in Physical Education* 22: 69–85.

Dyson, B.P., Linehan Rhodes, N. and Hastie, P.A. (2010). The ecology of Cooperative Learning in elementary school physical education classes. *Journal of Teaching in Physical Education* 29: 113–30.

Estes, C. (2004). Promoting student-centered learning in experiential education. *Journal of Experiential Education* 27(2): 141–60.

Estes, G.A. and Tomb, S. (1995). Is cheese food really food? A.k.a. some conscious alternatives to overprocessing experience. Paper presented at the International Conference on Outdoor Recreation and Education, Ithaca, NY, 26–28 October. ERIC Document Reproduction Service no. ED404080.

Frank, L. (2004). *Journey toward the caring classroom: using adventure to create community in the classroom.* Oklahoma City, OK: Wood 'N' Barnes Publishing.

Gass, M.A. and Stevens, C.A. (2007). Facilitating the adventure process. In D. Prouty, J. Panicucci and R. Collinson (eds), *Adventure education: theory and applications*, 101–23. Champaign, IL: Human Kinetics.

Johnson, D.W. and Johnson, R.T. (1989). Cooperation and competition: theory and research. Edina, MN: Interaction Book Company.

Johnson, D.W. and Johnson, R.T. (1994). Learning together. In S. Sharan (ed.), *Handbook of Cooperative Learning methods*, 51–81. Westport, CT: Greenwood Press.

Johnson, D.W. and Johnson, R.T. (1999). *Learning together and alone: cooperative, competitive and individualistic learning*, 5th edn. Boston, MA: Allyn and Bacon.

Johnson, D.W. and Johnson, F.P. (2009a). *Joining together: group theory and group skills*, 10th edn. Upper Saddle River, NJ: Pearson Education.

Johnson, D.W. and Johnson, R.T. (2009b). An educational psychology success story: social interdependence theory and Cooperative Learning. *Educational Researcher* 38: 365–79. DOI: 10.3102/0013189X09339057.

Johnson, D.W., Johnson, R.T. and Johnson Holubec, E. (1993). *Circles of learning: cooperation in the classroom*, 4th edn. Edina, MN: Interaction Book Company.

Johnson, D.W., Johnson, R., Stanne, M. and Garibaldi, A. (1990). The impact of leader and member group processing on achievement in cooperative groups. *Journal of Social Psychology* 130: 507–16.

Joplin, L. (1995). On defining experiential education. In K. Warren, M. Sakofs and J.S. Hunt, Jr. (eds), *The theory of experiential education*, 15–22. Boulder, CO: Association for Experiential Education.

Kagan, S. (1994). *Cooperative Learning*, 2nd edn. San Juan Capistrano, CA: Kagan Cooperative Learning.

Kolb, D.A. (1984). *Experiential learning*. Englewood Cliffs, NJ: Prentice-Hall.

Luckner, J.L. and Nadler, R.S. (1997). *Processing the experience: strategies to enhance and generalize learning*, 2nd edn. Dubuque, IA: Kendall Hunt Publishing.

National Association for Sport and Physical Education (2004). *Moving into the future: national standards for physical education*, 2nd edn. New York: McGraw-Hill.

Panicucci, J. (2007). Cornerstones of adventure education. In D. Prouty, J. Panicucci and R. Collinson (eds), *Adventure education: theory and applications*, 33–48. Champaign, IL: Human Kinetics.

Pfeiffer, J.W. and Jones, J.E. (1980). *The 1980 annual handbook for group facilitators*. San Diego: University Associates.

Priest, S. (1990). The semantics of adventure programming. In J.C. Miles and S. Priest (eds), *Adventure programming*, 111–14. State College, PA: Venture.

Priest, S. and Gass, M.A. (1997). *Effective leadership in adventure programming*. Champaign, IL: Human Kinetics

Putnam, J., Rynders, J., Johnson, D.W. and Johnson, R. (1989). Collaborative skill instruction for promoting positive interactions between mentally handicapped and nonhandicapped children. *Exceptional Children* 55: 550–57.

Strahm, M. (2007). Cooperative Learning: group processing and students needs for self-worth and belonging. *Alberta Journal of Educational Research* 53(1): 63–76.

Stuhr, P.T, Sutherland, S., Lorson, K., Ressler, J. and Psimopoulos, C. (2010). A debrief model for adventure-based learning [Abstract]. *Research Quarterly for Exercise and Sport* 81(1): A-72.

Sugarman, D., Doherty, K., Garvey, D. and Gass, M. (2000). *Reflective learning: theory and practice*. Dubuque, IA: Kendall Hunt Publishing.

Sutherland, S., Ressler, J. and Stuhr, P.T. (2009a). Adventure-based learning and reflection: the journey of one cohort of teacher candidates. Paper presented at the Annual Meeting of the American Educational Research Association, San Diego, CA, 13–17 April.

Sutherland, S., Ressler, J., Stuhr, P.T. and Psimopoulos, C. (2009b). Understanding the debrief process in adventure-based learning [Abstract]. *Research Quarterly for Exercise and Sport* 80(1): A-78.

Sutherland, S., Stuhr, P.T. and Ressler, J. (in press). The Sunday Afternoon Drive debrief model. In *Conference proceedings, world conference on physical education and sport: challenges and future directions*.

Villa, R.A., Thousand, J.S. and Nevin, A.I. (2010). *Collaborating with students in instruction and decision making: the untapped resource*. Thousand Oaks, CA: Corwin.

Yager, S., Johnson, D.W. and Johnson, R. (1986). Oral discussion, group-to-individual transfer, and achievement in Cooperative Learning groups. *Journal of Educational Psychology* 77: 60–6.

8 The Cooperative Learning model as an inclusive pedagogical practice in physical education

Michelle Grenier and Pat Yeaton

Key terms: students with disabilities, inclusion, medical model, social model, natural supports

---

Introduction

Within this chapter, it is suggested that Cooperative Learning is a potent pedagogical model enriched by the task-related processes that facilitate student engagement, particularly for students lacking age-appropriate physical or social skill competencies. Differentiated learning is promoted through explicit, concrete direction while a balanced mentor–mentee process of support emerges from the completion of group goals. Through the use of natural supports, Cooperative Learning promotes equal relationships by establishing conditions that encourage students to work together in ways that address the individualized learning needs of all students.

In Western cultures, the confluence of medicine and science has had a profound effect on how society fails to support individual differences (Wendell, 1996). From a medical perspective, it is easy to assume that nature has an accepted course of action and that a 'failed' human condition is the result of pathological states. People with disabilities are viewed as deviations from the norm, particularly when physical or psychological dispositions fall outside established codes of behaviour (Linton, 1998; Oliver, 1990; Shogan, 1998). Differences translate into deficits (Davis, 1997). Disability is essentialized as a trait, reinforced through social structures that promote a categorical superiority of intellectual and physical functioning (Jones, 1996).

The practice of Cooperative Learning challenges the historical socialization of teachers that prioritizes a medical model for treating differences as deficits and prescribes teaching strategies that often isolate individuals with disabilities (Barnes, 1996; Grenier, 2007; Lipsky and Gartner, 1997). In general, the success of the special education system has been the appropriation of medical terminology, which authorizes the 'management and control of those, who in one way or another, trouble the social order' (Rapley, 2004, p. 43). Students become tracked into a system that defines identity in relation to disability, thereby normalizing the special education label. In many cases, the disability concretizes identities that limit the full potential of the student (Gergen *et al.*, 1996). While some favour labelling as a means for accessing services, there is a trade-off between support and the negative effects of labelling which locates students in subordinate positions to their peers. This medical model has populated teacher thought to such an extent that today, almost 30 years after the Education for All Handicapped Act (EHA) was enacted, the dilemma of coupling the concept of equality with the need for efficiency remains at the centre of educational discussions. The result is displayed in the negative attitudes and what MacIntyre (1999) labels a 'failure of imagination' to inclusively educate students with disabilities (p. 75).

There are unintended consequences that emanate from the deficit, medical model. Student disability is foregrounded as the essential feature, which implies that 'the problem' is not limited to a particular domain of his or her life but is generalized across all situations (Gergen, 1994; Grenier, 2007). Consequently, there is little expectation that all students qualifying for specialized services will be fully integrated. Rather students are integrated according to the circumstances of their disability, with little attention to teaching and learning assumptions that guide practice.

In contrast to the medical model that encourages explanations in terms of the features of an individual's body, the social model regards characteristics of social organization that serve to disable people who have impairments because of structural and attitudinal barriers (Oliver, 1996). It centres on the concept of accommodation and the need to restructure mainstream schooling practices to ensure that all learners belong to an educational community (Grenier, 2007). While the social model does not deny the existence of impairments and/or physiological differences, judgments are not imbued with the sense of good and bad displayed by the medical model. These tensions give rise to approaches on how an inclusive classroom should be structured and the teaching practices that are adopted.

Inclusionary scholars call for an analysis of the way in which teachers create and sustain practices to confront the inequities within the school culture, particularly in the area of physical education. As a way to examine inclusive practices, discussions should emanate from a perspective of inclusivity that centres on who is *not* successful in the classroom (Baglieri and Knopf, 2004). Whose learning goals are not being met? Who struggles in the class? Often, it is the student with a disability who is marginalized and excluded (Goodwin and Watkinson, 2000). Cooperative Learning allows students to support each other in ways that promote meaningful relationships and mutual caring. It is a form of pedagogical practice premised on the notion that human functioning has its origins in social relationships that support equal status among students as a relational pedagogy (Noddings, 1984).

The essentials of Cooperative Learning

For students with disabilities, Cooperative Learning is effective in promoting equitable peer relationships through positive interdependence and shared responsibility for learning (Johnson and Johnson, 1989; Dyson *et al.*, 2010). Whether students are identified as 'typical', 'at-risk' or 'gifted', Cooperative Learning encourages respect and reduces prejudice (Sapon-Shevin *et al.*, 1994). The accomplishment of group goals and tasks demands that students work together for a common, communal interest. When arrangements are created which cater to individual students, disruption occurs with the inequitable boundaries so prevalent in physical education. Students' voices are heard, valued and supported as a relational ontology of acceptance (Baglieri and Knopf, 2004).

Natural supports

Cooperative Learning engages students within the day-to-day context of the classroom through natural supports that promote equal relationships and minimize differences. As a pedagogical model, Cooperative Learning sets up conditions through a shared commitment to learning that individually centred types of instruction do not provide. The rationale for Cooperative Learning is explained by Robert Slavin (1990, pp. 13–14):

> [C]ooperative structures create a situation in which the only way group members can attain their own personal goals is if the group is successful. Therefore, to meet their personal goals, group members must help their group mates do what helps the group succeed, and perhaps more important, encourage their group mates to exert maximum effort.

Five essential components are necessary for the Cooperative Learning Model to be effective in the classroom: positive interdependence, individual accountability, face-to-face interaction, interpersonal and small-group skills and group processing (Johnson and Johnson, 1989; Putnam, 1998). These elements combine to capitalize on students' skills by promoting a positive climate of learning through active engagement of the students, encouraging a conceptual shift from the individual student capabilities to a cooperative construction of learning between students in their engaged groups. Positive interdependence is contingent on the dependence of all group members and coordinating their actions. Individual accountability necessitates individual contributions to group goals accomplished through student or teacher evaluations. Face-to-face interactions occur through the dynamics of the small groupings among students, verbally and non-verbally. These negotiations between students encourage students to listen and work with classmates of varying abilities. Because of this, adaptations and individualized criteria for success are more easily incorporated into the group goals. Interpersonal and small-group skills are required for the productivity of the group. Students are taught the social skills through a clear understanding of the roles and responsibilities of each student. The assigned roles within the cooperative groups enable students to hear more explanations and be exposed to a variety of strategies for problem-solving (Johnson and Johnson, 1989). Lastly, students evaluate how well their group has functioned through group processing and student reflections. More importantly, students benefit from the actions by engaging in conversations that address necessary changes for the group's success (Putnam, 1998).

Cooperative Learning and students with disabilities

Cooperative Learning is a feasible pedagogical model, particularly for students with disabilities who may be excluded from whole-class activities that typically involve a command-style approach to teaching. It is equally effective for students lacking social skill competencies who do not always pick up on environmental or physical cues that direct learning. Within a well-developed programme of instruction, Cooperative Learning nourishes a climate of support (Johnson and Johnson, 1989). Studies involving students with moderate to severe disabilities demonstrated significantly higher levels of positive verbal interactions and academic gains than those achieved in traditional methods of instruction (Eichinger, 1990; Putnam and Farnsworth-Lunt, 1989; Wilcox *et al.*, 1987). Jones and Carter's (1994) study of mixed ability pairs found that low achievers were better able to accomplish the tasks and did not impede the performance of higher-achieving students. Putnam (1998) notes that higher-achieving students are sensitive to the efforts of their peers and tend to value their peers in multi-dimensional and dynamic ways. Klinger and Vaughn's (1998) research on Collaborative Strategy Reading (CSR) that utilized group roles to improve reading performance for students with disabilities found that students had more on-task behaviour and higher academic scores on evaluations. Students also expressed a preference for this instructional strategy. Haydon *et al.* (2010) found Cooperative Learning assisted fourth-grade students with autism. Responsive peers reinforced social skills as a direct result of the task structure and interactions between the students were frequent.

Although little research has been conducted with the Cooperative Learning model and students with disabilities in physical education settings, there is a growing body of literature focused on general physical education. Cooperative Learning has been found to improve motor skills and develop social skills in the accomplishment for elementary-aged students (Dyson, 2001, 2002; Dyson *et al.*, 2010). Students improved their social and group achievement skills while increasing motor performances (Barrett, 2000).

Research by Polvi and Telama (2000) demonstrated that students who use Cooperative Learning are able to provide psychological support and give instructions more effectively than those who do not. Students relied less on the teacher and more on each other, producing a 'caring' effect. This can have direct implications for peer support and mentoring, particularly when addressing the needs of heterogeneous groups.

Developing social skills

The Cooperative Learning model can be an effective strategy for teaching students on the autism spectrum (ASD). While most students learn in the gymnasium by watching the behaviours of others, students with ASD do not always pick up on the necessary cues for success. Therefore, it is important that they acquire appropriate social skills to effectively learn alongside their peers (Grenier and Yeaton, 2011).

Evidence suggests that students with ASD struggle with motor competencies and, as a general rule, score lower on standardized motor tests (Reid and Collier, 2002). While the social behaviours have typically taken precedence over physical skill instruction, Goodman and Williams (2007) note these behaviours can impede learning because they interfere with interpersonal relationships and may distance peers and adults. This lack of social engagement can further limit opportunities for students with ASD to successfully participate in physical activity (Pan, 2009). Therefore, attending to the students' motor development through the introduction of strategies that facilitate students' participation and learning in inclusive settings can have numerous benefits, including a reduced risk for a sedentary lifestyle (Todd and Reid, 2006).

Physical education practices

The way in which teachers design their programmes is dependent upon personal philosophy and curricular choices. The more traditional physical education programmes that subscribe to competitive practices, by their very nature reduce the number of students who can succeed. More importantly, they minimize students' engagement with the activity and consequently, the student's peers (Johnson and Johnson, 1989). Incorporating a Cooperative Learning approach into the physical education curriculum allows teachers to accommodate differences without compromising the challenges embedded within the activities (Grenier *et al.*, 2005).

Cooperative Learning through the STEPS process

Implementation of Cooperative Learning for students with disabilities requires commitment to the process of instruction. For the purposes of this chapter, the authors have outlined a STEPS process that can assist teachers as they begin developing lessons using Cooperative Learning.

Student

Knowledge of the student's skills and abilities is essential. When developing the lesson and assembling the groups, pay close attention to the behaviour characteristics of the student. The Individual Education Plan (IEP) is commonly used in the United States as a resource that provides specific and useful information on the student's disability and how that impacts his or her learning. Using Cooperative Learning allows the physical education teacher to help students meet annual measurable goals within their IEP. Consider the student who has this present level of academic achievement as described in the IEP:

> Jason has exhibited difficulties with verbal and nonverbal expression. His flat affect and awareness of others' perceptions, as well as initiating and engaging in dialogue with his teachers, has impacted his interactions within the class. Given that, his annual measurable goal would include demonstrating appropriate, pragmatic language skills for increased success throughout his school day. Benchmarks and short-term objectives elaborate on targeted behaviours: Jason will appropriately initiate and maintain a conversation on a non-preferred topic with an adult during a classroom activity; Jason will be able to understand how his body language affects his communication, and discuss how knowing this will help him in his interactions. These goals and benchmarks can readily be worked on during a Cooperative Learning lesson without any additional effort for the teacher. This is a natural part of the Cooperative Learning lesson that would help measure his progress towards the goals in his IEP. Related service providers such as the occupational, speech and physical therapist members may provide valuable input that can provide a more comprehensive picture when needed.

Tasks

Task structures can be developed in many ways and structured according to the Cooperative Learning approach adapted by the teacher. Most often, these are aligned according to the national learning standards and the objectives of the overall school curriculum. Once the initial tasks have been established for the class, the teacher can easily modify the task depending on the skills and abilities within the groups. Modification can be made on the number of completed tasks, how the task is performed, the amount of time spent on each task or the number of required repetitions. The teacher or the students themselves can provide modifications; however, the focus should remain on the students' successful completion of the tasks. Through trial and error, the students themselves can come up with ideas on modifications that are better suited to their skills. For example, Joey, a fifth-grade student with hemiplegic cerebral palsy, struggled with tossing a volleyball up when attempting to perform the underhand serve. Both his teacher and group members devised a technique where he would place the ball in the centre of a triangle made by tucking his arm close to his body. Lifting his arm, he would get the ball in the air while he struck the ball with his opposite, more mobile hand. While this was not standard procedure for serving a volleyball, it was an example of differentiating the instruction that accommodated Joey's abilities.

Recorder's Name _____ Team Color _____

Grade 3 Volleying Task Sheet
Lesson 1

The goals for today are:

1   To strike a lightweight ball upwards in self-space as many times in a row as you can.
2   To strike a lightly tossed ball back to your partner.

____1.   Stretches led by coach.

____2.   Coach will review volleying a ball underhand with Mrs Yeaton.

____3.   Underhand volley cues: **flat surface**
                                   extend to target
                                   quick feet

____4.   Stand inside a hoop in your team area. Have your partner watch you as you underhand volley the ball upward and you **catch it** without moving. They will give you corrective feedback. Try this 10 times and switch places.

____5.   How many times can you underhand volley the ball in a row without leaving the hoop or have it hit the ground? Record your # below. Did they perform the skill correctly? (+ = correct, – = incorrect)

Name	# of underhand volleys in a row	flat surface	extend to target	quick feet

____6.   Coach will learn the forearm pass from Mrs Yeaton.

____7.   Coach will teach the forearm pass to team.

____8.   Cues for the forearm pass: **flat surface (extend arms forward, forearms together)**
                                       extend to target
                                       quick feet

____9.   Your partner will lightly toss a ball to you. Forearm pass the ball back to your partner. Practice this 10 times and then switch.

____10. Have your coach watch you perform the forearm pass to your partner. They will watch you do 5 passes.

Figure 8.1 Grade 3 volleying task sheet 1.

Grade 3 Volleying Task Sheet
Lesson 1

The goals for today are:
1   To strike a lightweight ball upwards in self-space as many times in a row as you can.
2   To strike a lightly tossed ball back to your partner.

_____ 1.   Stretches led by coach.

_____ 2.   Coach will review volleying a ball underhand with Mrs Yeaton.

Cues: Extend to target   Quick feet
Flat surface

_____ 3.   Stand in hoop in team area. Underhand volley then catch the ball. Partner watches you. Do this 10 times then switch.

_____ 4.   How many times can you volley the ball and catch it? Record your answer below.

Name   _____   I can volley the ball   _____   times and catch it.

Name   _____   I can volley the ball   _____   times and catch it.

Name   _____   I can volley the ball   _____   times and catch it.

Name   _____   I can volley the ball   _____   times and catch it.

Name   _____   I can volley the ball   _____   times and catch it.

_____ 5.   Have Mrs Yeaton watch you perform the underhand volley 5 times.

_____ 6.   Coach will learn forearm pass from Mrs Yeaton and then teach it to the team.

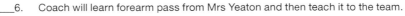

Cues: Extend to target   Quick feet
Flat surface

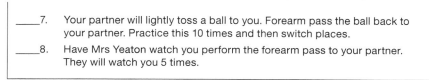

_____7.   Your partner will lightly toss a ball to you. Forearm pass the ball back to your partner. Practice this 10 times and then switch places.

_____8.   Have Mrs Yeaton watch you perform the forearm pass to your partner. They will watch you 5 times.

Figure 8.2 Grade 3 volleying task sheet 2.

Equipment

Appropriate equipment is essential when developing the tasks. Placing equipment in an area that is easily accessible and colour-coded makes the equipment manager's role much easier. When purchasing equipment, consider having enough equipment so that everyone in the class is able to have their own piece of equipment. This maximizes the opportunities to respond to the task structure and reduces waiting time. Equipment should be scaled to fit the students' needs, including the student with disabilities. Many companies offer specialized equipment that may be more suitable to the students' skill levels and performance abilities.

Personnel

Because Cooperative Learning encompasses group skills, it is important to consider the amount and level of peer support when designing instruction. When composing groups, discussion with other educators including the paraprofessionals and classroom teachers can provide insight into behaviours and compatible classmates. Mix genders, with no more than four to a team. It is also acceptable to create small groups of two if there is a student who has difficulty working in larger groups. This can minimize unwanted behaviours, particularly if he or she is matched with an empathetic student.

Outlining a set of behaviours in a visible area that students can employ if they have difficulty working together is also helpful. Work closely with the coaches to ensure that they understand the task and recognize potential ways to modify the task for the student with a disability. Encouraging students to take turns with a different combination of partners enhances students' social skills and group productivity.

Paraprofessional support

At times, it is preferable to have the support of a paraprofessional. Much will depend on the student's disability and the conditions of support. In cases where students have behavioural issues it is preferable to have the paraprofessional work with the group to monitor behaviours. As the teacher, it is your responsibility to instruct the paraprofessional how to guide *and not direct* the group in accomplishing the tasks. Paraprofessionals can also be instrumental in previewing learning material prior to the students' participation in physical education. Previewing represents a strategy for working with students whose learning goals include appropriate social engagement in inclusive settings. It is designed to improve on-task behaviours as well as physical and social skill development by presenting key information prior to the start of class that will help students' transition to physical education. For example, using a visual schedule that presents key information can help students make connections between movement skills and the sequence of progressions required to complete a task. Often these are pictorial representations of specific skills. Organizers can visually engage students by reinforcing positive psychosocial behaviours through teacher practices that model specific skills identified on the schedule. Paraprofessionals and occupational therapists can serve in these roles. In addition, previewing with the student gives the paraprofessional a chance to get better acquainted with the PE content area.

Teacher _____   **Team Color** _____

Members of our team:

1. _____
2. _____
3. _____
4. _____
5. _____

Team Contract

As a team we agree to:

    1. be nice to each other
    2. work together
    3. help each other learn the skills
    4. support each other when mistakes occur
    5. try to solve problems on our own

Sign your name below:

_____

Team Stickers

Figure 8.3 Team sheet.

Peer support

Establishing clear guidelines for behaviour is accomplished through the contract. If disputes or challenges occur within the group, the students should sit down and discuss the fact that they signed a contract and need to abide by it. The teacher can serve as a facilitator to assist the students in resolving the issues. The contract serves as the glue that commits students to the process of working together.

At times, efforts to learn and promote the group interdependence need to be positively reinforced. Stickers as well as other reward structures can be used as motivators for individual students to stay on-task or they may be designed for enhanced group performance. For example, when students clean up their team area, they get a sticker. If they fill out their task sheet, they get a sticker. For elementary-school students, stickers can be given for any number of behaviours and used as needed by the teacher.

Safety

Most often, safety concerns fall into two areas. The first is the students' themselves. Depending on the type of disability, attention should be on personal behaviours and/or physical safety. For example, the primary issue for students with autism is the unpredictability of behaviours. A particular piece of equipment can trigger negative behaviours that reflect the student's discomfort with the activity. At other times, a particular game may overstimulate the student, causing them to engage in perseverations. For students with physical disabilities, spatial concerns appear to be more of an issue. Establishing clear boundaries, both personal and general, is imperative. If a student uses a wheelchair, classmates should be cognizant of personal and self-space, while the student should be able to manage his or her mobility when using the chair.

Case study: applying Cooperative Learning for a student with a physical disability

Joey is pushed into the gymnasium by a classmate, who then wheels him over to a pile of equipment arranged in the corner. Joey has cerebral palsy (CP), which means he has limited use of his extremities and needs a motorized wheelchair for mobility. His spinal issues require him to wear a brace during the school day for support. Cognitively, Joey requires more time than his peers to process information and respond to requests. As a result, he has a difficult time, socially because of the fast-paced nature of the conversation. However, Joey is a very bright and outgoing boy who appears to comprehend the limitations of his disability.

Upon his arrival in the gymnasium, his classmate Kiel places four cones, a few balls and beanbags in Joey's lap and moves him to the far section of the gymnasium. At each corner Joey hands Kiel a cone as they mark the space for their Cooperative Learning groups.

Soon afterwards, two other group members join Kiel and Joey as they form a circle in the middle of their marked area. Facing each other for the warm-up, their

Cooperative Learning Team Roles

Coach

Teaches skills
Leads team in stretches
Keep team on task
Demonstrates
Helps/answers?
Starts/stops activity
Makes sure everyone is heard

Equipment Manager

sets up team area with
  cones
gets equipment for team
sets up equipment for
  tasks
picks up equipment at
  end of class

Encourager

sounds like:
  'nice try'
  'great job'
  'you can do it'
looks like:
  high 5
  thumbs up
  Pat on the back

Task Reader

Reads the task to team
Explains the task
Reads task out loud to team

Recorder

checks off tasks team has
  done
records team information

Date: _____   Date: _____

Coach _____   Coach _____

Equipment Manager _____   Equipment Manager _____

Encourager _____   Encourager _____

Task Reader _____   Task Reader _____

Recorder _____   Recorder _____

Date: _____   Date: _____

Coach _____   Coach _____

Equipment Manager _____   Equipment Manager _____

Encourager _____   Encourager _____

Task Reader _____   Task Reader _____

Recorder _____   Recorder _____

Date: _____   Date: _____

Coach _____   Coach _____

Equipment Manager _____   Equipment Manager _____

Task Reader _____   Task Reader _____

Recorder _____   Recorder _____

Recorder _____   Recorder _____

Figure 8.4 Cooperative Learning team roles.

laughing voices count out the stretches in unison. Joey self-adapts his movements in the warm-up, leaning over in his chair as the others stretch out their lower body. He extends his hands halfway down the top part of his legs. Joey's movements are slow by comparison to his peers, yet no one seems to notice.

Once the stretching is complete, another group member pushes Joey behind a red line in their square. Without prompting from the teacher, Joey begins his slow journey forward, wheeling his chair to a point 10 feet away. He performs his cardio-workout while his classmates run for two minutes, circling the outside of the cones.

With warm-ups complete, the reader for the day takes the folder from Joey's tray and describes the class activities, which include throwing and catching skills. As their designated coach, Joey reminds the others to throw, using the appropriate cues. His knowledge of the skills gives him a special privilege, and he enjoys the authority the role of coach affords him. Periodically, he refers to his lesson sheet to remind the students of the particulars for throwing.

Working their way through the tasks, the students come to the final activity – constructing a game using a few selected pieces of equipment. The children hunker down, brainstorming a list of possibilities. After several minutes of negotiations and compromises, the children come up with a modified game of baseball. Although Joey's skills are limited, the children compensate by using his lap as a target. When it is his turn to bat, the students will toss the ball to him and he will trap it with an oversize glove. He will then throw the ball and be pushed by a class member to the base.

The 45-minute class has come to an end, and the teacher gives the students a signal that it is time to clean up. The students respond by picking up the equipment in their areas. As equipment manager, Kiel gets help from Joey as she moves from corner to corner, dropping the cones into Joey's tray.

Applying the STEPS process

Student

Joey needs physical support and skill adaptations. Although he has good social skills, he requires a group of students who will help him with reading (as a coach) and securing the equipment when he is the equipment manager.

Task

The tasks were modified slightly to accommodate Joey's functional skills. Joey's limited ability to throw and catch required substantial changes to the typical throwing and catching games played by children. Although it took the better part of a class period, the group managed to create what they considered a game in which all members were included. The game design incorporated an oversize glove for Joey and someone who could push him to the base. As the ball was gently tossed onto Joey's lap, he trapped it with the glove. Another student in the group stood poised next to Joey, picking up the ball to 'pinch' throw for him. The student then pushed Joey to the base.

Equipment

No necessary equipment changes; however, Joey used an oversize glove to trap the ball. Students were given a variety of equipment-selection options.

Personnel

For most physical education classes, Joey's paraprofessional remains in the gymnasium, but circulates among the differing groups to provide any additional support that might be needed. Joey's teacher carefully assembled the students who comprised Joey's group to ensure there was a balance of social, cognitive and physical skills.

Safety

During warm-ups, Joey was able to manage himself as he modified the stretches. When it was time for the group running, one of Joey's group-mates wheeled him over to a line on the floor. From there, he propelled himself to a pre-established area 10 feet away. Most of the time, one of his group-mates was primarily responsible for wheeling him to the designated work areas. Because the students operate within the confines of a small-group area, Joey is able to safely navigate his chair without restriction.

Conclusion

Education, like all social institutions and processes, is a human creation, its nature and purpose determined by human values, history and changing patterns of power relationships. Thus, all educational objectives, emphases in curriculum content and classroom processes must necessarily be a selection of the culture from which curriculum planners and teachers make their selections of objectives, content, resources and teaching methods – and there is no rational way of making such selections without holding certain values to establish priorities (Fien, 1997, p. 437).

This chapter has identified ways in which conceptions of disability are representative of the larger discourses on the nature of ability and the underlying standpoint that informs competence. Given this perspective, Cooperative Learning serves as a vehicle to contest the construction of disability as a deficit discourse that can rejuvenate a definition of pedagogy as transformation by closing the gap between inclusion and exclusion for students with disabilities (Lusted, 1986). Rather than viewing students with disabilities as non-members of the classroom whose needs are intrinsically different, the use of Cooperative Learning promotes cultural sensitivity through the integrally bound relationships of the group. How individuals are socially situated in relation to one another is particularly meaningful when it is embedded within a practice that associates competence with culturally specific negotiations (Evans, 2004). Within the structure of Cooperative Learning, students work together towards group goals through the natural supports of peers and a shared understanding of the outcomes of their actions.

In order to consider the implications of the Cooperative Learning model for students with disabilities, it is important to return to a definition of inclusion as a place where diversity is prioritized and teachers have high expectations for all students. To move towards this realization, teachers should be sensitive to the conditions that support the learning needs of all students and committed to practices that promote equal status among peers (Lipsky and Gartner, 1997). The inclusive gymnasium allows students, irrespective of their particular skills, to exhibit forms of learning that parallel those of their peers. As a viable strategy that encourages students of diverse abilities to work together in the achievement of learning goals, Cooperative Learning can provide an opportunity for students to engage in reciprocal relationships when instruction is provided in a manner that fosters positive social interactions. Moving in this direction requires that we consider teaching as a relational resource for actions to emerge that promote an awareness of possibility rather than an adherence to limitation. In order to do this, educators must challenge the assumptions that inform many of the deficit-based practices of special education to create opportunities for students to learn and fully participate in the school culture. The advantage of utilizing Cooperative Learning as a pedagogical tool is that teachers are able to use their creative skills in order to meet the diversity of students' learning requirements.

References

Baglieri, S. and Knopf, J. (2004). Normalizing difference in inclusive teaching. *Journal of Learning Disabilities* 37(6): 525–9.

Barnes, C. (1996). Theories of disability and the origins of oppression of disabled people in western society. In L. Barton (ed.), *Disability and society: emerging issues and insights*, 43–60. London: Longman.

Barrett, T. (2000). Effects of two Cooperative Learning strategies on academic learning time, student performance, and social behavior of sixth grade physical education students. Unpublished doctoral dissertation, University of Nebraska, Lincoln.

Carrington, S. and Robinson, R. (2004). A case study of inclusive school development: a journey of learning. *International Journal of Inclusive Education* 8(2): 141–53.

Davis, L.J. (1997). *Constructing normalcy: the disabilities studies reader.* New York: Routledge.

Dyson, B. (2001). Cooperative Learning in an elementary physical education program. *Journal of Teaching in Physical Education* 20: 264–81.

Dyson, B. (2002). The implementation of Cooperative Learning in an elementary physical education program. *Journal of Teaching in Physical Education* 22: 69–86.

Dyson, B.P., Linehan, N.R. and Hastie, P.A. (2010). The ecology of Cooperative Learning in elementary school physical education classes. *Journal of Teaching in Physical Education* 29: 113–30.

Eichinger, J. (1990). Effects of goal structures on social interaction between elementary level nondisabled students and students with severe disabilities. *Exceptional Children* 56: 408–17.

Evans, J. (2004). Making a difference? Education and 'ability' in physical education. *European Physical Education Review* 10(1): 95–108.

Fien, J. (1997). Learning to care: a focus for values in health and environmental education. *Health Education Research* 12(4): 437–47.

Gergen, K. (1994). *Realities and relationships: soundings in social construction.* Cambridge, MA: Harvard University Press.

Gergen, K., Hoffman, L. and Anderson, H. (1996). Is diagnosis a disaster? A constructionist dialogue. In F. Kaslow (ed.), *Handbook for relational diagnosis*, 102–18. New York: Wiley.

Goodman, G. and Williams, C. (2007). Interventions for increasing the academic engagement of students with autism spectrum disorders in inclusive classrooms. *Teaching Exceptional Children* 39(6): 53–61.

Goodwin, D. and Watkinson, E. (2000). Inclusive physical education from the perspective of students with physical disabilities. *Adapted Physical Activity Quarterly* 17: 144–60.

Grenier, M. (2007). Inclusion in physical education: from the medical model to social constructionism. *Quest* 59(3): 298–310.

Grenier, M., Dyson, B.P. and Yeaton, P. (2005). Cooperative Learning that includes students with disabilities. *Journal of Health, Physical Education, Recreation and Dance* 76(6): 29–35.

Grenier, M. and Yeaton, P. (2011). Previewing: a successful strategy for students with autism. *Journal of Physical Education, Recreation and Dance* 82(1): 28–33.

Haydon, T., Maheady, L. and Hunter, W. (2010). Effects of numbered heads together on the daily quiz scores and on-task behavior of students with disabilities. *Journal of Behavioral Education* 19(3): 222–38.

Johnson, D.W. and Johnson, R. (1989). *Cooperation and competition: theory and research.* Edina, MN: Interaction Book Co.

Jones, S. (1996). Toward inclusive theory: disability as social construction. *NASPA Journal* 33(4): 347–55.

Jones, M.G. and Carter, G.C. (1994). Verbal and non-verbal behavior of ability-grouped dyads. *Journal of Research in Science Teaching* 31(6): 603–20.

Klinger, J.K. and Vaughn, S. (1998). Using collaborative strategy reading. *Teaching Exceptional Children* 30(6): 32–7.

Linton, S. (1998). *Claiming disability.* New York: New York University Press.

Lipsky, D. and Gartner, A. (1997). *Inclusion and school reform.* Baltimore, MD: Brookes.

Lusted, D. (1986). Why pedagogy? *Screen* 27: 2–14.

MacIntyre, A. (1999). *Dependent rational animals: why human beings need virtue.* Chicago: Open Court Press.

Noddings, N. (1984). *Caring: a feminine approach to ethics and moral education.* Berkeley: University of California Press.

Oliver, M. (1990). *The politics of disablement.* New York: St. Martin's Press.

Oliver, M. (1996). *Understanding disability: from theory to practice.* Basingstoke: Palgrave.

Pan, C.Y. (2009). Age, social engagement, and physical activity in children with autism spectrum disorders. *Research in Autism Spectrum Disorders* 3: 22–31.

Putnam, J.A. (1998). *Cooperative Learning and strategies for inclusion.* Baltimore, MD: Brookes.

Putnam, J.A. and Farnsworth-Lunt, J. (1989). Cooperative Learning and the integration of students with learning disabilities. *Journal of Social Psychology* 13(6): 741–53.

Polvi, S. and Telama, R. (2000). The use of Cooperative Learning as a social enhancer in physical education. *Scandinavian Journal of Educational Research* 44(1): 105–15.

Rapley, M. (2004). *The social construction of intellectual disability.* Cambridge: Cambridge University Press.

Reid, G. and Collier, D. (2002). Motor behavior and the autism spectrum disorders. *Palaestra* 18(4): 20–7.

Sapon-Shevin, M., Ayres, B. and Duncan, J. (1994). Cooperative Learning and inclusion. In J. Thousand, R. Villa and A. Nevin (eds), *Creativity and collaborative learning: a practical guide to empowering students and teachers*, 45–58. Baltimore, MD: Brookes.

Shogan, D. (1998). The social construction of disability: the impact of statistics and technology. *Adapted Physical Activity Quarterly* 15: 269–77.

Slavin, R.E. (1990). *Cooperative Learning: theory, research, and practice.* Boston: Allyn and Bacon.

Todd, T. and Reid, G. (2006). Increasing physical activity in individuals with autism. *Focus on Autism and Other Developmental Disabilities* 21(3): 167–76.

Wendell, S. (1996). *The rejected body.* New York: Routledge.

Wilcox, J., Sbardellati, E. and Nevin, A. (1987). Cooperative Learning groups aid integration. *Teaching Exceptional Children* 20(1): 61–3.

9 Cooperative Learning and tutoring in sports and physical activities

Lucile Lafont

Key terms: social skills, conversation, verbal analysis

Perspectives of Cooperative Learning, the motivational and developmental approaches and the importance of interactions

Cooperative Learning is a pedagogical model in which students work together in small, structured, heterogeneous groups to complete group tasks and in which group members help each other learn while achieving group goals (Dyson *et al.*, 2010). This chapter demonstrates the role of analysing verbal interaction between peers within cooperative groups or dyads. First, the author explains how French physical education curricula can stimulate physical education teachers to implement Cooperative Learning situations, which are devoted to enhancing students' social roles through their work in small groups. Then, following Slavin's perspective, a European theoretical framework for the study of peer interactions is developed. Finally, the author presents four qualitative analyses of verbal interactions between peers in small groups conducted with French students across four different sports during physical education lessons. These analyses support previously published results in basketball and handball (Lafont *et al.*, 2007; Darnis and Lafont, 2008), and further show how verbal exchanges in small groups allow students to develop both increased understanding and acquisition of games strategies. Moreover, using the cases of acrobatics and table tennis reported in this chapter, the author provides an explanation of motor learning and cooperative processes in Cooperative Learning classrooms (Lafont and Capmartin, 2010).

Slavin (1987) described two major complementary theoretical perspectives: motivational and developmental. Motivational perspectives emphasize rewards that favour individual accountability, related efforts and reciprocal help (Johnson and Johnson, 1989; Slavin, 1990). They focus primarily on goal structures according to Deutsch's definitions (1949). Deutsch held that a situation is cooperative when attainment of a goal by one individual is positively correlated with attainment of that goal by other members of the group (for example, making a pyramid in acrobatic gymnastics). The developmental perspective is a European one and is based on the social psychology of cognitive development, integrating Piagetian and Vygotskian theoretical frameworks on peer collaboration. So, from the neo-Piagetian approach, Mugny and Doise (1978) incorporated peer interactions into Piagetian constructivism. The authors showed that working in small groups or in dyads (two partners) is better for cognitive structure than working alone. Studies by Doise and Mugny (1997), among others, have provided evidence of the importance of socio-cognitive conflict. Socio-cognitive conflict is a mechanism of cognitive regulation that occurs when two partners bring their two opposing solutions to a problem into confrontation and when they coordinate them into a new approach better adapted to solving the problem (Doise, 1989; Perret-Clermont, 1979).

Socio-cognitive conflict occurs under two essential conditions: the partners in the interaction must be at the same level, and their responses must be opposing. It is the inter-individual disagreement that later upsets the equilibrium at the intra-individual level. The functional social psychologists Gilly *et al.* (1988) and Gilly (1989) expanded this notion by suggesting that socio-cognitive conflict is no longer the only mechanism that accounts for progress during peer interaction and they defined four modes of active cooperation (acquiescent mode co-elaboration, co-construction, confrontations without disagreement, contradictory confrontations). Sorsana (1999) complemented their classification by adding parallel behaviours or non-collaborative behaviours. Finally, Darnis and Lafont (2008) added tutoring behaviours and were able to define six types of co-elaboration:

1   parallel behaviours when there are no co-elaboration behaviours: there is no communication but only a juxtaposition of individual speech;
2   acquiescent mode co-elaboration: one out of two individuals finds a solution alone, and his partner accepts it without modification;
3   co-construction: each partner provides one part of the solution, the contributions alternate and gradually lead to the construction or to a common adoption of a solution;
4   confrontations without disagreement corresponding to non-discussed disagreement;
5   contradictory confrontations defined by the presence of argued disagreements, opposite answers or different solutions which can lead to a socio-cognitive conflict;
6   tutoring behaviours when one of the partners assumes a partial solution by helping or advising the other partner and so allowing him to progress.

On the other hand, studies based on Vygotsky's thinking stress the importance of dissymmetrical relations and interactions. Symmetrical situations may occur when partners have the same skill level. Conversely, dissymmetrical (or asymmetrical) relations exist when a member of the dyad is more skilled or older or has a higher status than his or her partner. These relations are based on the notions of guidance and interactive tutoring (Bruner, 1983). Tutoring refers to dissymmetrical exchanges in learning and knowledge transmission situations where the interventions of a tutor enable a novice to progress (Winnykamen, 1990). In the classroom setting, asymmetric interaction may take place between the teacher and a student or between students of different skill levels for various domains (motor or academic, for example). Beaudichon *et al.* (1988) reported that the ecological system of classroom life involves a multiplicity of relational and interactive mechanisms, conflicts, collaboration and different forms of guidance all coexisting within the classroom. Furthermore, many authors insist on the importance of interactions between members to ensure effective cooperation (see Cohen, 1994; Johnson and Johnson, 1989). In physical education the interaction between group members usually takes two different forms: on the one hand, interactions during the task; and on the other, discussions, debate ideas and mutual advice after the task. Moreover, interactions such as conversations, and discussions for the development of group actions within cooperative groups or within dyads have also been investigated (Darnis and Lafont, 2008; Lafont *et al.*, 2007).

Therefore, the multidimensional nature of peer interactions must be stressed so that these interactions can be examined and explored in different ways, as this chapter will show later. The chapter demonstrates the complementarities between quantitative and qualitative analyses in the case of physical education, as already discussed in academic and cognitive tasks by Olry-Louis and Soidet (2003). The analysis and categorization of verbal exchanges in small cooperative groups or in dyads is termed 'qualitative analysis (or approach)', that is, when the partners speak about game strategies or an action project.

French curricula in physical education

In France, Cooperative Learning is often used in elementary schools. Teachers implement 'study groups' or 'work teams' where pupils are assigned a task for their team, and the members are encouraged to help their partners to learn. The reward is collective but is based on the sum of the members' individual performances or progress. Slavin's cooperative groups fall into this category. In physical education, cooperation is often present for two reasons: (i) the type of physical activity or sport and (ii) classroom organization chosen by the teacher.

Different sports and activities can be classified according to different criteria (Lafont and Winnykamen, 1999). First, collective sports (such as rugby and hockey) include within their logic a collective or dual dimension, which can be used as a basis for a cooperative situation: that is, the partners of the group or the dyad share a common goal. Other sports and aesthetic activities, such as acrobatic gymnastics, dance and rhythmic gymnastics, involve both individual and collective dimensions of cooperation. These collective aspects of activities (that include an artistic dimension) have been particularly promoted in France as a result of the introduction of new physical education programmes in middle schools (Bulletin Officiel de l'Education Nationale spécial, 2008). Second, physical education constitutes an outstanding opportunity for cooperative organization of the class in sport as a whole, through the different roles assumed by pupils (such as recorder, coach and so on). Physical education therefore seems well suited to contributing to the development of social competences related to a common grounding, which is to grant one's own and others' safety and self-involvement in various social roles. These competences or roles can be used in different activities alongside the development of motor tasks such as helping a team-mate, reciprocal assessment, debate and/or co-observation. These competences, originally developed by Lafont and Winnykamen (1999), can now be rethought in the light of these new physical education programmes. On the basis of the expected skills defined in these programmes, Table 9.1 presents a grouping of sports and physical activities according to these different tasks.

These skills and social roles can be complemented by tasks accompanying the motor tasks defined by Lafont and Winnykamen (1999): managing, advising, choosing an action project in groups and regulating it, setting up an apprenticeship system and regulating it, preventing, helping by physical guidance,

Table 9.1 Expected skills relating to social roles in physical education programmes in middle schools in France

Sports grouping	Sport	Role and tasks accompanying motor tasks
Achieve maximal and measurable motor performance with an environmental goal or given deadline	In individual sport athletics, swimming	To play the part of an observer, timekeeper or peer assessment Collect reliable data Develop a tactical project with team mates in a relay race
To move according to various and uncertain environments	In outdoor sports climbing, sailing	Mutual aid and collective or mutual safety
To achieve a physical performance with an artistic or acrobatic aim	Aerobic	Conceive and present a collective synchronized routine Design a collective production
	Acrobatic sport	Assemble and dismantle a pyramid Play the part of a carrier or acrobat-helper Construct and use a common code Evaluate performances according to simple criteria
	Gymnastics, rhythmic gymnastics	Design and present acrobatic series in duo, trio or quad Assess according to commonly defined code
	Circus Art	Compose and present a collective act
	Dance	Compose and present a collective choreography
To lead and master an individual or collective contest	Collective sports Racket Dual sports like judo	Enrol in a simple game project Observe and co-referee Score counting and filling in an observation sheet Manage a contest and help a partner to analyse his game in order to win

demonstrating and explaining movements or strategies. Therefore, within the scope of Cooperative Learning in physical education, individual sports such as gymnastics include numerous social roles which can lead to the cooperative organization of the physical education class.

Dancing, acrobatic gymnastics and/or rhythmic gymnastics all involve an artistic dimension, which fosters creative activity and collective performance. When these activities are organized through Cooperative Learning then the interdependence of students can be deliberately enhanced as they seek to stimulate, drive or even constrain the activity. All these tasks require the following general skills: observation, analysis, decision-making, negotiation and evaluation. Some tasks are assumed by an individual in relation to a group (such as refereeing in a collective sport) or towards individuals (dual meetings: refereeing and management in the case of combat or racket sports). Other tasks are collective, referred to as 'strategizing' by Dyson *et al.* (2010). Examples include students choosing a strategy in collective sports or constructing series of common actions in rhythmic gymnastics or contemporary dance. In summary, there are many implicit opportunities in physical education to develop collaborative skills. However, through the clear use of Cooperative Learning, these assumed facets of 'mutual cooperation' become explicit and are hardwired into the students' learning experiences.

Cooperative Learning or tutoring in physical education?

Cooperative Learning and the tutoring of peers refer to different pedagogical practices. In the first, the work is collective and may operate without attributing specific roles (except in the case of groups of experts, where the relationships are by nature asymmetrical and when the skills are specialized), the objective is common and the actions positively inter-correlated. In the latter, the work is performed in dyads and two scenarios can be identified. On one hand, there is fixed tutoring where the roles are differentiated (and they never change), the tutor's task consists in helping his or her partner, the relations are asymmetrical (or dissymmetrical) and the tutor has a higher skill level (or age or status) than the tutee. On the other hand, reciprocal tutoring supposes strict and reasoned turn-taking, which means a more symmetrical skill level. However, observation of cooperative classes shows the continuity between tutoring and working in cooperative groups, which is the subject of Dyson's studies (2001, 2002), when the coaching roles are assumed by pupils organized in reciprocal tutoring or small groups.

In France, the research team in sport at the Université Bordeaux Segalen (among others) has conducted studies on the acquisition of motor skills through social interaction and verbal exchanges. They have demonstrated the efficiency of these interactions by measuring motor performance in quasi-experimental situations (quantitative research). Besides these studies, Grehaigne *et al.* (2001) introduced the notion of 'the debate of ideas' in building game strategies. Moreover, in the theoretical framework of situated learning, Bourbousson *et al.* (2010) show how students can coordinate their actions in collective situations like basketball.

The qualitative analysis of verbal (and sometimes non-verbal) interactions covers several functions:

1   explaining skill and knowledge acquisitions in dyads or groups;
2   evaluating the participation of each member of the group or dyad in the common project;
3   linking the relations between the partners and the acquisitions;
4   evaluating improvements and relations between knowledge and know-how as the task is performed;
5   understanding more precisely the dynamics of the learning process and/or social relationships.

In undertaking this analysis, these researchers endeavoured to gather data concerning verbalization about motor tasks and action projects in an approach different from Dyson's (2001, 2002) work. Dyson conducted qualitative studies on the experiences of pupils and teachers in lessons with a Cooperative Learning format. Data were collected by interviewing teachers and pupils, and by observing and using field notes. This analysis showed strong support for Cooperative Learning. The pupils particularly appreciated reciprocal help and having to play the coach's role, as well as their individual accountability within the group. The Bordeaux studies extend this work to focus not only on the benefits of Cooperative Learning but also on verbal exchanges in relation to the collective purpose, that is, the success of the tasks. Drawing on Gilly *et al.*'s (1988) and Gilly's (1989) framework of analysis, which has been further complemented by applying pragmatics to the analysis of verbal interactions, the researchers have sought to shed light on how knowledge arises from interactions. Every speech act is considered as a social act (i.e. making somebody do something (Searle and Vanderveken, 1985)). In this way this chapter presents the results of some studies of conversations, interactive dynamics and speaking turns to develop a better understanding of how communications within small groups and within dyads develop and enhance learning. Consequently, the author now seeks to examine the construction of game strategies during the time devoted to verbal interactions in alternation with motor tasks. These data are then related to acquisitions and/or to social relationships and to individual participation in the collective product.

Study one: past actions and building game strategies

The first study examines the peer interactions that occurred during discussions in small groups in a basketball-type ball game. These discussions were understood as cooperative situations between peers. The option chosen for the teachers' intervention consisted of instigating verbal exchanges between pupils. The quantitative analysis (Lafont *et al.*, 2007) consisted of comparing an experimental condition utilizing cooperation in a small group with a control condition with students working in groups but without verbal exchanges and with students completing individual tasks.

Fourteen children in a third/fourth-grade class (average 9.4 years old) participated in the study. The participants were divided into three teams of similar motor performance levels according to a pre-test in a game context. During an intervention session of 12 lessons they were in teams, and were alternately involved in phases of the game and short discussions about the game. The motor tasks involved students in basketball sequences with adapted rules (four players, smaller space).

Previous studies have shown that this condition of cooperation through verbal exchanges had positive effects in relation to participation in the game and efficiency in attack compared to a control group who participated in individual motor tasks instead of collective discussions (Lafont *et al.*, 2007). The findings demonstrated that groups that had frequent discussions between the sequences of playing (intervention group) turned out to be more effective than those who just performed the activity without discussion (control group). Verbal interactions were analysed in terms of: the interactive dynamics within each group, the contents of the verbal interactions and every team member's participation in each of the discussions. The longitudinal observation of each discussion allowed the researchers to highlight the temporal dynamics of participation in these verbal exchanges. The discussions within three teams were videotaped, transcribed verbatim and then analysed.

The ways in which students interacted and the focus of their conversations differed appreciably from one group to another, particularly within groups at the beginning and the end of the unit. The inductive categorization of the students' conversations showed that they mainly concerned the 'score of the matches', the 'partners of the team ', 'the task' and techniques associated with the ball (passes, shots). At the end of the unit, the exchanges mainly focused on 'tactical considerations related to the organization of the team and to occupation of the playing area', 'the organization of the attack', 'the behaviour of the opponents', 'the defence' as well as the 'benefits of the meetings'. Finally, moral issues (e.g. 'it is not good to be bad losers' – student interview, Jane) and opinions about the atmosphere of the group were also discussed within one team.

The contents of the exchanges predominately concerned (88.8 per cent) characteristics of the game (partners' actions , tactics, technique, scores). Only 6.7 per cent concerned the analysis of the atmosphere within the team ('we are not interdependent enough'). Three interactive dynamic types (following, for example, Gilly *et al.*'s (1988) definitions) were identified from the analysis of the three teams.

1   Seven contradictory confrontations defined by the presence of opposites able to initiate a socio-cognitive conflict (including five during the third discussion).

2   Nine co-constructions without discrepancy (someone gives an idea to the group, another player adds another idea) (including seven during the third conversation).

3   Eighteen episodes of non co-elaboration: parallel behaviours where there was no communication but only a juxtaposition of individual speech. These

episodes were of two types: (a) criticisms (of partners, tactical choices) in three teams; (b) individual proposals of solutions.

The main forms of communication consisted in descriptive reports of what happened during the match, in explanations or in answers to the teacher's questions: 'Lar made a pass to Maud and then she took a shot'; 'if we want to win, we must be more interdependent'; 'Lar must go here and Jo must be on the left'. On a linguistic level, the things students talked about in their groups evolved during the intervention. Conversations became more complex and centred more and more on game strategies. Frequently, the researchers observed other forms of non-conflictual discussion in which various arguments were formulated and then the participants co-constructed their own solutions to team problems. This was a matter of cooperation in the sense that several members of the team took turns in providing part of the solution to the problem (which should be considered as 'group processing'). Finally, other modes of intervention were individual and juxtaposed (parallel behaviours: see Gilly's categorization above). As with earlier studies, this study showed that confrontation between peers seldom leads to opposing views or co-constructed solutions and therefore allows for better motor performance in the game.

Study two: Cooperative Learning in acrobatics

In this study a number of Cooperative Learning groups were formed based on differing criteria (e.g. competence level, relationships, gender) for a group task to build a pyramid in acrobatics (Lafont and Chaze-Capmartin, 2010). The researchers used a model to study qualitative interactions in small groups for an artistic and acrobatic sport: a model already explored in team sports (Darnis and Lafont, 2008; Lafont *et al.*, 2007).

Participants in the study were 24 third- and fourth-grade (average 8.11 years old) children in elementary school in the urban community of Bordeaux (France). The class group consisted of 13 boys and 11 girls. Participants had to learn elements of acrobatics and then build a series of pyramid schemes in small groups of four students and present their work at the end of the unit. Six groups of four students were formed, taking into account existing peer relationships in the sociogram (both positive (= attraction) and negative (= rejection)) and gender. The six groups had the same competence levels at the pre-test. A sociogram was created in order to form the groups. It evaluated attractions and rejections between peers. An identical sociogram was completed at the beginning and the end of the unit of work. The unit lasted six weeks (one lesson plus one discussion each week).

Discussions within intervention groups, as shown in Table 9.2, were recorded and analysed. The data showed homogeneity between the groups, that is, no significant difference was found. The number of speaking turns (ST) (i.e. when each member of the group speaks to another member) per group ranged from 42 to 55. Groups 1 and 3 (positive relationships in the sociogram) had no more verbal exchanges and ST than groups 2 and 4 (neutral relationships in the

Table 9.2 Groups following criteria: with/without discussion, relationships and gender

	G1	G2	G3	G4	G5	G6
Discussion of game strategies	Yes	Yes	Yes	Yes	No	No
Attraction/rejection (sociogram)	Yes +7	No −2	Yes +4	+1	Yes +8	Yes +3
Gender	Girls	Boys	Boys	Mixed	Girls	Mixed

sociogram). Qualitative analysis of 'local' verbal interactions was conducted using the framework defined by Gilly (1989) (see above). For example, the interactive dynamic dominant in group 4 was the 'co-construction' group communication in which many verbalizations demonstrated the attention paid to the speech of other children in the group. Moreover, each member of the group proposed a part of the solution to the problem or gave instructions to other teammates. What follows is a co-construction discussion from lesson 2 in group 4 (note: the four children are practising for their routine and trying to remember a pyramid).

Agy: Now, remember the beginning.
Arn: Oh, yes! What is the beginning?
Agy: Ah, yes, yes! Anthony and I were behind, it was the shoulder stand and you two [to Arn and L], you did other things there!
L: [This] must be the beginning. It starts here.
Agy: Go!
A: OK! We'll take it from the beginning.
L: Then we made the wheel. But, Cons, you have to shoot away [he said to Lou] because I have to go there like this [he shows the movement].
(They get ready for the start; the boys each make an attitude; Lou makes a plank and L performs three wheels.)
Agy: So now for the pyramid, right? First pyramid!

The example shows how each partner added complementary and necessary information, items were recalled by one person, the instructions were given successively by others and then the first speaker obtained the consent of the others before issuing an instruction. In other words we can observe here the progressive co-construction of the solution, that is, the contributions alternate and gradually lead to the construction of a solution. This verbal exchange shows how speaking turns are shared and how each partner cooperates to achieve the final goal: the pyramids. Finally the results show a relationship between the final production and the conversations that occurred within 'intervention groups'.

With specific regard to the final motor output, groups G2 and G3 (intervention groups of boys who used either an acquiescent co-elaboration mode of verbalization or one out of two individuals finds a solution alone and his partner accepts it without modification) showed greater success with regard to guidance and timing of actions. Following Gilly's previous observation this success was unexpected, as we had hypothesized that verbal interaction such as 'co-construction' would be more favourable than other types of interaction to improve skills This was perhaps because groups working on acquiescent co-elaboration (G2 and G3, see above) were more effective in achieving the different elements of the tasks. In the absence of opposition and conflict, the choices were made more quickly. It would be of interest to examine whether these groups experienced a more intense form of physical activity. Moreover, it was the groups (G1 and G4) which worked most in a co-constructive modality (ST were shared and each partner cooperated) who scored the highest with regard to the criteria of difficulty and originality. Our results indicate that co-construction leads to students undertaking more risky, more difficult and ultimately more creative activity. In addition, the changes in the sociogram between the beginning and the end of the unit for all six groups demonstrated that verbal exchanges strengthened the links between peers and the network affinities (for intervention groups G1, 2, 3 and 4 only). This shows that verbal cognitive processes are interlinked with social relationships within small cooperative groups.

Moreover, this study showed the value of implementing acrobatics content in the early years of primary school. Practice and collective goals led to a better network of affinity. However, the response time (only four recorded sessions) was a limitation of this study, as were the data collection procedures, because collaborative skills are complex and require more sustained practice. In terms of the methodology of studying cooperation in physical education, this study provides additional insights into measures of motor acquisition, social relations and analysis of conversational dynamics.

Study three: learning in dyads in handball and table tennis

Darnis and Lafont's study (2008) compared symmetric and slightly asymmetrical dyads (where one partner is just a little more competent than the other) in the resolution of a motor problem in handball. Fifty-two girls from 11 to 12 years old (pupils in the first year of secondary school) participated in the study. The intervention created a motor situation of attacking with two players against one defender in half of the playing area (two against one-plus-one). The rules of handball were used. To analyse verbal exchanges in a situation of co-construction of action rules in collective sports, the authors chose the Gilly framework (1989) (see the beginning of this chapter: parallel behaviours; the acquiescent mode co-elaboration (one out of two individuals finds a solution alone and his partner accepts it without modification); co-construction where each partner provides one part of the solution; confrontations without disagreement corresponding to non-discussed disagreement; and contradictory confrontations with socio-cognitive conflict).

Improvements in relation to game strategies, as well as to choice-relevance, seemed to be more positively linked with co-construction dynamics, including confrontations without disagreement and tutoring interactions. This means that the dyads who co-constructed the action rules had higher levels of improvement.

These interlocutory modalities seemed to be the most relevant for obtaining progress regarding the knowledge and the skills required by the task. Moreover, the most revealing interactive dynamic regarding competences seems to be spontaneous tutoring interaction, which specifically is the case in asymmetrical dyads.

The value of reciprocal peer tutoring (RPT) is widely recognized today by researchers in education (Ward and Lee, 2005). Some recent studies in France (which explored individual activities and cooperation in table tennis) focused on the conditions of efficiency of RPT related to motor skills acquisition in published research (Ensergueix and Lafont, 2010). Together, these studies underlined the importance of specific training of pupils in their coach or coached role. According to work on fixed tutoring (Cicero and Lafont, 2007), such training is thought to improve the sensitivity of the pupil towards the particular needs of his or her partner (player) when practising the function of coach. Beyond the comparative analysis of such mechanisms, the point here was to compare the nature of verbal exchanges between pupils aged between 14 and 15 trained or not in RPT. The quantitative data partly confirmed the authors' expectations by indicating the superiority of the trained to the untrained condition for motor performance and tactical choice with reference to whether the trajectory of the ball is high or low, that is, whether to use a smash or simple forehand. Interlocutory analysis allowed them to better understand the helping and advising processes during these alternating coaching situations.

In dyads not prepared for interaction, speaking turns were few in number irrespective of who the coach was (1 to 6 ST for each verbal exchange), statements were very short and the speech acts were requests, formulated as commands: 'Pay attention to the ball!' The authors also found declarative speech acts: 'Your racket is too open.' The contents of the exchanges were limited to one or two different pieces of information, more often given by the coach to the performer.

In trained dyads, the authors noted alternate speaking, for example, the player sometimes asked the coach questions. The statements made by the coach were longer (between 4 and 8 ST) and better linked with each other by logic connectors (i.e. 'if ... then'). The speech acts from students were declarative and directive, and the content was very different. For example, these terms were used: pivots, replacements, surges, smashes, disguised shots, targets, racket, force and distance from the table. Finally, they noted formulations of action rules adapted to the context with connectors such as 'if', 'when'.

The following is an example of a trained dyad. M is the coach, and J is the performer:

M: That's right. You must try to aim even more at the side zones because you aimed at the central zone. Usually, you aim more at the side zones. You should close your racket just a little more so that the ball lands well on the table when you aim at the side zones.

J: So, do I have to close more?

M: Yeah, close your racket a little more. Otherwise the position: you go back rather fast except from time to time when you play a backhand smash, that is when you are on the left, at the end of the table; you don't always stand back fast enough, for example if the ball goes rather to the right, later in the zone ... for example having had a smash in zone 1. So yeah, you must go back faster to the centre.

J: Also, I forgot to look at the racket ...

M: The racket, yeah, just a little. That's it. Otherwise, it's not bad, your position was fine, you smashed well.

J: OK.

These findings explore innovative techniques for analysing the interactions verbatim in situations of reciprocal tutoring. The examination of verbal exchanges provides support for the positive effects of training in tutoring. It seems that the efficiency of training in tutoring allows improvements in knowledge and subsequently facilitates gains in efficiency when performing actions.

Conclusion

With reference to Slavin (1987), who reconciled organizational and developmental approaches in Cooperative Learning, the chapter demonstrates how a qualitative analysis of verbal exchanges between peers in physical education can be applied to four different sports (basketball, handball, acrobatics and table tennis). This approach is situated within the perspective developed by Lafont and Winnykamen (1999), who define three successive levels of cooperation: shared goal; shared goal with synchronization of actions; and 'activities accompanying motor tasks' such as debate, physical guidance, co-observation, peer assessment.

Among these tasks the authors chose to analyse the construction of strategies in a team performing an artistic and acrobatic activity, acrobatic gymnastics, as well as in game strategies in collective sports (team and dyads). Furthermore, verbal exchanges were also analysed within two types of dyads (spontaneous/trained) of reciprocal tutoring in a racket sport. The analysis of interactive dynamics, speaking turns and contents of verbal exchanges led to better understanding of the evolution of motor skills related to cognitive progress. Subsequently they were able to verify individual participation in the construction and regulation of action projects. The analysis also showed various interaction modes (discrepancies, co-construction, tutoring) as well as the difficulty of managing controversies, particularly within a small group. It appears that in the Cooperative Learning perspective, the analysis of interactions in small groups or in dyads is a complementary means of understanding the benefits of Cooperative Learning in relation to different social roles in a physical education class.

From a methodological point of view, the European perspective of Cooperative Learning mainly uses developmental or functional social psychology. Interlocutory analysis leads to progress in the qualitative approach specifically for dyads. However, to be successful, sessions must be long enough (two or three minutes) and specifically devoted to verbal exchanges.

Finally, the chapter has endeavoured to explain the developmental perspective of Cooperative Learning applied to physical education specifically in France. This European theoretical framework makes it possible to analyse verbal interactions and debate over ideas in small groups or dyads. Focusing on this approach has emphasized some characteristics of Cooperative Learning: face-to-face, group or dyad processing, shared goal and collective strategies. Moreover, it has explained how qualitative analysis of verbal exchanges during motor acquisition complements quantitative measures of motor performance and tactical choices.

In this perspective, face-to-face interaction and group processing through verbal exchanges appear to be essential for Cooperative Learning in physical education in order to share ideas (ways of thinking) so as to reach a common goal and develop motor skills. Moreover, the best interactive dynamics seem to be socio-cognitive conflict, co-construction and tutoring.

References

Beaudichon, J., Verba, M. and Winnykamen, F. (1988). Interactions sociales et acquisition de connaissances chez l'enfant: une approche pluridimensionnelle. *Revue Internationale de Psychologie Sociale* 1(1): 129–41.

Bourbousson J., Poizat, G., Saury, J. and Seve, C. (2010). Team coordination in basketball: description of the cognitive connections among teammates. *Journal of Applied Sport Psychology* 22: 150–66.

Bruner, J.S. (1983). *Le développement de l'enfant: savoir faire, savoir dire*. Paris: Presses Universitaires de France.

Bulletin Officiel de l'Education Nationale spécial (2008). Programme de l'enseignement d'éducation physique et sportive pour les classes de sixième, de cinquième, de quatrième et de troisième du college. No. 6, 28 August.

Cicero, C. and Lafont, L. (2007). Interaction de tutelle et imitation modélisation interactive entre élèves: l'effet de la formation d'élèves-tuteurs en gymnastique sportive. *Bulletin de Psychologie* 60: 335–48.

Cohen, E.G. (1994). Restructuring the classroom: conditions for productive small groups. *Review of Educational Research* 64: 1–35.

Darnis, F. and Lafont, L. (2008). Effets de la dissymétrie de compétence pour un apprentissage coopératif en dyades en Education Physique et Sportive. *Cahiers Internationaux de Psychologie Sociale* 79: 69–83.

Deutsch, M. (1949). A theory of co-operation and competition. *Human Relations* 2(2): 129–52.

Doise, W. (1989). Constructivism in social psychology. *European Journal of Social Psychology* 19: 389–400.

Doise, W. and Mugny, G. (1997). *Psychologie sociale et développement cognitif*. Paris: Armand Colin.

Dyson, B. (2001). Cooperative Learning in an elementary school physical education program. *Journal of Teaching in Physical Education* 20: 264–81.

Dyson, B. (2002). The implementation of Cooperative Learning in an elementary physical education program. *Journal of Teaching in Physical Education* 22: 69–85.

Dyson, B., Linehan, N.R. and Hastie, P.A. (2010). The ecology of Cooperative Learning in elementary physical education classes. *Journal of Teaching in Physical Education* 29: 113–30.

Ensergueix, P. and Lafont, L. (2010). Reciprocal peer tutoring in a physical education setting: influence of peer-tutor training and gender on motor performance and self-efficacy outcomes. *European Journal of Psychology of Education* 25: 222–42.

Gilly, M. (1989). The psychosocial mechanisms of cognitive constructions: experimental research and teaching perspectives. *International Journal of Educational Research* 13(6): 607–18.

Gilly, M., Fraisse, J.C. and Roux, J.P. (1988). Résolution de problèmes en dyades et progrès cognitifs chez des enfants de 11 à 13 ans: dynamiques interactives et mécanismes sociocognitifs. In A.N. Perret-Clermont and M. Nicolet (eds), *Interagir et connaître: enjeux et régulations sociales dans le développement cognitif*, 73–92. Fribourg: Del Val.

Grehaigne, J.F., Godbout, P. and Bouthier, D. (2001). The teaching and learning of decision-making in team sports. *Quest* 53: 59–76.

Johnson, D.W. and Johnson, R.T. (1989). *Cooperation and competition: theory and research*. Edina, MN: Interaction Book Co.

Lafont, L. and Chaze-Capmartin, S. (2010). La cooperación entre iguales y la adquisición de habilidades motrices en la dimensión artística: complementariedad entre aproximaciones cuantitativa y cualitativa, el ejemplo del acrosport. Actas del VII congreso international de actividades físicas cooperativas, Valladolid, 30 June–3 July.

Lafont, L., Proeres, M. and Vallet, C. (2007). Cooperative group learning in a team game: role of verbal exchanges between peers. *Social Psychology of Education* 10: 93–113.

Lafont, L. and Winnykamen, F. (1999). Cooperation and competition in children and adolescents. In Y. Vauden Auweele, F. Bakker, S. Biddle, M. Durand and R. Seiler (eds), *Psychology for physical educators*, 379–404. Champaign, IL: Human Kinetics.

Mugny, G. and Doise, W. (1978). Socio-cognitive conflict and structure of individual and collective performances. *European Journal of Social Psychology* 8: 181–92.

Olry-Louis, I. and Soidet, I. (2003). Coopérer pour co-construire des savoirs: une approche différentielle. *L'Orientation Scolaire et Professionnelle* 32: 503–35.

Perret-Clermont, A.N. (1979). *La construction de l'intelligence dans l'interaction sociale*. Berne: Peter Lang.

Searle, J.R. and Vanderveken, D. (1985). *Foundations of illocutionary logic*. Cambridge: Cambridge University Press.

Slavin, R.E. (1987). Developmental and motivational perspectives on Cooperative Learning: a reconciliation. *Child Development* 58: 1161–7.

Slavin, R.E. (1990). Comprehensive Cooperative Learning models: embedding Cooperative Learning in the curriculum and school. In S. Sharan (ed.), *Cooperative Learning: theory and research*, 261–88. New York: Praeger.

Sorsana, C. (1999). Stratégies socio-cognitives dans la résolution de la tour de Hanoï. In M. Gilly, J.P. Roux and A. Trognon (eds), *Apprendre dans l'interaction: analyse des médiations sémiotiques*, 143–59. Nancy: Presses Universitaires de Nancy.

Ward, P. and Lee, M.A. (2005). Peer-assisted learning in physical education: a review of theory and research. *Journal of Teaching in Physical Education* 24: 205–25.

Winnykamen, F. (1990). *Apprendre en imitant?* Paris: Presses Universitaires de France.

10 Cooperative Learning and interactions in inclusive secondary-school physical education classes in Australia

Wendy Dowler

> With all the quiet kids now, like one certain student, he doesn't really like to talk, he always is shy and doesn't say much. When we had to interact with our peers and all that, he started to get better with communication and all that and he is starting to talk to us. He is getting better with communicating with other people.
>
> Student comment after being in groups for three lessons in 2011

Key terms: inclusive schooling, social interactions, inclusive physical education, mild intellectual disability, personal development, health and physical education

---

Introduction

This chapter explores the notion of utilizing the Cooperative Learning model as a teaching tool to foster social interaction between students with a mild intellectual disability and their peers without a disability. Specific examples from research currently being conducted in the Australian context will be used to highlight how preparing for and implementing Cooperative Learning in a secondary-school inclusive physical education class can promote or discourage interactions. Providing a framework for this discussion will be the literature from Allport's (1954) contact theory. My observations of the research so far, alongside the perspectives of the teacher and students, will be presented and initial observations for moving forward in the Australian context for the use of the Cooperative Learning model in an inclusive physical education class will be discussed.

This chapter is based on two studies (Dowler, 2010, 2011). The first case study collected qualitative data on the implementation of Cooperative Learning in an inclusive physical education class that included one student with a mild intellectual disability. The study was specifically looking at the interactions between this student and their peers without a disability. Case study two is part of a larger single-subject multiple baseline design study that is collecting both quantitative and qualitative data on the impact of Cooperative Learning on the social interaction behaviours of students with a mild disability in three inclusive secondary-school physical education classes. As this is ongoing research, this chapter will report on the qualitative data from case study one and selected quantitative data of case study two. The following section will present several definitions that will provide background for the rest of the study.

Definitions

1   Social interaction. A student 'producing verbal or nonverbal behaviour directed toward another within the context of a mutual activity' (Hughes *et al.*, 2002, p. 392), for example, gestures, facial expressions, speech, conversational topic, initiation and greeting and/or smiling.
2   Inclusive physical education. For the purposes of this study this occurs when a student(s) with a disability is/are in a typical physical education class of peers without a disability. This is compared to a class that consists of all students with a disability (Block, 2000).
3   Mild intellectual disability. To meet criteria for mild intellectual disability, students must have a full-scale IQ score of approximately two to three standard deviations below the mean on an approved individual test of intelligence. There must be information on the assessment of adaptive skills and school performance (where applicable) consistent with or below this range of scores (New South Wales Department of Education and Training, 2003).
4   Personal Development, Health and Physical Education (PDHPE) teacher. PDHPE teachers are equivalent to physical education teachers internationally. In New South Wales, Australia these teachers are required to teach classroom-based personal development and health lessons to students as well as physical education.

The Australian context

The inclusion of students with a mild intellectual disability in secondary-school physical education classes has become more prevalent in recent years, with 45 per cent of Australian students with an intellectual disability attending an ordinary class in a mainstream school (Australian Institute of Health and Welfare (AIHW), 2008). Driven by the Disability Discrimination Act 1992, Disability Education Standards 2005 and the policy of the various state Departments of Education in Australia, inclusion is increasingly seen as good practice in the provision of physical education for students with a mild intellectual disability (Block, 1998; Commonwealth of Australia, 2002; Department of Education, Science and Training, 2005; Sherrill, 1998). However, despite the legislation and the strong commitment to a policy of inclusion there seems to be a discrepancy between this policy and practice.

While academic, vocational, behavioural and specifically motor skills in physical education are all considered important dimensions to develop for students with a mild intellectual disability, the social interaction skills of these students are consistently reported as an area of difficulty in their daily life (Leffert and Siperstein, 2002). Compounding this, teenage peers without a disability have difficulty knowing how to interact with students with a disability (Carter and

Hughes, 2005; Copeland *et al.*, 2004; Cutts and Sigafoos, 2001). Furthermore, in secondary-school physical education there is a growing body of research high-lighting the fact that interactions between students with a mild intellectual disa-bility and their peers without a disability in the secondary setting are occurring infrequently (Block and Obrusnikova, 2007; Butler and Hodge, 2004; Carter and Hughes, 2005; Cutts and Sigafoos, 2001). Concurrently the research suggests that students with a mild intellectual disability are less accepted and more frequently rejected than peers without a disability (Gresham and MacMillan, 1997).

Support for students with mild intellectual disabilities to be included alongside peers without a disability is not guaranteed, with 28 per cent of students with intellectual disabilities not receiving special support at schools in 2003 (AIHW, 2008). In addition physical education teaching strategies are also creating envi-ronments that lead to limited interactions between students with and without disabilities (Block and Obrusnikova, 2007). To this end Cooperative Learning, which advocates numerous social benefits (Dyson 2001), was chosen as the teaching strategy for the two studies to ascertain how Cooperative Learning may impact social interactions between the two groups of students.

Cooperative Learning and inclusive physical education

Cooperative Learning has been considered promising as an approach for inclu-sion. However, there is limited research on its impact on social interactions for students with a mild intellectual disability in inclusive physical education settings (Grenier, 2006; Nyit and Hsieh, 2004). The strongest support for using Cooperative Learning strategies to improve the social interactions of students with a mild intellectual disability was reported in a Taiwanese study by Nyit and Hsieh (2004). The study investigated the effects of Cooperative Learning on teacher–student interactions and peer relationships of a student with mild intel-lectual challenges in a fifth-grade inclusive physical education class. In relation to student and peer relationships the study found that Cooperative Learning: (a) had the potential to increase the social status and peer relationships of the student with intellectual challenges and (b) had the potential to increase the initiative behaviour of peer relationships for the students with intellectual challenges.

Whilst this is the only study conducted with students with a mild intellectual disability, other research by Wong (2008) and Grenier (2006) does provide some support for Cooperative Learning in the inclusive physical education setting with other students with a disability. Wong examined the effect of mainstreaming on the attitudes of peers without a disability, in a secondary school, toward students with a variety of disabilities including three students with autism. Wong (2008) noted that cooperative activities in the physical and adventure settings led to positive interactions and more meaningful experiences between students with and without a disability. They also emphasized the importance of the guidance and supervision of the teacher in fostering this reaction.

Similar findings were discussed in a study by Grenier (2006), where a third-grade physical education class including a child with cerebral palsy was observed over a six-month period. The teacher interviewed in the study commented that

Cooperative Learning, although successful most of the time, had its challenging days. This study uncovered three themes related to inclusion:

1   the teacher's belief in the development of social skills for all students;
2   the teacher's use of purposeful strategies to accommodate students with disabilities;
3   the student's learning was shaped by personal experience.

The primary-level setting of this study does not generalize to a secondary setting but one could argue that this research evidence is transferable to secondary. This suggests that further research is needed to examine the implementation of Cooperative Learning in this domain, where students are older and more able to understand group structures. For educators to be confident that Cooperative Learning may work in their own settings, research in the Australian setting was required to provide solid evidence of its impact on social interactions in the inclusive physical education setting. Aside from the research by Gillies (2003, 2004) on the use of Cooperative Learning in the classroom setting, no research in Australia in the inclusive physical education setting has been conducted.

Preparing for Cooperative Learning in inclusive physical education

It is generally accepted by researchers that preparing students for Cooperative Learning is important so that students can contribute positively to Cooperative Learning structures (Gillies and Ashman, 1996; Terwel *et al.*, 2001). There is an emphasis on the need to teach social skills such as listening, negotiating and problem-solving (Sapon-Shevin, 1994) and providing appropriate feedback (Dyson *et al.*, 2010). Additionally, leadership, decision-making, trust-building, communication and conflict management were considered important (Stevahn *et al.*, 2002). Other studies have found that students with a disability or who were socially rejected were perceived more positively when they had been involved in collaborative skills training with their peers without a disability (Asher, 1983; Putnam *et al.*, 1996). Focusing on physical education, research has suggested that all students be provided with social skills training early in the year and be explicitly taught the skills to undertake their role in a group, with appropriate reinforcement (Dyson, 2002; Dyson and Grineski, 2001; Grenier, 2006). To this end both studies incorporated a period of time to prepare all students in the groups for participation in Cooperative Learning.

Theoretical background

To guide the two studies and to complement the analysis of the data collected, the elements of contact theory (Allport, 1954) were applied to ascertain how the Cooperative Learning model could address the interaction problems in the inclusive physical education setting discussed earlier. The principles of contact theory guided the use of Cooperative Learning as the teaching strategy for the studies above all strategies. The theory proposes that to create favourable interactions between majority and minority groups there is a need for equal-status contacts in the interactions between participants, and the community involved must sanction and support the equal-status interactions. Participants should also be involved in the pursuit of common goals and 'common interests and common humanity should be perceived between members of the two groups' (Allport, 1954, p. 281).

The elements of Cooperative Learning explained earlier in this book align closely to the principles of contact theory. Equal status, the pursuit of common goals and common interests can be found in Cooperative Learning structures where students are grouped in small heterogeneous groups, contributing equally, depending on each other and interacting face to face as they strive to achieve common goals. The equal status contacts between the students can be sanctioned by the teacher as he or she supports the students to achieve the goals and reflect on their performance as a cohesive group. The methods used in the following two case studies were designed to examine how the Cooperative Learning elements may impact equal-status interactions between students with a mild intellectual disability and their peers without a disability.

Case study one

1   Participants. The participants in this case study were students and a teacher from a secondary school in New South Wales, Australia. The school was chosen using a convenience sampling technique (Patton, 1990). A Year 8 mixed-ability and mixed-gender physical education class in the school was chosen because it included a student diagnosed with a mild intellectual disability. This student was a 14-year-old female (target student), and an expert teacher from the school targeted the student for the study because of the limited social interaction observed with her peers without a disability. The female teacher, who volunteered to be part of the study, was head of the physical education faculty at the school with 10 years' teaching experience.

2   Preparation of teacher and students. Both the teacher and the students in the class were given time to prepare for Cooperative Learning. The teacher was provided with professional development on the Cooperative Learning model and a programme to implement and was supported throughout the study. The class was provided with two health and one physical education preparation lesson that focused on developing students' interpersonal and small-group skills. Students were then asked to apply the skills they had learned in three physical education lessons.

3   Cooperative Learning structures. The students, from the beginning, were placed in six heterogeneous groups (based on gender and ability) of four and one group of three students. A variety of Cooperative Learning structures such as co-op play, learning teams, performer-coach and jigsaw techniques were used in both the preparation and application phases of the study (Dyson and Grineski, 2001).

4   Data collection. Data were collected through interviews, a focus group, a teacher journal and observations incorporating field notes. The

semi-structured interviews were with the teacher and individually with the four students in the group that included the student with a disability. A focus group of six students was conducted with randomly chosen students from each of the other five groups in the class. After each lesson the teacher commented in a journal. The researcher observed the lessons, collecting qualitative data on the interaction behaviours of the target student. Data were analysed by systematically sorting and coding data to establish categories. The findings were then compared to the theoretical propositions of contact theory (Brantlinger *et al.*, 2005).

Case study two

1   Participants. As with case study one, the participants were students and a teacher from a secondary school in New South Wales, Australia, chosen using a purposive sampling technique (Patton, 1990). A Year 8 graded (based on ability) and single-sex (male) physical education class was chosen because it included a student with a mild disability. This student was a 14-year-old male (target student) diagnosed with a learning disability with a borderline intellectual disability IQ score. The student was observed by an expert teacher as having limited social interaction with his peers without a disability. The male teacher, who volunteered to be part of the study, had eight years' teaching experience and participated in extra-curricular welfare activities within the school.

2   Preparation of teachers and students. Both the teacher and the students in the class were given time to prepare for Cooperative Learning. The teacher was provided with professional development on the Cooperative Learning model and a programme to implement and was supported throughout the study. The class was provided with eight alternating health and physical education classes that focused on developing students' interpersonal and small-group skills. Students were then asked to apply the skills they had learned in five subsequent physical education lessons.

3   Cooperative Learning structures. After the fourth preparation lesson the students were placed in six heterogeneous groups (based on physical and intellectual ability) of four. The lessons started with simpler structures such as round robin, inside–outside circle (Kagan and Kagan, 2009), think–pair–share, co-op play and a modified jigsaw and progressed to learning teams, performer-coach and co-op play.

4   Data collection. Qualitative data were collected through interviews, a focus group, a teacher journal and observations incorporating field notes. Quantitative data were collected through a social interaction data collection instrument (SIDCI) before and after the Cooperative Learning intervention. The SIDCI instrument was specifically developed for the study after examination of two instruments already established and validated for social interaction and inclusion. These instruments are AIPE-S (Place and Hodge, 2001) and an instrument describing the social interaction of students with an intellectual disability (Hughes *et al.*, 2002).

The format and structure of the SIDCI were adapted from SOFIT: system for observing fitness instruction time (McKenzie *et al.*, 1991). Data on frequency, length, initiation and type of interaction were collected for all the lessons. These data were collected via partial interval recording utilizing a 20-second observe/20-second record method (Richards *et al.*, 1999). For the purposes of this study it was decided that the short interactions would be one or two word, facial expression or gesture exchanges, for example, smile, 'hi' or nod, or one sentence with no response. Long interactions continued with one or more people for the entire 20-second observe interval. Medium interactions were a sentence with a response and reciprocating interactions more than once, with a period of time of no interaction in the observation interval.

The following section presents the results from the two case studies. Considering, however, that data collection from case study two has just been completed only the quantitative results from the study will be presented in this chapter, with some comments from the students and teacher. These quantitative results across the baseline (before Cooperative Learning intervention), preparation and application phases will be displayed in graphical form.

Results from both case studies

The major categories that emerged from case study one were (a) the impact of group members on group success and cohesion, (b) the need to prepare students' social skills for Cooperative Learning, (c) the benefits and pitfalls of activity design and implementation of Cooperative Learning to impact interactions, (d) the provision of support for the student with a disability and (e) the use and access of Cooperative Learning resources. These categories all impacted how much the target student interacted with her peers.

The frequency of interactions from case study two across the baseline, preparation and application phases was variable, with an increasing trend of interactions as the lessons progressed (see Figure 10.1). Interactions in the baseline phase started higher as the target student was paired with his best friend, however this dropped toward the end of this phase when he was in the lesson without his friend. To allow comparison to these last two baseline lessons the target student was placed in a group without his best friend for the rest of the preparation and application lessons. Although interaction dropped slightly when groups were formed in lesson 10, they rebounded to their highest level in the next preparation lesson. Overall the length of interactions in the preparation phase increased. Figure 10.2 illustrates the percentage of short, medium and long interactions, with the percentage of short interactions decreasing during the preparation phase from the highs in the baseline phase. It was hypothesized before the study that interactions would initially decrease in the application phase when the groups were asked to more independently apply the skills they learnt in the preparation phase. This is evident in the first lesson of the application phase (14) where interaction frequency and percentage of long interactions decreased. This decrease

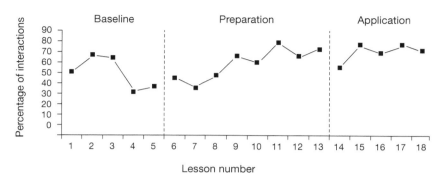

Figure 10.1 Percentage of interactions in inclusive physical education lessons. Interactions were between the student with a mild intellectual disability, his peers without a disability and the teacher during the baseline, preparation and application lessons. Classroom-based health lessons were 6, 7, 10 and 12.

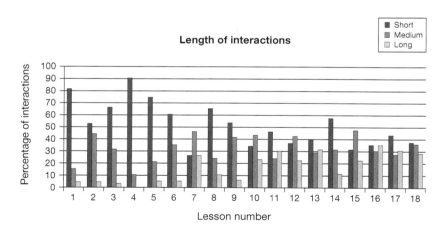

Figure 10.2 Percentage of short, medium and long interactions in inclusive physical education lessons. Interactions were between the student with a mild disability, his peers without a disability and the teacher during the baseline, preparation and application lessons. Classroom-based health lessons were 6, 7, 10 and 12.

was not long-lasting with interaction frequency and percentage of long interactions rebounding in the later four application lessons.

A search of medium, long and medium and long interactions clustered together was undertaken in order to uncover the Cooperative Learning structures and situations that promoted interactions. Conversely a search of 'no' interactions was undertaken to ascertain how interactions were discouraged. The following discussion will present these findings alongside the major themes that emerged from case study one.

Promoting interactions

The most prominent structures and situations that promoted interactions were found when the target students and their group members were required to either problem-solve, explain, bond or choose roles. Furthermore, it became apparent that the worksheets and task cards, proximity to group members and teacher's feedback also promoted longer interactions. Although some of the above structures and situations were evident in both studies, differences were found between the two target students.

Problem-solving

The frequency and length of interactions were at their highest in case study two when the students were asked to problem-solve. In a co-op play activity the groups were given a map of the field set-up and were asked to complete the task given on the map together. To decipher the map students huddled together, and even though the attempt at the task was not completed according to instructions, the group continued to interact as they worked together to attempt the task.

Explaining

Jigsaw structures where students had to explain a skill technique or explain information not known to other group members promoted longer interactions in case study two. Pairs and groups were made accountable for explaining by either (a) withholding equipment until all students could display a technique (it did not have to be the 'correct' technique, but an attempt), (b) being able to perform a novel challenge where technique was displayed, (c) being responsible for group-member improvement in a skill required for a game, (d) unveiling of the product of their explanation to each other or the class or (e) a game could only commence once all students had explained unknown information about the rules and scoring to each other.

Cooperative Learning roles

Once groups were formed students had to choose what role they would play for each lesson or activity. This choice usually created longer discussions as students negotiated what role they would play. The target student in case study two was always keen to be the group organizer and stated this in the final interview when asked what role he liked the most. The target student in case study one also preferred the group organizer role, and her interactions were livelier during this time. This liveliness with her group members was also observed in structures that promoted the sharing and interdependence of roles. An example was a co-op play warm-up activity that required the group to swap the roles of leader and supporter throughout the game. The target student and the group were motivated to interact with each other as they strived to complete the task before other groups (field notes).

Group bonding

During the preparation lessons students were given opportunities to bond with their partner or group members through Cooperative Learning structures. The students had to talk about themselves, their weekend and holiday adventures, find things in common, develop a group colour and group name and talk about group progress. These opportunities were generally in the health lessons, with group processing occurring in physical education lessons as well. In the first preparation lesson both target students were reluctant to engage in these types of activities. However, as the preparation lessons continued they became more relaxed with their group members. In case study one the target student's interactions were more prevalent when they had to create a name for their group. The teacher commented, 'I observed two times during the roles activity she was interacting with her group. Her role was "encourager" when I was observing and she was talking with her group saying things such as "good idea" and "well done"' (teacher journal, after lesson 2).

Teacher feedback

Interactions between the target students and their group were longer when the teacher connected with their group. This connection occurred in both case studies when the teacher guided the group as they developed a group colour and group name. Similar interactions were found in later application lessons in case study two, where feedback from the teacher on the group's progress in the task and clarification of the task combined with a time limit for completion were observed.

Positioning of students

The Cooperative Learning element of face-to-face interaction was important for fostering equal-status interactions as students were positioned to contribute equally, to observe others and gain confirmation of their contribution. In most of the structures mentioned above the group members were in close proximity to each other and were huddled together in a circle formation. In case study one, when the teacher positioned groups in the physical education lessons in huddles and away from other groups, the target student interacted more with her group members. Similarly in case study two, when students were required to huddle together longer interactions were also promoted. These huddles occurred when choosing roles, during structures such as jigsaw, performer-coach and utilizing the Cooperative Learning element of group processing.

Resources

To further promote face-to-face interactions and to assist students to work through the tasks either worksheets or task cards, usually found in a group folder, were employed in lessons. These resources created a focus and structure for the group to follow, and results from both studies illustrate that they assisted with the promotion of interactions for both target students. They were both drawn to the folder on many occasions, asked the teacher questions about the task cards and interacted with their group to work out the written tasks. The teacher in case study two commented: 'Task cards and the worksheets allowed him [target student] to have something concrete in front of him and it didn't force him to generate his own discussion to start with' (teacher interview, 1 July 2011).

Combination of concepts

The performer-coach structure was employed in lesson 17 in case study two and continued for most of the lesson. This created the second-highest lesson interaction for the target student with his group. The activity combined expla-nation, problem-solving, worksheets, close proximity and teacher feedback and guidance. The class was informed that the skills being practised, for example, bowling and pitching, would be included in the final game in the next lesson, giving the activity a context for the lesson. The group shared the roles of coach, checker, performer and catcher. When the target student was either the coach or checker more noticeable medium and longer interactions occurred, as both roles had to work together to provide feedback to the performer.

What discouraged interactions

In both case studies the most prominent structures and situations that discour-aged interactions were found when groups were not positioned to interact, other students in the class needed to be managed and instruction time was longer. Additional situations and structures were found in case study one in relation to group selection, gender pairing, non-verbal communication and lack of access to resources.

Positioning

Students are not always in a position to interact in physical education lessons. For example, in some of the application lessons in case study two students were continually moving and spread out on the field and consequently interactions became shorter. Although they were responsible for working together as a group in the field their opportunity to interact for longer periods of time was reduced. Similarly, in case study one students were sometimes waiting in lines with their backs to each other, as was recorded in the field notes: 'Activity finished – all four students sit down in a line. [There is] an opportunity to talk to each other but there is no communication' (field note, lesson 5, 17 March 2010). It is noted that the teacher did not ask for lines but the students automatically placed themselves in this position, which made it difficult to foster face-to-face interactions. Waiting in lines is potentially a previously learned behaviour.

Instruction and behaviour management

In both studies the need for the teacher to manage the behaviour of other students in other groups inadvertently impacted interactions. The teacher in case study one commented:

> A lot of the time [the students with a mild intellectual disability] do not ask questions, they do as they are asked and they are not a discipline problem. They then tend to get lost in the room as you focus your attention on other issues in the classroom. This is one of the frustrating aspects of teaching – that your attention is often drawn away from students who need it the most.
>
> (Teacher interview, 11 May 2010)

The time students had to interact with each other was also directly impacted by the amount of time devoted to instruction in the lesson. Early in the preparation phase of both studies instructions were more prevalent, as students were learning how to participate in Cooperative Learning structures. Combined with the management of other students' behaviour, interaction frequency was variable. However, as the lessons progressed in case study two, instruction and management time decreased and interaction increased. This is a similar finding to that of Dyson *et al.* (2010).

Access to resources

The most prominent situation that stifled interactions in case study one was the lack of access to resources found in the performer-coach activity. It was noted that the target student did not have access to the skill description sheet. Her group was split up (a decision made by one member of the group, not the teacher) and the target student was paired with another student from another group. Her interaction with this student and her own group was non-existent, as she did not know what to do.

Group selection

Group-member selection and subsequent presence of subtle negative non-verbal communication by a particular group member emerged as one of the major themes in case study one that impacted interaction. The other female in the group with the target student at times isolated herself from the group socially. The teacher noted:

> [The other female in the group] I feel was at times uninterested in the activities and more concerned in looking out for her peer group. This I feel had an impact on [the target student] as she then became more reserved (e.g. 2 on 2 volleyball activity).
>
> (Teacher journal, lesson 4)

Non-verbal communication

The non-verbal communication exhibited by the other female in the group became a barrier to interaction, particularly between her and the target student. Many examples in the field notes highlighted the other female displaying behaviours that pointedly ignored the target student and at times the whole group. These included having her back to the target student and the group, not looking at the target student, playing with objects and walking away from the group during an activity.

Gender pairing

Interactions were also stifled for the target student when gender pairing emerged. The target student was more interactive with the male members of the group but as the teacher gave the groups more autonomy throughout the lessons gender pairing emerged. If the activity design did not include other pairing options and the teacher did not intervene, the target student was regularly paired with the other female in the group and interaction was stifled. Field notes repeatedly referred to the gender pairing and the following is an example in the game of fielding end ball:

> Boys at front, girls at the back. [Target student] with her hands on her hips. The two boys are talking only to each other and [the target student and the other female] are not getting involved in the game much at all as the boys are stopping the ball before it goes to them.
>
> (Field note, lesson 5, 17 March 2010)

Conclusion

Based on the research conducted to date, the Cooperative Learning model is showing potential as a teaching tool to improve interactions between students with a mild intellectual disability and their peers without a disability. The Cooperative Learning model seems to be reinforcing the principles of contact theory as equal-status interactions are promoted when students contribute equally and share roles and resources as they pursue common goals in a Cooperative Learning task. Students are supported within these tasks by the teacher and other students sanctioning the use of equal-status interactions. Students are also able to perceive commonalities between themselves as they participate in team-bonding activities and are given time to connect and process as a group.

Conversely, when time is restricted as a result of instruction and management of other students, the ability of the teacher to support equal-status interactions is reduced. The teacher has less time to observe what might be required for groups to display equal-status interactions such as access to resources, pairing options and how students are positioned to interact. However, with Cooperative Learning students can be encouraged to improve their interactions either by the teacher or by a group member or peer in their class. Additionally, Allport (1954) cautions that 'certain personalities resist the influences of contact' (p. 279). This was evident when students displayed negative non-verbal communication and behavioural issues. Combating these situations is required for the benefits of Cooperative Learning for inclusive physical education classes to be realized.

Although contact theory was adequate to explain how to promote favourable interactions, it was not sufficient to understand the process of interaction. A more in-depth theoretical framework from social interaction theories would be beneficial to interpret the findings from both studies. Replicating case study two in other physical education classes will also provide more solid evidence for the success of the Cooperative Learning model in improving interactions in inclusive physical education classes. In this research context, it seems that for Cooperative Learning to be successful both (a) devoting time to preparing students to participate equally in Cooperative Learning structures and (b) being persistent as a teacher with students as they learn this new way of learning are important for promoting favourable interactions. Although the teachers in these studies received some training on the Cooperative Learning model the process of implementation was not always smooth in the earlier lessons. The teacher in the 2011 study commented on using Cooperative Learning in the future:

> The fact this was your [research], if it was just me trying this new teaching, I probably would have lasted two or three lessons. I would have been going this is not working with the kids because they were not doing it as I had seen it. At the end of 13 lessons you sit back and evaluate it, they did pretty good. Part of it is through perseverance and patience, that's just the key to it. It is not a learning style that you are going to get instant results with ... I did not realize how good a class they were.
>
> (Teacher interview, 1 July 2011)

Further support of teachers as they begin to use the Cooperative Learning model in their classes seems necessary if PDHPE teachers are to realize the improvement in interactions not only for students with a mild intellectual disability but for their peers as well.

Acknowledgement

I would like to thank all the teachers who have worked so hard and the students for being so enlightening.

References

Allport, G.W. (1954). *The nature of prejudice*, 25th anniversary edn. Cambridge, MA: Addison-Wesley.

Asher, S. (1983). Social competence and peer status: recent advances and future directions. *Child Development* 54: 1427–34.

Australian Institute of Health and Welfare (2008). *Disability in Australia: intellectual disability. AIHW Bulletin* no. 67, cat. no. AUS 110. Online. Available HTTP: <http://www.aihw.gov.au/publication-detail/?id=6442468183&tab=2>, accessed 15 December 2011.

Block, M.E. (1998). Don't forget about the social aspects of inclusion. *Strategies* 12(2): 30–4.

Block, M.E. and Obrusnikova, I. (2007). Inclusion in physical education: a review of the literature from 1995–2005. *Adapted Physical Activity Quarterly* 24: 103–24.

Brantlinger, E., Jimenez, R., Klinger, J., Pugach, M. and Richardson, V. (2005). Qualitative studies in special education. *Exceptional Children* 71(2): 195–207.

Butler, R.S. and Hodge, S.R. (2004). Social inclusion of students with disabilities in middle school physical education classes [electronic version]. *Research in Middle Level Education Online* 27. Online. Available HTTP: <http://www.nmsa.org/Publications/RMLEOnline/tabid/101/Default.aspx>, accessed 11 November 2007.

Carter, E.W. and Hughes, C. (2005). Increasing social interaction among adolescents with intellectual disabilities and their general education peers: effective interventions. *Research and Practice for Persons with Severe Disabilities* 30(4), 179–93.

Commonwealth of Australia (2002). *Education of students with disabilities*. Online. Available HTTP: <http://www.aph.gov.au/Senate/Committee/EET_CTTE/completed_inquiries/2002-04/ed_students_withdisabilities/index.htm>, accessed 24 November 2008.

Copeland, S.R., Hughes, C., Carter, E.W., Guth, C., Presley, J.A., Williams, C.R. *et al.* (2004). Increasing access to general education. *Remedial and Special Education* 25(6): 342–52.

Cutts, S. and Sigafoos, J. (2001). Social competence and peer interactions of students with intellectual disability in an inclusive high school. *Journal of Intellectual and Developmental Disability* 26(2): 127–41.

Department of Education, Science and Training (2005). *Disability standards for education*. Online. Available HTTP: <http://www.ag.gov.au/www/agd/agd.nsf/Page/Humanrightsandanti-discrimination_DisabilityStandardsforEducation>, accessed 4 February 2009.

Dowler, W. (2010). Cooperative Learning in the inclusive physical education setting. Paper presented at the International Association for the Study of Cooperation in Education conference on Cooperative Learning: Pedagogy, Policy and Practice.

Dowler, W. (2011). Cooperative Learning, social interaction and inclusive physical education. Unpublished dissertation, University of Wollongong.

Dyson, B. (2001). Cooperative learning in an elementary physical education program. *Journal of Teaching in Physical Education* 20(3): 264–81.

Dyson, B. (2002). The implementation of Cooperative Learning in an elementary physical education program. *Journal of Teaching in Physical Education* 22(1): 69–85.

Dyson, B. and Grineski, S. (2001). Using Cooperative Learning structures in physical education. *Journal of Physical Education, Recreation and Dance* 72(2): 28–31.

Dyson, B.P., Linehan, N.R. and Hastie, P.A. (2010). The ecology of Cooperative Learning in elementary physical education classes. *Journal of Teaching in Physical Education* 29: 113–30.

Gillies, R.M. (2003). Structuring cooperative group work in classrooms. *International Journal of Educational Research* 39: 35–49.

Gillies, R.M. (2004). The effects of Cooperative Learning on junior high school students during small-group learning. *Learning and Instruction* 14: 197–213.

Gillies, R.M. and Ashman, A.F. (1996). Teaching collaborative skills to primary school children in classroom-based work groups. *Learning and Instruction* 6(3): 187–200.

Grenier, M. (2006). A social constructionist perspective of teaching and learning in inclusive physical education. *Adapted Physical Activity Quarterly* 23: 245–60.

Gresham, F.M. and MacMillan, D.L. (1997). Social competence and affective characteristics of students with mild disabilities. *Review of Educational Research* 67(4): 377–415.

Hughes, C., Copeland, S.R., Wehmeyer, M.L., Agran, M., Cai, X. and Hwang, B. (2002). Increasing social interaction between general education high school students and their peers with mental retardation. *Journal of Developmental and Physical Disabilities* 14(4): 387–402.

Kagan, S. and Kagan, M. (2009). *Kagan Cooperative Learning*. San Clemente, CA: Kagan Publishing.

Leffert, J.S. and Siperstein, G.N. (2002). Social cognition: a key to understanding adaptive behaviour in individuals with mild mental retardation. *International Review of Research in Mental Retardation* 25: 135–81.

McKenzie, T.L., Sallis, J.F. and Nadar, P.R. (1991). SOFIT: system for observing fitness instruction time. *Journal of Teaching in Physical Education* 11: 195–205.

New South Wales Department of Education and Training (2003). *Disability criteria*. Online. Available HTTP: <http://www.schools.nsw.edu.au/media/downloads/schoolsweb/student-support/programs/disabilitypgrms/disabcriteria.doc>, accessed 15 December 2011.

Nyit, C.K. and Hsieh, Y.T. (2004). The effects of Co-operative Learning on teacher–student interactions and peer relationships: a case study of a student with mild intellectual challenges. Unpublished dissertation, National Taiwan Normal University.

Patton, M.Q. (1990). *Qualitative evaluation and research methods*, 2nd edn. Newbury, CA: Sage.

Place, K. and Hodge, S.R. (2001). Social inclusion of students with physical disabilities in GPE: a behavioural analysis. *Adapted Physical Activity Quarterly* 18: 389–404.

Putnam, J., Markovchick, K., Johnson, D.W. and Johnson, R.T. (1996). Cooperative Learning and peer acceptance of students with learning disabilities. *Journal of Social Psychology* 136(6): 741–52.

Richards, S.B., Taylor, R.L., Ramasamy, R. and Richards, R.Y. (1999). *Single subject research: applications in educational and clinical settings*. San Diego: Singular Publishing Group, Inc.

Sapon-Shevin, M. (1994). Cooperative Learning and middle schools: what would it take to really do it right? *Theory into Practice* 33(3): 183–90.

Sherrill, C. (1998). *Adapted physical activity, recreation and sport: crossdisciplinary and lifespan*, 5th edn. Dubuque, IA: WCB/McGraw-Hill.

Stevahn, L., Johnson, D.W., Johnson, R.T. and Schultz, R. (2002). Effects of conflict resolution training integrated into high school social studies curriculum. *Journal of Social Psychology* 142(3): 305–31.

Terwel, J., Gillies, R.M., Eeden, P. and Hock, D. (2001). Cooperative Learning processes of students: a longitudinal multilevel perspective. *British Journal of Educational Psychology* 71: 619–45.

Wong, D.K.P. (2008). Do contacts make a difference? The effects of mainstreaming on students' attitudes toward people with disabilities. *Research in Developmental Disabilities* 29: 70–82.

Conclusion

Cooperative Learning in physical education

Ashley Casey and Ben Dyson

> A situation is cooperative when attainment of a goal by one individual is positively correlated with attainment of that goal by other members of the group.
>
> Deutsch (1949, cited in Lafont, this volume)

Key terms: non-negotiables, self-active students, academic and social learning, social interdependence, social cultural significance of human movement

---

The Cooperative Learning model has a long history in classroom-based instruction (Slavin *et al.*, 1985; Johnson and Johnson, 2009) but it is only in the last decade that it has developed a growing level of recognition in the physical education community. In many ways its emergence into the practices of physical education teachers has been through the increasing exposure of pre-service teachers to the model as part of their teacher education programmes. Yet, until recently, our understanding of Cooperative Learning has been limited to the lessons we have drawn from the classroom practices of other subject areas and from the developing body of literature in our field. This book has allowed us the opportunity to develop that literature base and to consolidate the learning from a number of countries into one place. This final chapter now seeks to bring those ideas and experiences together and begin to define the characteristics of Cooperative Learning in physical education. Our intention is to draw together the themes that have emerged from the preceding chapters from eight different countries and to explore explicit characteristics or the 'non-negotiables' that we would expect to see when teachers and teacher educators profess to implement the Cooperative Learning model within a physical education context.

Developing a Cooperative Learning classroom

Benner (2001) suggests that schools and teachers should be creators of spaces where students can be self-active. This idea is supported by Bähr and Wibowo (this volume) and seems to exemplify the long-term goals of Cooperative Learning in physical education, that is, that students are involved as individuals and groups in the development of physical and social understanding. The paradox for teachers and other educators is that, while this is the eventual aim of such self-activity, by its very nature the decision to engage with the content must be made by the student. Accordingly, it is the responsibility of teachers to create the conditions conducive to self-activity. Therefore it is important to examine inclusive practices and to develop Cooperative Learning as one approach to teaching in physical education that emanates from a perspective of inclusivity.

In order to rephrase the nature of learning so that we invite students to be self-active rather than telling them how and where to be involved we need to reconsider the role of the teacher. As Sutherland (this volume) suggested, when students are self-involved as learners then they have the opportunity to discover what they have learned for themselves. In contrast teacher-coerced/expected engagement creates a 'situation where the student does not learn how to learn from their own experience, but rather is told what (s)he learned' (Sutherland, this volume). Yet for this to happen we need to encourage a sense of physical education that values more than team sports and competition, which by its inherent nature reduces the number of students who can achieve and who are therefore engaged.

Instead, in physical education, we argue for an innovative approach that is purposeful and meaningful and which seeks to develop attributes of cooperation that are discussed in the professional literature and often 'talked about' yet appear as unproven outcomes of physical education (Gordon, 2010; Hellison, 2003). However, as Lafont (this volume) argued, physical education should be a natural site for cooperation, because many activities or team sports require teamwork and collaboration. Yet do teachers actually plan for these implicit outcomes in physical education (such as cooperation, leadership and teamwork) if they are treated as the foregone conclusions of the subject? We would argue that the Cooperative Learning model explicitly offers these outcomes to physical educationalists because they are outcomes that are actively considered for within the lesson plan and Cooperative Learning structures. Indeed, the Cooperative Learning model deliberately gives equality of outcome to both academic and social learning. It is this mix of academic and social learning that marks Cooperative Learning out from other teaching strategies such as working in groups, cooperative games or team-building activities (Velázquez-Callado, this volume).

The Cooperative Learning model was defined in the Introduction as a pedagogical approach because it does not seek to position the teacher or the content as the dominant contributor to the learning environment. Instead Cooperative Learning is an approach that places its emphasis on bringing together the triad of: (1) learning, (2) teaching and (3) content, or in other words pedagogy (Haerens *et al.*, 2011). In the next three sections we will explore the outcomes reported in the preceding chapters that relate to these elements of pedagogy.

Learning

We have deliberately placed learning at the top of the pedagogical triangle as we believe, in the words of John Dewey, that the learner 'becomes the sun around which the appliances of education revolve; he is the centre about which they are organised' (Dewey, 1900, p. 51). Unlike Dewey we do not exclusively see the child as the learner in education but instead, as many of our authors have suggested, teachers also need to learn how to teach through the Cooperative Learning model. Indeed, in Casey's (this volume) chapter he deliberately positions himself as a learner and suggests that to use Cooperative Learning successfully he had to fully engage with the five elements of Cooperative Learning himself. Similarly, Ovens *et al.* (this volume) and Velázquez-Callado (this volume) with school children, and Zach and Cohen (this volume) with pre-service teachers all found that when the Cooperative Learning model is first used in classrooms teachers need to learn about the model before they can teach through this approach.

Conversely, while the current dominance of an asymmetrical relationship (one in which one party plays the dominant role) between teachers and students exists (Lafont, this volume), there is a reported need for teachers to learn alternative pedagogies (Kirk, 2010; Metzler, 2005, Metzler and McCullick, 2008). The unevenness of classroom interaction goes a long way to ensuring that the teacher maintains the dominant role in the classroom, regardless of a practitioner's desire for change (Casey, 2010). Such dominance is deliberately addressed in the Cooperative Learning model. Furthermore, other hierarchical situations are challenged and overcome when students are able to look and act beyond societal expectations around ability and physical competence (Ovens *et al.*, this volume) and especially with regard to disabilities (Dowler, this volume; Grenier and Yeaton, this volume). Indeed Cooperative Learning has been shown to promote cultural sensitivity and to be a culturally responsive pedagogical model through the integrally bound relationships of the groups it forms amongst students (Grenier and Yeaton, this volume). The model, as Dowler (this volume) shows, has also allowed students who have previously been socially excluded to be more positively perceived as a consequence of being involved in collaborative skills training with peers without a disability. By including all students then the practices undertaken in the name of physical education have begun to further and value intentions and outcomes that 'promote an awareness of possibility rather than an adherence to limitation' (Grenier and Yeaton, this volume) that is, as discussed by Dowler (this volume), a belief in what cannot be achieved by a certain 'type' of student rather than what could be achieved by any student in an appropriate positive learning environment.

At a micro-level of teaching, Lafont (this volume) shows how student social interaction evolved during a series of Cooperative Learning interventions. She found that conversations between students were more complex, more focused on thinking about physical education, and were increasingly free from conflict, in which participants co-constructed their own solutions. The ability of students to correct their own mistakes, learn from them and regulate their own conflicts is something explicit within the Cooperative Learning model (Velázquez-Callado, this volume) and is reported in the literature (Dyson, 2001; Dyson *et al.*, 2010). While a number of authors gave reasons for this, Bähr and Wibowo (this volume) suggest that it emerges most strongly out of the teachers' willingness to let their students explore dead ends, false leads and misconceptions during their learning. Indeed Bähr and Wibowo (this volume) and Sutherland (this volume) both describe the learning journey (or the Sunday Afternoon Drive) as potentially more significant than the eventual or intended outcome.

Cooperative Learning is a pedagogical model that can foster social interaction between students with mild intellectual disability and their peers (Dowler, this volume). Equally, though, it is a model that foregrounds the needs of individual students as they seek to expand their movement possibilities (Bähr and Wibowo, this volume). It has been shown to have the potential to overcome the established, maybe even preordained, hierarchy in physical education based on ability (Pill, 2008). It has long been argued that being 'good' at physical education means being good at the techniques that currently define the subject area (Kirk, 2010). Yet we argue in this book that this technocratic focus is not enough. In contrast, as Lafont's (this volume) chapter shows, when students are taught how to engage in meaningful and educative conversations through their engagement in the Cooperative Learning model, there are positive effects on game participation and efficiency in attack – and not just by those already considered to be technically good. As one of the teachers in New Zealand (Ovens *et al.*, this volume) suggested, 'children should be active and interactive. I think it links and that they'll learn best by doing and trying out for themselves and just creating things themselves and problem solving.' This is a key issue, because if children do learn best when they have a meaningful and well-established role to play in their own learning then we must work harder as educators to achieve this. However, to make this a reality, as we will explore in the next section, the act of teaching is an equally important component.

Teaching

In Germany, *Erziehung* (or education) is the job of the teacher, while it is widely considered that learning is the responsibility of the student. However, learning is not something that just occurs in a classroom. In fact, many educators argue that 'mediocrity' and 'rote' learning are norms of instruction in today's schools (Doyle, 1992; Siedentop *et al.*, 1994). In fact, 20 years ago Larry Locke (1992) stated that 'non-teaching' proliferated in physical education. Instead, the teacher must create, with his or her pedagogy, the environment for students to be learners. We are promoting a positive and 'inviting' student-driven teaching environment that motivates students to learn compared to a teacher-driven 'direct instruction' (Metzler, 2005) that plagues many of our school systems.

This book has shown that the Cooperative Learning model enhances student learning – both for those who normally engage in physical education (Casey, this volume; Ovens *et al.*, this volume) and students who have been excluded. Unfortunately students are excluded from physical education as a consequence of what they are seen *not* to be able to do because of learning difficulties (Dowler, this volume), disabilities (Grenier and Yeaton, this volume), gender (Fernández-Río and Méndez-Giménez, this volume) and/or poor motor development. Yet as Zach and Cohen (this volume) and Casey (this volume) highlighted, learning to teach through the Cooperative Learning model is not straightforward. Cooperative Learning is an innovative pedagogical approach for physical education and to learn to use it requires time and effort (Dyson *et al.*, 2004). Unfortunately the initial engagement of the model can, in the case of the pre-service teachers in Zach and Cohen's (this volume) study, result in lower teacher efficacy. Additionally it can lead to confusion on the part of teachers, especially when they are required to develop a new pedagogical approach while also trying to develop their knowledge of a new subject area (Ovens *et al.*, this volume; Casey, 2010).

The demands on teaching should not be overlooked and perhaps it is time to re-consider the ways in which Cooperative Learning is introduced to teachers and to students (Casey, this volume). In his chapter Velázquez-Callado (this volume) deliberately positions cooperative games and the Cooperative Learning model in an asymmetrical relationship. He suggests that while cooperative games generally do not adhere to the five elements of Cooperative Learning, they can serve as a useful 'stepping stone' into the development of the full model. Similarly Casey (this volume) shows how he slowly developed his use and understanding of the model as he learned to use it alongside his students. These examples of practice serve us as a reminder that teachers and students alike need help when using the model. Indeed, Dyson (2001, 2002) and Dyson *et al.* (2010) indicated that the meaningful adoption of the Cooperative Learning model in physical education was not something that was achieved quickly.

A clear message emerging from a number of the chapters is the importance of group processing in developing an inclusive and progressive form of student-centred learning. Yet, as Casey *et al.* (2009) found, this is a time-consuming process that is difficult to justify in short lessons. However, the strength of argument put forward by a number of our authors (Dowler, this volume; Ovens *et al.*, this volume; Grenier and Yeaton, this volume; Sutherland, this volume) suggests that its importance is such that time should be found. It was argued a decade ago that the problem-solving and reflective tasks inherent in adventure education would serve as an appropriate foundation for the eventual construction of a Cooperative Learning pedagogy (Dyson, 2001, 2002). A similar argument has been made in this book, and yet the focus seems to have shifted more towards the importance of group processing as the central element of the Cooperative Learning model: the first non-negotiable. This is compared to a more 'evaluation'-oriented group processing that is described in the generic literature (Johnson and Johnson, 1989). The notion of group processing featured in this book could serve as the fulcrum for the other four non-negotiable elements of Cooperative Learning in physical education (positive interdependence, individual accountability, face-to-face interaction and interpersonal and small-group skills) that have featured heavily here and in the wider literature. Furthermore, the foregrounding of this element allows teachers and students the time to reconsider the hierarchical structures that currently exist in the classroom and encourage the use of 'I' statements rather than placing blame through the 'You' statements (Sutherland, this volume) that often emerge in haphazard and poorly constructed teaching situations.

If, as Fernández-Río and Méndez-Giménez (this volume) and many more before them suggest (e.g. Cohen and Latham, 1997; Dyson, 2002), the Cooperative

Learning model has close links with the theories and practice of constructivism and constructivist teaching, then teachers must be guided to see in a convergent manner that there are many appropriate responses to the problems they set. We strongly advocate a role for physical education where education is the key objective and the intended outcome rather than current notion that our profession's subject matter is based on an exposure curriculum, competitive sport or fitness (Kretchmar, 1994; Metzler, 2005). The call to student-generated activity from the German concept of *Bildung* requires the teacher to create an environment where the possibility of self-generated activity exists (see Bähr and Wibowo, this volume). Fundamentally this requires the teacher to rethink teaching and learning, and as Dyson *et al.* (2004) suggested, it is a 'conceptual shift' that occurs in a chaotic and complex manner. In itself this is not either an easier or an effortless process. It requires considerable work on the teacher's part, as Casey (this volume) found, and needs to be carried out in a purposeful and systematic process over time.

Content

We believe that it is important to consider how the Cooperative Learning model has been successfully adopted in a number of international contexts and then adapted to a number of settings and subject areas. This book, in its ten chapters, has reported on interventions in Spain, France, Germany, the UK, New Zealand, Australia, Israel and the USA. Moreover, it has shown successful interventions at primary, secondary and university level and in a diverse range of content, from swimming and aesthetic disciplines to adventure education and individual and team games. In a subject area traditionally represented by 'the larger discourses on the nature of ability and the underlying standpoint that informs [performance] competence' (Grenier and Yeaton, this volume), Cooperative Learning offers an alternative standpoint that can rejuvenate the typical pedagogy that represents physical education.

In their chapter Dyson *et al.* (this volume) examine the processes in which university faculty and teachers engaged in co-constructing and restructuring their teaching and learning processes in light of a reconceptualized national curriculum in New Zealand. Similarly, Casey (this volume) deliberately sought to move away from the traditional approach to teaching regularly described by critics such as Metzler (2005), Kirk (2010) and Tinning (2010). He did this within the context of the UK national curriculum, which professes to place value on the roles that students undertook in lessons other than those of performer. In their work on self-made materials Fernández-Río and Méndez-Giménez (this volume) explored the potential of Cooperative Learning in embracing and harnessing the mantra of 'reduce, reuse and recycle' in modern Spain's 'throw away' society. In countries that are culturally and socially very different, Grenier and Yeaton (this volume) in the USA and Dowler (this volume) in Australia both showed how Cooperative Learning was a potent pedagogical model to facilitate the engagement of students with physical and/or social disabilities.

In many cases there seems to be an expectation that physical education is a site where social interaction and learning thrive. Yet, as a number of these chapters have clearly illustrated, the structures and contextual limitations that occur in physical education are not always conducive to enriched student engagement (Tinning, 2010). Indeed, many students (and, we would argue, teachers) lack appropriate social skills, because they are asked to succeed in an environment that historically focuses almost exclusively on the psychomotor domain (Kirk, 2010). Consequently students and/or groups of students need to be deliberately positioned and structured to interact with one another. This book has shown that when this is achieved students are better placed to engage in their tasks and the tasks of their peers. When meaningful student interaction does occur then greater management and instruction time is needed to allow them to adequately engage in learning (Dowler, this volume; Ovens *et al.*, this volume; Grenier and Yeaton this volume; Lafont, this volume).

What is Cooperative Learning in physical education?

One of the intended outcomes of this book was to explore the use of the Cooperative Learning model in physical education and then propose a definition that is similar to but different from the classroom-based model of Cooperative Learning from which it was derived. Our intent, therefore, is to define Cooperative Learning as a pedagogical model in physical education.

We argue that the five elements inherent in the Cooperative Learning model and illuminated in each of the chapters are the non-negotiables of Cooperative Learning in physical education – regardless of the content or age of the students. These elements should be regarded as the ultimate aim of those seeking to use the model in any context (Johnson and Johnson, 2009). However, as we have suggested in this book, the presence of group processing appears to be the underlying goal that provides the foundation for the Cooperative Learning model as a pedagogical practice in physical education. Lafont (this volume) posited that groups that engage in frequent social interactions between sequences of play turned out to be more effective than those who just performed the activity without discussion. She felt that the best interactions contain elements of socio-cognitive conflict, co-construction and peer tutoring. Similarly, it was these forms of interaction that Dowler (this volume) stated were the areas that students with mild intellectual disability reported the most difficulty developing. Social interactions are an inherent part of physical education and teamwork in the gymnasium and much less common in the generic classroom. We suggest that group work discussed by Velázquez-Callado (this volume) is common in team activities and in physical education. However, our vision of Cooperative Learning in physical education moves group work from the random and short-term associations commonly formed in the gymnasiums where the subject is taught and towards a state of 'social interdependence' that is developed in a structured and purposeful manner. This requires a deliberate decision by the teacher to change his or her role in the classroom and in the learning process. Furthermore it requires the teacher to reconsider their practices in light of the expectations of the school, of colleagues and of the subject area (Casey, in press).

The notion that students need to engage in discussions about physical education is part of changing expectations about what it means to teach physical education (Casey, in press). It is a purposeful decision to move away from a notion of physical education as something where students engage predominantly in physical activity and is a shift away from the inherent skills-orientated philosophy of learning in physical education (Kirk, 2010). It moves the emphasis towards a philosophy of physical education that values students' experiences ahead of outcomes. Yet suggesting physical education as a site of social interaction is not new. Zach and Cohen (this volume) indicated that physical education should be considered a place where social interaction and social processes constantly occur in competitive ball games, performance in gymnastics, encouraging each other in outdoor training or creatively in dance. Indeed, Lafont (this volume) suggests that verbal interactions allowed students to better construct game strategies and Fernández-Río and Méndez-Giménez (this volume) use social interactions to guide students to create their own equipment. Similarly, Bähr and Wibowo (this volume), Ovens *et al.* (this volume) and Fernández-Río and Méndez-Giménez (this volume) all place social interaction at the heart of the Cooperative Learning model in physical education. Between them these authors report high levels of girls' participation, highlight collaboration as the central carrier of the educational potential in physical education, show how the model enhanced student motivation, improved behaviour, facilitated higher-quality cognitive and physical involvement, improved social interaction and led to an increased sense of empowerment and responsibility. This consensus of opinion suggests that Cooperative Learning in physical education is a pedagogical approach that allows students to make decisions to be involved at a deep and meaningful level (Bähr and Wibowo, this volume; Ovens *et al.*, this volume). We agree with Larsson and Quennerstedt's (2010) position that movement is a socio-cultural act that involves exploration of what human movement means, and how it is significant within a specific context. In the case of Cooperative Learning, this means that human movement is something that is undertaken within a cooperative relationship with others (including students and teachers). Therefore, Cooperative Learning in physical education could be tentatively defined as:

> A pedagogical model that, through its five elements, explores the social-cultural significance of human movement through the use of individual and group learning outcomes to enhance student development, interaction and task-mastery within the physical, cognitive and affective domains.

As Casey (this volume) suggests at the end of his chapter, defining Cooperative Learning in physical education in this way moves this pedagogical approach away from Kirk's (2010) notion of teaching in our subject as 'Physical-Education-As-Sport-Techniques'. It is about challenging teachers to make physical education an aesthetic, pleasurable and pedagogical experience for their students by thinking about human movement in different ways (Pringle, 2010). More importantly, it is about inviting them to be co-participants in the learning journey regardless of content. Furthermore, educators in the twenty-first century realize that if our students are to be successful in the workplace of the future, we must educate for social skills and the capability to work with diversity.

References

Casey, A. (2010). Practitioner research in physical education: teacher transformation through pedagogical and curricular change. Unpublished PhD thesis, Leeds Metropolitan University.

Casey, A. (in press). A self study using action research: changing site expectations and practice stereotypes. *Educational Action Research*.

Casey, A., Dyson, B. and Campbell, A. (2009). Action research in physical education: focusing beyond myself through Cooperative Learning. *Educational Action Research* 17: 407–23.

Cohen, E.G. and Latham, R.A. (1997). *Working for equity in heterogeneous classrooms: sociological theory in practice*. New York: Teachers College Press.

Dewey, J. (1900). *The school and society: being three lectures*. Chicago, IL: University of Chicago Press.

Doyle, W. (1992). Curriculum and pedagogy. In P.W. Jackson (ed.), *Handbook of research on curriculum*, 486–516. New York: Macmillan.

Dyson, B. (2001). Cooperative Learning in an elementary school physical education program. *Journal of Teaching in Physical Education* 20: 264–81.

Dyson, B. (2002). The implementation of Cooperative Learning in an elementary school physical education program. *Journal of Teaching in Physical Education* 22: 69–85.

Dyson, B., Griffin, L. and Hastie, P. (2004). Sport education, tactical games, and Cooperative Learning: Theoretical and pedagogical considerations. *Quest* 56: 226–40.

Dyson, B.P., Linehan, N.R. and Hastie, P.A. (2010). The ecology of Cooperative Learning in elementary school physical education classes. *Journal of Teaching in Physical Education* 29: 113–30.

Gordon, B. (2010). An examination of the responsibility model in a New Zealand secondary school physical education programme. *Journal of Teaching in Physical Education* 29: 21–37.

Haerens, L., Kirk, D., Cardon, G. and De Bourdeaudhuij, I. (2011). Toward the development of a pedagogical model for health-based physical education. *Quest* 63: 321–38.

Hellison, D.R. (2003). *Teaching responsibility through physical activity*. Leeds: Human Kinetics.

Johnson, D.W. and Johnson, R.T. (1989) *Cooperation and competition: theory and research*. Edina, MN: Interaction Book Co.

Johnson. D.W. and Johnson, R.T. (2009). An educational psychology success story: social interdependence theory and Cooperative Learning. *Educational Researcher* 38: 365–79.

Kirk, D. (2010). *Physical education futures*. London, Routledge.

Kretchmar, R.S. (1994). *Practical philosophy of sport*. Leeds: Human Kinetics.

Larsson, H. and Quennerstedt, M. (2010). Understanding movement: a socio-cultural approach to analysing human movement. Paper presented at the Australian Association for Research in Education (AARE) Conference, Melbourne, 28 November–2 December 2010.

Locke, L (1992). Changing secondary school physical education. *Quest* 44: 361–72.

Metzler, M.W. (2005). *Instructional models for physical education*, 2nd edn. Scottsdale, AZ: Holcomb Hathaway.

Metzler, M.W. and McCullick, B.A. (2008). Introducing innovation to those who matter most: the P-12 pupils' perceptions of the model-based instruction. *Journal of Teaching in Physical Education* 27: 512–28.

Pill, S. (2008). A teacher's perceptions of the Sport Education model as an alternative for upper primary school physical education. *ACHPER Australia Healthy Lifestyles Journal* 55(2): 23–9.

Pringle, R. (2010). Finding pleasure in physical education: a critical examination of the educative value of positive movement affects. *Quest* 62: 119–34.

Siedentop, D., Doutis, P., Tsangaridou, N., Ward, P. and Rauschenbach, J. (1994). Don't sweat gym: an analysis of curriculum and instruction. *Journal of Teaching in Physical Education* 13: 375–94.

Slavin, R., Sharan, S., Kagan, S., Hertz Lazarowitz, R., Webb, C. and Schmuck, R. (1985). (eds), *Learning to cooperate, cooperating to learn*. New York: Plenum.

Tinning, R. (2010). *Pedagogy and human movement: theory, practice, research.* Abingdon: Routledge.

Index

Printed in the USA/Agawam, MA
June 4, 2012

566327.040